THE USDA
COMPLETE GUIDE TO
HOME CANNING

THE USDA'S HANDBOOK FOR
PRESERVING, PICKLING, AND FERMENTING
VEGETABLES, FRUITS, AND MEATS

- BULLETIN 539 -

BY U.S. DEPARTMENT OF AGRICULTURE

REVISED 2015
AGRICULTURE INFORMATION BULLETIN NO. 539

LEGACY EDITION

THE DOUBLEBIT
TRADITIONAL FOOD PRESERVER'S LIBRARY
BOOK 2

Doublebit Press
Eugene, OR

New content, introduction, and annotations
Copyright © 2020 by Doublebit Press. All rights reserved.

Doublebit Press is an imprint of Eagle Nest Press
www.doublebitpress.com | Eugene, OR, USA

Original content under the public domain. Originally published in 2015 by the U.S. Department of Agriculture.

This title and other Doublebit Press books are available at a volume discount for youth groups, outdoors clubs, or reading groups. Contact at info@doublebitpress.com for more information.

Doublebit Press Legacy Edition ISBNs
Hardcover: 978-1-64389-145-3
Paperback: 978-1-64389-146-0

Disclaimer: Because of its age and historic context, this text could contain content on present-day inappropriate methods, activities, outdated medical information, unsafe chemical and mechanical processes, or culturally and racially insensitive content. Doublebit Press, or its employees, authors, and other affiliates, assume no liability for any actions performed by readers or any damages that might be related to information contained in this book. This text has been published for historical study and for personal literary enrichment toward the goal of preserving the American handcraft tradition, timeless trade skills, and traditional artisanal knowledge.

First Doublebit Press Legacy Edition Printing, 2020

Printed in the United States of America
when purchased at retail in the USA

INTRODUCTION
To The Doublebit Press Legacy Edition

The old experts of artisanal trades, country and homestead knowledge, and the woods and mountains taught timeless principles and skills for centuries. Through their timeless books, the old experts offered rich descriptions of how the world works and encouraged learning through personal experiences *by doing*. Over the last 125 years, manufacturing, farming, and construction have substantially changed. Of course, many things have gotten simpler as equipment and technology have improved. In addition, some activities of pre-digital times are now no longer in vogue, or are even outright considered inappropriate or illegal. However, despite many of the positive changes in manufacturing and crafting methods that have occurred over the years, *there are many other skills and much knowledge that have been forgotten.*

By publishing *Doublebit Legacy Editions*, it is our goal at Doublebit Press to do what we can to preserve and share the works from forgotten teachers that form the cornerstone of the history of the American artisans and traditional crafts. Through remastered reprint editions of timeless classics, perhaps we can regain some of this lost knowledge for future generations.

This book is an important contribution traditional handcraft and country skills literature and has important historical and collector value toward preserving the American handcraft and outdoors tradition. The knowledge it holds is an invaluable reference for practicing skills and hand craft methods. Its chapters thoroughly discuss some of the essential building blocks of knowledge that are fundamental but may have been forgotten as equipment gets fancier and technology gets smarter. In short, this book was chosen for Legacy Edition printing because much of the basic skills and knowledge it contains has been forgotten or put to the wayside in trade for more modern conveniences and methods.

With technology playing a major role in everyday life, sometimes we need to take a step back in time to find those basic building blocks used for gaining mastery – the things that we have luckily not completely lost and has been recorded in books over the last two centuries. These skills aren't forgotten, they've just been shelved. *It's time to unshelve them once again and reclaim the lost knowledge of self-sufficiency.*

Based on this commitment to preserving our outdoors and handcraft artisanal heritage, we have taken great pride in publishing this book as a complete original work. We hope it is worthy of both study and collection by outdoors folk in the modern era of outdoors and traditional skills life.

Unlike many other photocopy reproductions of classic books that are common on the market, this Legacy Edition does not simply place poor photography of old texts on our pages and use error-prone optical scanning or computer-generated text. We want our work to speak for itself, and reflect the quality demanded by our customers who spend their hard-earned money. With this in mind, each Legacy Edition book that has been chosen for publication is carefully remastered from original print books, *with the Doublebit Legacy Edition printed and laid out in the exact way that it was presented at its original publication.* We provide a beautiful, memorable experience that is as true to the original text as best as possible, but with the aid of modern technology to make as beautiful a reading experience as possible for books that can be over a century old.

Because of its age and because it is presented in its original form, the book may contain misspellings, inking errors from print plates, and other printing blemishes that were common for the age. However, these are exactly the things that we feel give the book its character, which we preserved in this Legacy Edition. During digitization, we ensured that each illustration in the text was clean and sharp with the least amount of loss from being copied and digitized as possible. Full-page plate illustrations are presented as they were found, often including the extra blank page that was often behind a plate. For the covers, we use the original cover design to give the book its original feel. We are sure you'll appreciate the fine touches and attention to detail that your Legacy Edition has to offer.

For traditional handcrafters and classic artisanal enthusiasts who demand the best from their equipment, this Doublebit Press Legacy Edition reprint was made with you in mind. Both important and minor details have equally both been accounted for by our publishing staff, down to the cover, font, layout, and images. It is the goal of Doublebit Legacy Edition series to be worthy of collection in any outdoorsperson's library and that can be passed to future generations.

Every book selected to be in this series offers unique views and instruction on important skills, advice, tips, tidbits, anecdotes, stories, and experiences that will enrich the repertoire of any person who enjoys escaping a bit from today's modern technology-based, cookie-cutter, and highly industrialized skills. Instead, folks seeking to make things with their hands like the old days may find great value from these resurrected instructional manuals from the past. These books were not simply written to be shelved in a library – they contain our history and forgotten methods to make things with real character and energy with a *human* component.

Therefore, to learn the most basic building blocks of a craft leads to mastery of all its aspects. We hope this book helps you along this path with its rich descriptions and illustrations!

United States
Department of
Agriculture

National Institute
of Food
and Agriculture

Revised 2015

**Agriculture Information
Bulletin No. 539**

Complete Guide to
Home Canning

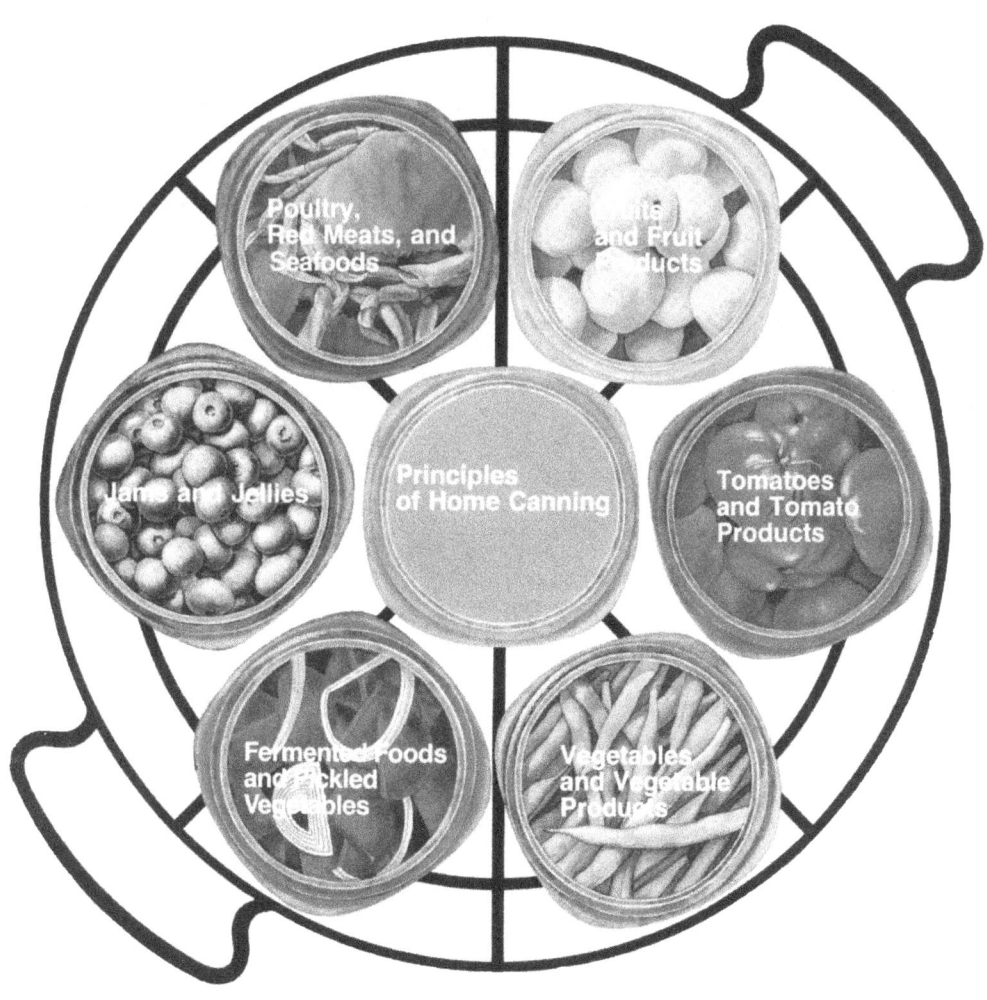

Acknowledgments

The creation of an Extension Service Center for Excellence at the Penn State University in the 1980s made it possible to conduct the research necessary to revise four previously published bulletins for canning foods in the home. The Center was the cooperative effort of the Extension Service, Cooperative State Research Service, and the Penn State University with Gerald D. Kuhn, PhD, of the Penn State University as Director. A National Center for Home Food Processing and Preservation was established in 2000 as a cooperative effort of the National Institute of Food and Agriculture (formerly the Cooperative State Research, Education, and Extension Service) and the University of Georgia as the lead institution in a multi-state activity with Elizabeth L. Andress, PhD, as Project Director. This Center conducted research that made it possible to include some new products in this revised guide.

The National Institute of Food and Agriculture wishes to credit the primary development of this guide to Gerald D. Kuhn (Penn State University), Elizabeth L. Andress (University of Georgia), and Thomas S. Dimick (Penn State University). USDA staff who assisted in preparing the original *Complete Guide to Home Canning* include Milton P. Baldauf, Catherine E. Adams, Nancy T. Sowers, and Vincent G. Hughes. Others who have assisted in later revisions include Kenneth N. Hall (University of Connecticut), Thomas W. Poore (USDA), Judy A. Harrison, Elaine M. D'sa and Mark A. Harrison (all at the University of Georgia). Research for the smoked fish recommendation was conducted by Carolyn Raab and Ken Hilderbrand (Oregon State University) with partial funding from the OSU Extension Sea Grant Program. Research for the fish in quart jars recommendation was conducted by Kristy Long and Chuck Crapo (University of Alaska). Research for six of the salsa recommendations was conducted by Richard H. Dougherty and Virginia N. Hillers (Washington State University). The research on acidification of home canned Asian pears and figs was conducted by Margy Woodburn (Oregon State University). All have contributed significant ideas and time in making this guide a truly up-to-date research-based publication.

This project was partially funded through a grant from the National Integrated Food Safety Initiative (Grant No. 00-51110-9762) of the National Institute of Food and Agriculture, U.S. Department of Agriculture.

December 2009
Revised 2015

Agriculture Information Bulletin No. 539

Complete Guide to Home Canning

Caution: All home-canned foods should be canned according to the procedures in this Guide. Low-acid and tomato foods not canned according to the recommendations in this publication or according to other USDA-endorsed recommendations present a risk of botulism. If it is possible that any deviation from the USDA-endorsed methods occurred, to prevent the risk of botulism, low-acid and tomato foods should be boiled in a saucepan before consuming even if you detect no signs of spoilage. At altitudes below 1,000 ft, boil foods for 10 minutes. Add an additional minute of boiling time for each additional 1,000 ft elevation. However, this is not intended to serve as a recommendation for consuming foods known to be significantly underprocessed according to current standards and recommended methods. It is not a guarantee that all possible defects and hazards with non-recommended methods can be overcome by this boiling process. The recommendation is to only can low-acid and tomato foods according to the procedures in this Guide.

Reference to commercial products and services is made with the understanding that no discrimination is intended and no endorsement by the U.S. Department of Agriculture is implied. Clear Jel® and Splenda® are mentioned because they are the only suitable products presently available to the general public for the stated purposes in given products.

The U.S. Department of Agriculture (USDA) prohibits discrimination in all its programs and activities on the basis of race, color, national origin, age, disability, and where applicable, sex, marital status, familial status, parental status, religion, sexual orientation, genetic information, political beliefs, reprisal, or because all or part of an individual's income is derived from any public assistance program. (Not all prohibited bases apply to all programs.) Persons with disabilities who require alternative means for communication of program information (Braille, large print, audiotape, etc.) should contact USDA's TARGET Center at 202-720-2600 (voice and TDD). To file a complaint of discrimination, write to USDA, Director, Office of Civil Rights, 1400 Independence Avenue, S.W., Washington, DC 20250-9410, or call 800-795-3272 (voice) or 202-720-6382 (TDD). USDA is an equal opportunity provider and employer.

Preface

Home canning has changed greatly in the 180 years since it was introduced as a way to preserve food. Scientists have found ways to produce safer, higher quality products. The first part of this publication explains the scientific principles on which canning techniques are based, discusses canning equipment, and describes the proper use of jars and lids. It describes basic canning ingredients and procedures and how to use them to achieve safe, high-quality canned products. Finally, it helps you decide whether or not and how much to can.

The second part of this publication is a series of canning guides for specific foods. These guides offer detailed directions for making sugar syrups; and for canning fruits and fruit products, tomatoes and tomato products, vegetables, red meats, poultry, seafoods, and pickles and relishes. Handy guidelines for choosing the right quantities and quality of raw foods accompany each set of directions for fruits, tomatoes, and vegetables. Most recipes are designed to yield a full canner load of pints or quarts. Finally, processing adjustments for altitudes above sea level are given for each food.

This publication contains many new research-based recommendations for canning safer and better quality food at home. It is an invaluable resource book for persons who are canning food for the first time. Experienced canners will find updated information to help them improve their canning practices.

Research is continually being conducted in areas that affect food preservation recommendations. Make sure your food preservation information is always current with up-to-date tested guidelines.

This publication supersedes four USDA Home and Garden Bulletins: Number 8—"Home Canning of Fruits and Vegetables"; Number 56—"How to Make Jellies, Jams, and Preserves at Home"; Number 92—"Making Pickles and Relishes at Home"; and Number 106—"Home Canning of Meat and Poultry."

For Safety's Sake

Pressure canning is the only recommended method for canning meat, poultry, seafood, and vegetables. The bacterium *Clostridium botulinum* is destroyed in low-acid foods when they are processed at the correct time and pressure in pressure canners. Using boiling water canners for these foods poses a real risk of botulism poisoning.

If *Clostridium botulinum* bacteria survive and grow inside a sealed jar of food, they can produce a poisonous toxin. Even a taste of food containing this toxin can be fatal. Boiling food 10 minutes at altitudes below 1,000 ft should destroy this poison when it is present. For altitudes at and above 1,000 ft, add 1 additional minute per 1,000 ft additional elevation. **Caution:** To prevent the risk of botulism, low-acid and tomato foods not canned according to the recommendations in this publication or according to other USDA-endorsed recommendations should be boiled as above, in a saucepan before consuming, even if you detect no signs of spoilage. This is not intended to serve as a recommendation for consuming foods known to be significantly underprocessed according to current standards and recommended methods. It is not a guarantee that all possible defects and hazards with other methods can be overcome by this boiling process. All low-acid foods canned according to the approved recommendations may be eaten without boiling them when you are sure of all the following:
- Food was processed in a pressure canner.
- Gauge of the pressure canner was accurate.
- Up-to-date researched process times and pressures were used for the size of jar, style of pack, and kind of food being canned.
- The process time and pressure recommended for sterilizing the food at your altitude was followed.
- Jar lid is firmly sealed and concave.
- Nothing has leaked from jar.
- No liquid spurts out when jar is opened.
- No unnatural or "off" odors can be detected.

Do Your Canned Foods Pass This Test?

Overall appearance
- Good proportion of solid to liquid
- Full pack with proper headspace
- Liquid just covering solid
- Free of air bubbles
- Free of imperfections—stems, cores, seeds
- Good seals
- Practical pack that is done quickly and easily

Fruit and vegetables
- Pieces uniform in size and shape
- Characteristic, uniform color
- Shape retained—not broken or mushy
- Proper maturity

Liquid or syrup
- Clear and free from sediment

Determining Your Altitude Above Sea Level

It is important to know your approximate elevation or altitude above sea level in order to determine a safe processing time for canned foods. Since the boiling temperature of liquid is lower at higher elevations, it is critical that additional time be given for the safe processing of foods at altitudes above sea level.

It is not practical to include a list of altitudes in this guide, since there is wide variation within a State and even a county. For example, the State of Kansas has areas with altitudes varying between 75 ft to 4,039 ft above sea level. Kansas is not generally thought to have high altitudes, but there are many areas of the State where adjustments for altitude must be considered. Colorado, on the other hand, has people living in areas between 3,000 and 10,000 ft above sea level. They tend to be more conscious of the need to make altitude adjustments in the various processing schedules. To list altitudes for specific counties may actually be misleading, due to the differences in geographic terrain within a county.

If you are unsure about the altitude where you will be canning foods, consult your county Extension agent. An alternative source of information would be your local district conservationist with the Soil Conservation Service.

Table of Contents

Section .... Page

Acknowledgments .... not numbered
Preface ii
For Safety's Sake iii
Do Your Canned Foods Pass This Test? iii
Determining Your Altitude Above Sea Level iv

Guide 1. Principles of Home Canning 1-3

Why can foods? 1-5
How canning preserves foods 1-5
Ensuring safe canned foods 1-6
Ensuring high-quality canned foods 1-11
Jars and lids 1-13
Recommended canners 1-17
Selecting the correct processing time 1-22
Cooling jars 1-25
Testing jar seals 1-25
Reprocessing unsealed jars 1-26
Storing canned food 1-26
Identifying and handling spoiled canned food 1-26
Preparing pickled and fermented foods 1-27
Preparing butters, jams, jellies, and marmalades 1-29
Canned foods for special diets 1-31
Canning fruit-based baby foods 1-31
How much should you can? 1-32

Glossary of Terms 1-33

Index of Foods 1-36

Guide 2. Selecting, Preparing, and Canning Fruit and Fruit Products 2-3

General 2-5
Preparing and using syrups 2-5
Apple butter 2-6
Apple juice 2-6
Apples—sliced 2-7
Applesauce 2-7
Spiced apple rings 2-8
Spiced crab apples 2-9
Apricots—halved or sliced 2-9
Berries—whole 2-10
Berry syrup 2-10
Cantaloupe pickles 2-11
Cantaloupe pickles, no sugar added 2-12
Cherries—whole 2-12

Cranberry orange chutney	2-13
Figs	2-14
Fruit purees	2-14
Grapefruit and orange sections	2-15
Grape juice	2-15
Grapes—whole	2-16
Mango chutney	2-16
Mango sauce	2-17
Mixed fruit cocktail	2-18
Nectarines—halved or sliced	2-18
Peaches—halved or sliced	2-19
Pears—halved	2-19
Pears, Asian—halved or sliced	2-20
Pineapple	2-21
Plums—halved or whole	2-21
Rhubarb—stewed	2-22
Zucchini-pineapple	2-22
Fruit Salsas	**2-23**
Spicy cranberry salsa	2-23
Mango salsa	2-24
Peach salsa	2-24
Peach apple salsa	2-25
Pie Fillings	**2-25**
Apple pie filling	2-26
Blueberry pie filling	2-27
Cherry pie filling	2-27
Festive mincemeat	2-28
Green tomato pie filling	2-29
Peach pie filling	2-30
Process times for some acid foods in a dial-gauge pressure canner	2-31
Process times for some acid foods in a weighted-gauge pressure canner	2-32

Guide 3. Selecting, Preparing, and Canning Tomatoes and Tomato Products ... 3-3

General	3-5
Tomato juice	3-5
Tomato and vegetable juice blend	3-6
Tomatoes—crushed	3-7
Standard tomato sauce	3-8
Tomatoes—whole or halved (packed in water)	3-9
Tomatoes—whole or halved (packed in tomato juice)	3-10
Tomatoes—whole or halved (packed raw without added liquid)	3-11
Tomatoes with okra or zucchini	3-12
Tomatillos	3-13
Spaghetti sauce without meat	3-13
Spaghetti sauce with meat	3-14
Mexican tomato sauce	3-15
Easy hot sauce	3-16
Cayenne pepper sauce	3-17

Tomato ketchup 3-17
Country western ketchup 3-18
Blender ketchup 3-18

Salsa Recipes 3-19
Selection and preparation of ingredients 3-19
Chile salsa (hot tomato-pepper sauce) 3-21
Chile salsa II 3-22
Tomatillo green salsa 3-22
Tomato salsa using paste tomatoes 3-23
Tomato salsa using slicing tomatoes 3-24
Tomato/green chile salsa 3-24
Tomato/tomato paste salsa 3-25
Tomato taco sauce 3-26

Guide 4.
Selecting, Preparing, and Canning Vegetables and Vegetable Products 4-3

Asparagus—spears or pieces..4-5
Beans or peas—shelled, dried 4-5
Beans, baked 4-6
Beans, dry, with tomato or molasses sauce 4-6
Beans, fresh lima—shelled 4-7
Beans, snap and Italian—pieces 4-8
Beets—whole, cubed, or sliced 4-9
Carrots—sliced or diced 4-10
Corn—cream style 4-10
Corn—whole kernel 4-11
Mixed vegetables 4-12
Mushrooms—whole or sliced 4-13
Okra 4-14
Peas, green or English—shelled 4-14
Peppers 4-15
Potatoes, sweet—pieces or whole 4-16
Potatoes, white—cubed or whole 4-17
Pumpkins and winter squash—cubed 4-18
Soups 4-18
Spinach and other greens 4-19
Squash, winter—cubed 4-20
Succotash 4-20

Guide 5. Preparing and Canning Poultry, Red Meats, and Seafoods 5-3

Chicken or rabbit 5-5
Ground or chopped meat 5-6
Strips, cubes, or chunks of meat 5-6
Meat stock (broth) 5-7
Chile con carne 5-8
Clams 5-9
King and Dungeness crab meat 5-9
Fish in pint jars 5-10

Fish in quart jars 5-11
Oysters 5-12
Smoked fish 5-13
Tuna 5-14

Guide 6. Preparing and Canning Fermented Foods and Pickled Vegetables 6-3
Selection of Fresh Cucumbers 6-5
Low-temperature pasteurization treatment 6-5
Suitable containers, covers, and weights for fermenting food 6-6
Salts used in pickling 6-7

Fermented Foods 6-7
Dill pickles 6-7
Sauerkraut 6-8

Cucumber Pickles 6-9
Bread-and-butter pickles 6-9
Quick fresh-pack dill pickles 6-10
Sweet gherkin pickles 6-10
14-day sweet pickles 6-11
Quick sweet pickles 6-12

Other Vegetable Pickles 6-13
Pickled asparagus 6-13
Pickled dilled beans 6-14
Pickled three-bean salad 6-14
Pickled beets 6-15
Pickled carrots 6-16
Pickled baby carrots 6-16
Pickled cauliflower or Brussels sprouts 6-17
Chayote and jicama slaw 6-17
Bread-and-butter pickled jicama 6-18
Marinated whole mushrooms 6-18
Pickled dilled okra 6-19
Pickled pearl onions 6-20
Marinated peppers 6-20
Pickled bell peppers 6-21
Pickled hot peppers 6-22
Pickled jalapeño pepper rings 6-23
Pickled yellow pepper rings 6-24
Pickled sweet green tomatoes 6-24
Pickled mixed vegetables 6-25
Pickled bread-and-butter zucchini 6-26

Pickled Vegetable Relishes 6-26
Chayote and pear relish 6-26
Piccalilli 6-27
Pickle relish 6-28
Pickled corn relish 6-28
Pickled green tomato relish 6-29
Pickled horseradish sauce 6-30
Pickled pepper-onion relish 6-30

Spicy jicama relish 6-30
Tangy tomatillo relish 6-31

Pickled Foods for Special Diets 6-32
No sugar added pickled beets 6-32
No sugar added sweet pickle cucumber slices 6-33
Reduced-sodium sliced dill pickles 6-34
Reduced-sodium sliced sweet pickles 6-34

Guide 7. Preparing and Canning Jams and Jellies 7-3
Making jelly without added pectin 7-5
Extracting juices and making jelly 7-5
Making jam without added pectin 7-6

Making jams and jellies with added pectin 7-7
Pear-apple jam 7-8
Strawberry-rhubarb jelly 7-8
Blueberry-spice jam 7-9
Grape-plum jelly 7-10
Golden pepper jelly 7-10

Making reduced-sugar fruit spreads 7-11
Peach-pineapple spread 7-11
Refrigerated apple spread (made with gelatin) 7-12
Refrigerated grape spread (made with gelatin) 7-12
Remaking soft jellies 7-13

Complete Guide to
Home Canning

United States Department of Agriculture

National Institute of Food and Agriculture

Guide 1
Principles of Home Canning

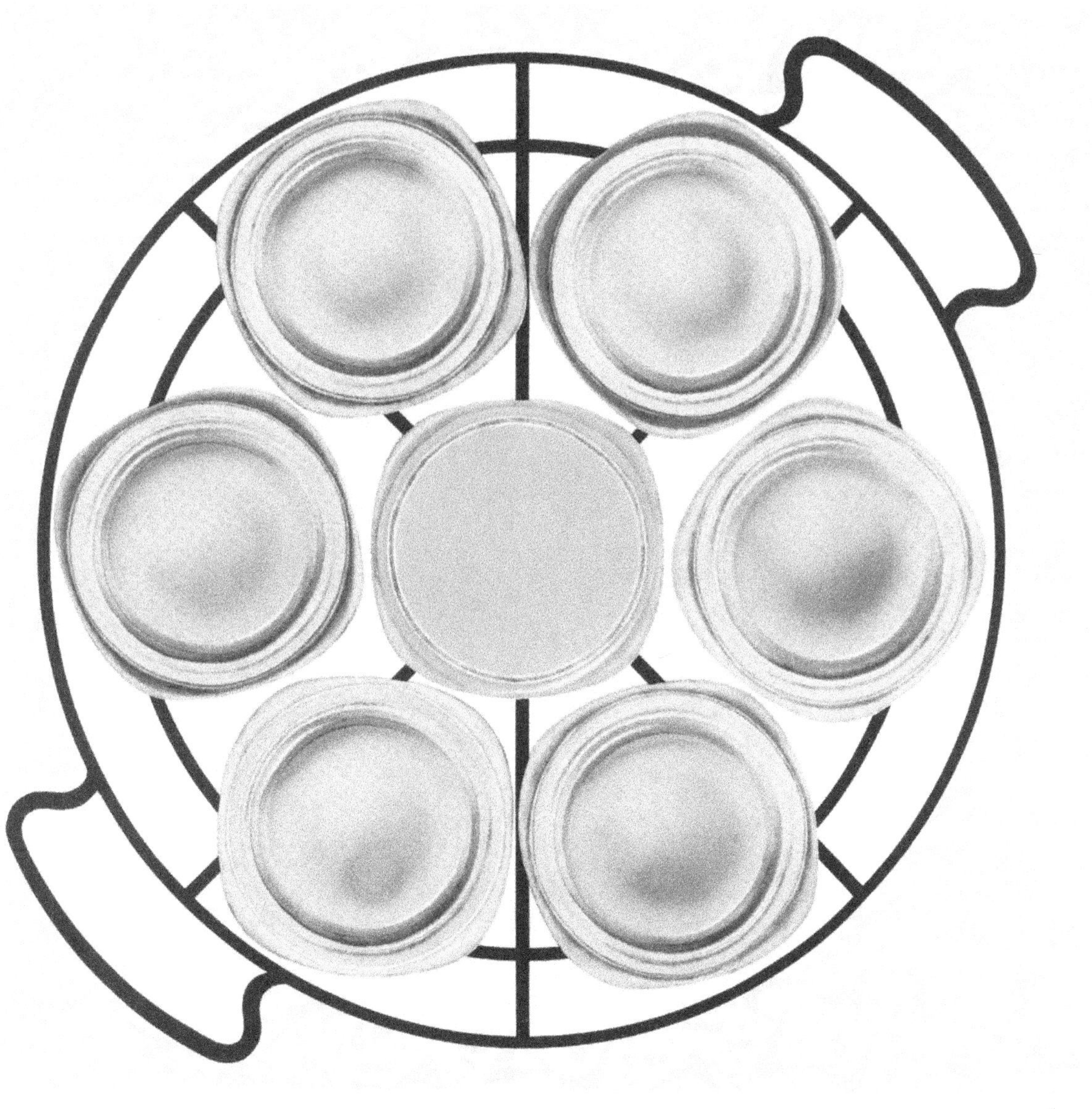

Guide 1
Principles of Home Canning

Table of Contents

Section	Page
Why can foods?	1-5
How canning preserves foods	1-5
Ensuring safe canned foods	1-6
Food acidity and processing methods	1-8
Process adjustments at high altitudes	1-10
Equipment and methods not recommended	1-10
Ensuring high-quality canned foods	1-11
Maintaining color and flavor in canned food	1-11
Advantages of hot packing	1-12
Controlling headspace	1-13
Jars and lids	1-13
Jar cleaning and preparation	1-14
Sterilization of empty jars	1-14
Lid selection, preparation, and use	1-15
Recommended canners	1-17
Boiling-water canners	1-18
Using boiling-water canners	1-18
Pressure canners	1-19
Using pressure canners	1-21
Selecting the correct processing time	1-22
Example of using tables for determining proper process time	1-23
Cooling jars	1-25
Testing jar seals	1-25
Reprocessing unsealed jars	1-26
Storing canned food	1-26
Identifying and handling spoiled canned food	1-26
Preparing pickled and fermented foods	1-27
Ingredients	1-28
Pickles with reduced salt content	1-28
Firming agents	1-28
Preventing spoilage	1-29
Preparing butters, jams, jellies, and marmalades	1-29
Ingredients	1-29
Jams and jellies with reduced sugar	1-30
Preventing spoilage	1-30
Methods of making jams and jellies	1-30
Canned foods for special diets	1-31
Canning without sugar	1-31
Canning without salt (reduced sodium)	1-31
Canning fruit-based baby foods	1-31
How much should you can?	1-32
Glossary of Terms	1-33
Index of Foods	1-36

Why can foods?

Canning can be a safe and economical way to preserve quality food at home. Disregarding the value of your labor, canning homegrown food may save you half the cost of buying commercially canned food. Canning favorite and special products to be enjoyed by family and friends is a fulfilling experience and a source of pride for many people.

Many vegetables begin losing some of their vitamins when harvested. Nearly half the vitamins may be lost within a few days unless the fresh produce is cooled or preserved. Within 1 to 2 weeks, even refrigerated produce loses half or more of some of its vitamins. The heating process during canning destroys from one-third to one-half of vitamins A and C, thiamin, and riboflavin. Once canned, additional losses of these sensitive vitamins are from 5 to 20 percent each year. The amounts of other vitamins, however, are only slightly lower in canned compared with fresh food. If vegetables are handled properly and canned promptly after harvest, they can be more nutritious than fresh produce sold in local stores.

The advantages of home canning are lost when you start with poor quality fresh foods; when jars fail to seal properly; when food spoils; and when flavors, texture, color, and nutrients deteriorate during prolonged storage.

The information and guides that follow explain many of these problems and recommend ways to minimize them.

How canning preserves foods

The high percentage of water in most fresh foods makes them very perishable. They spoil or lose their quality for several reasons:
- growth of undesirable microorganisms—bacteria, molds, and yeasts,
- activity of food enzymes,
- reactions with oxygen,
- moisture loss.

Microorganisms live and multiply quickly on the surfaces of fresh food and on the inside of bruised, insect-damaged, and diseased food. Oxygen and enzymes are present throughout fresh food tissues.

Proper canning practices include:
- carefully selecting and washing fresh food,
- peeling some fresh foods,
- hot packing many foods,
- adding acids (lemon juice or vinegar) to some foods,
- using acceptable jars and self-sealing lids,
- processing jars in a boiling-water or pressure canner for the correct period of time.

Collectively, these practices remove oxygen; destroy enzymes; prevent the growth of undesirable bacteria, yeasts, and molds; and help form a high vacuum in jars. Good vacuums form tight seals which keep liquid in and air and microorganisms out.

Ensuring safe canned foods

Growth of the bacterium *Clostridium botulinum* in canned food may cause botulism—a deadly form of food poisoning. These bacteria exist either as spores or as vegetative cells. The spores, which are comparable to plant seeds, can survive harmlessly in soil and water for many years. When ideal conditions exist for growth, the spores produce vegetative cells which multiply rapidly and may produce a deadly toxin within 3 to 4 days of growth in an environment consisting of:
- a moist, low-acid food
- a temperature between 40° and 120°F
- less than 2 percent oxygen.

Botulinum spores are on most fresh food surfaces. Because they grow only in the absence of air, they are harmless on fresh foods.

Most bacteria, yeasts, and molds are difficult to remove from food surfaces. Washing fresh food reduces their numbers only slightly. Peeling root crops, underground stem crops, and tomatoes reduces their numbers greatly. Blanching also helps, but the vital controls are the method of canning and making sure the recommended research-based process times, found in these guides, are used.

The processing times in these guides ensure destruction of the largest expected number of heat-resistant microorganisms in home-canned foods. Properly sterilized canned food will be free of spoilage if lids seal and jars are stored below 95°F. Storing jars at 50° to 70°F enhances retention of quality.

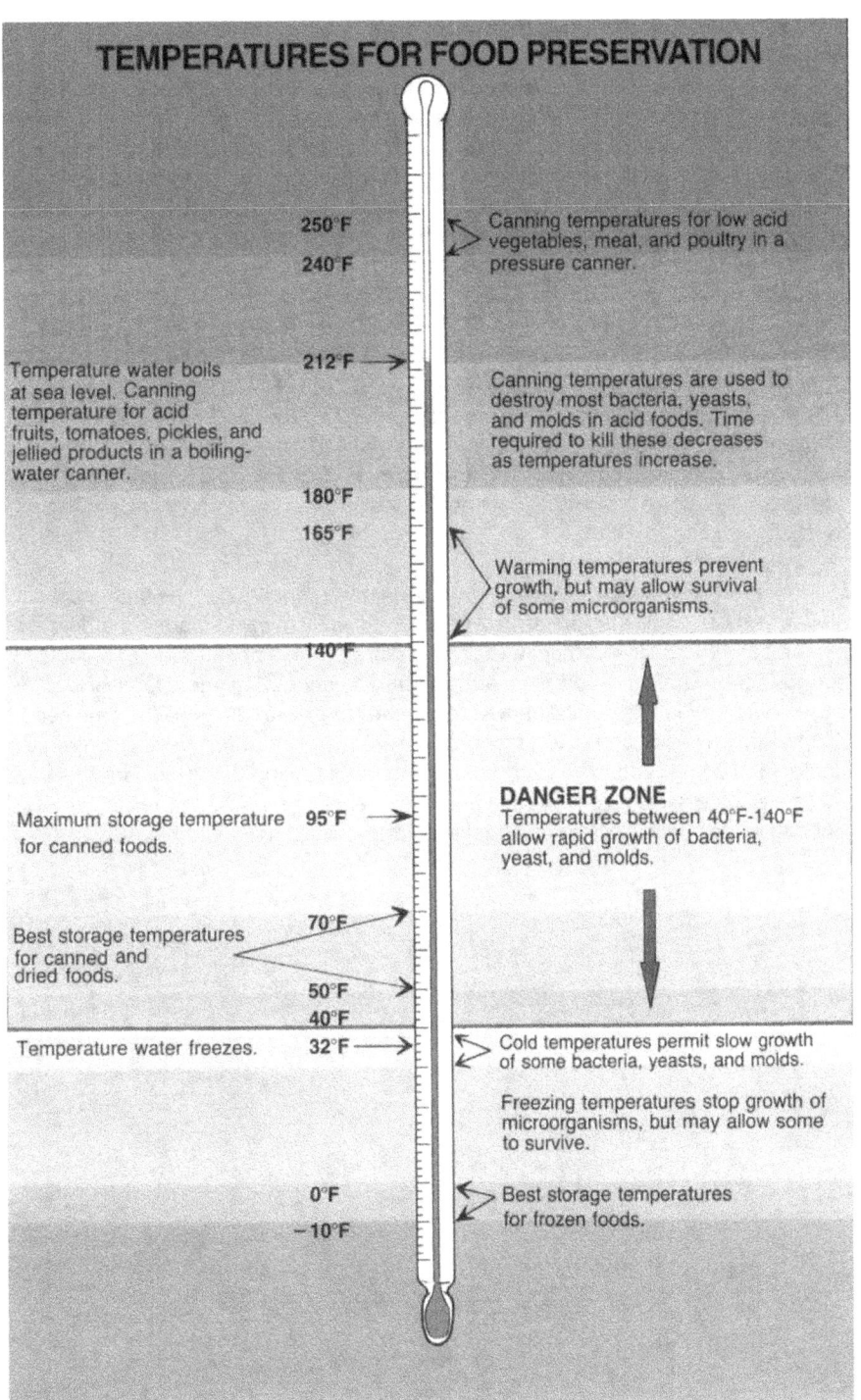

Food acidity and processing methods

Whether food should be processed in a pressure canner or boiling-water canner to control botulinum bacteria depends on the acidity of the food. Acidity may be natural, as in most fruits, or added, as in pickled food. *Low-acid* canned foods are not acidic enough to prevent the growth of these bacteria. *Acid* foods contain enough acid to block their growth, or destroy them more rapidly when heated. The term "pH" is a measure of acidity; the lower its value, the more acid the food. The acidity level in foods can be increased by adding lemon juice, citric acid, or vinegar.

Low-acid foods have pH values higher than 4.6. They include red meats, seafood, poultry, milk, and all fresh vegetables except for most tomatoes. Most mixtures of low-acid and acid foods also have pH values above 4.6 unless their recipes include enough lemon juice, citric acid, or vinegar to make them acid foods. Acid foods have a pH of 4.6 or lower. They include fruits, pickles, sauerkraut, jams, jellies, marmalades, and fruit butters.

Although tomatoes usually are considered an acid food, some are now known to have pH values slightly above 4.6. Figs also have pH values slightly above 4.6. Therefore, if they are to be canned as acid foods, these products must be acidified to a pH of 4.6 or lower with lemon juice or citric acid. Properly acidified tomatoes and figs are acid foods and can be safely processed in a boiling-water canner.

Botulinum spores are very hard to destroy at boiling-water temperatures; the higher the canner temperature, the more easily they are destroyed. Therefore, all low-acid foods should be sterilized at temperatures of 240° to 250°F, attainable with pressure canners operated at 10 to 15 PSIG. PSIG means pounds per square inch of pressure as measured by gauge. The more familiar "PSI" designation is used hereafter in this publication. At temperatures of 240° to 250°F, the time needed to destroy bacteria in low-acid canned food ranges from 20 to 100 minutes. The exact time depends on the kind of food being canned, the way it is packed into jars, and the size of jars. The time needed to safely process low-acid foods in a boiling-water canner ranges from 7 to 11 hours; the time needed to process acid foods in boiling water varies from 5 to 85 minutes.

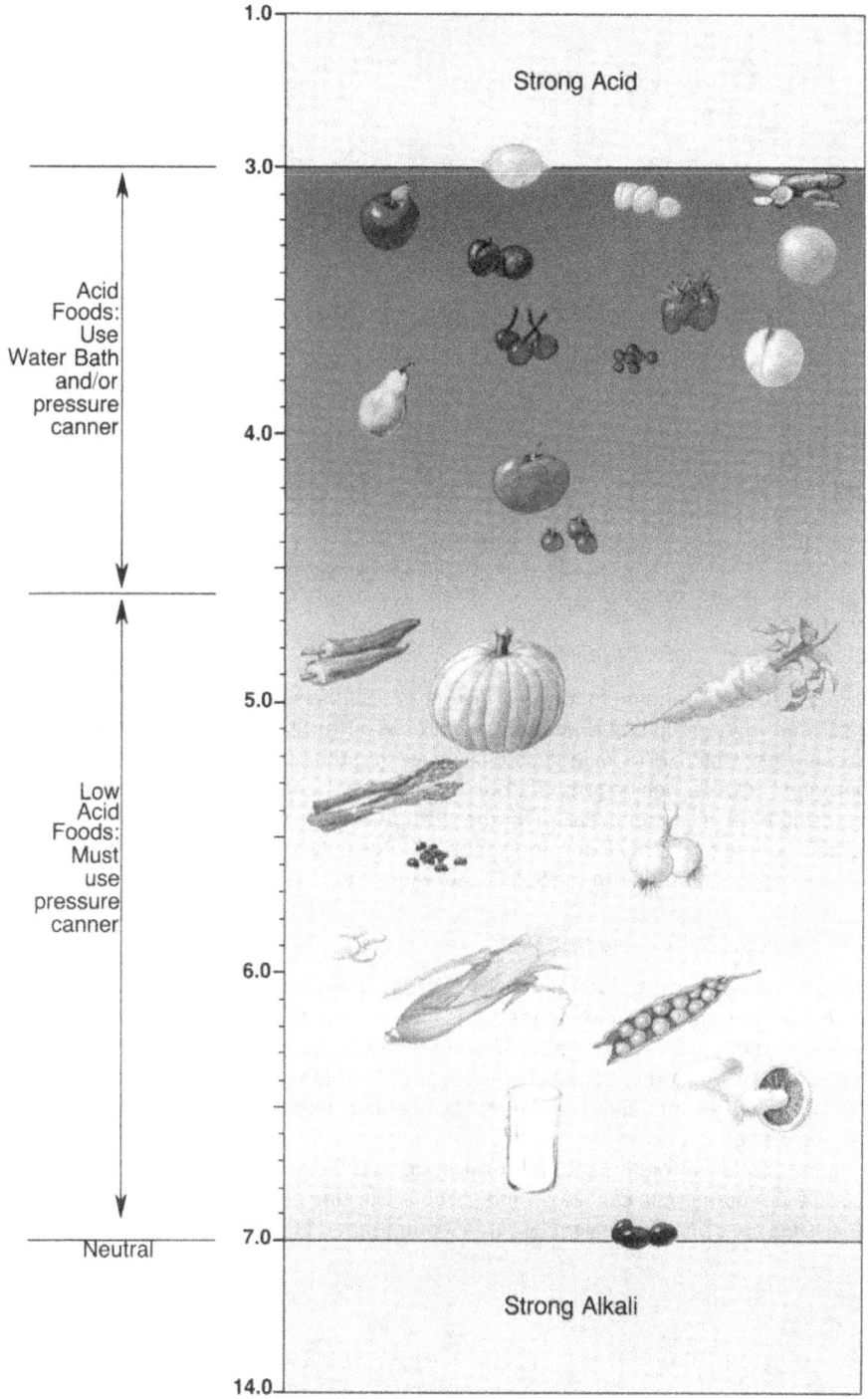

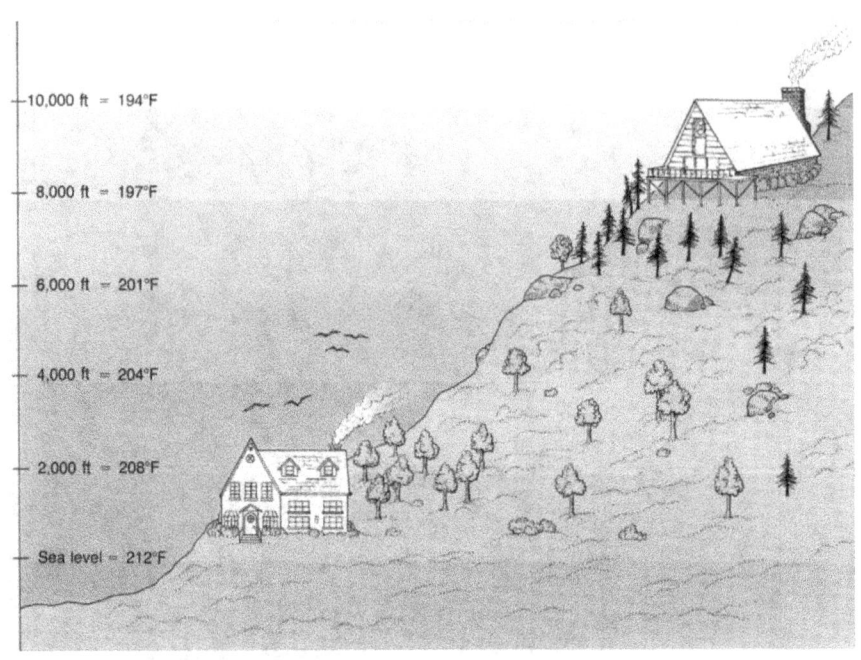

Process adjustments at high altitudes

Using the process time for canning food at sea level may result in spoilage if you live at altitudes of 1,000 feet or more. Water boils at lower temperatures as altitude increases. Lower boiling temperatures are less effective for killing bacteria. Increasing the process time or canner pressure compensates for lower boiling temperatures. Therefore, when you use the guides, select the proper processing time or canner pressure for the altitude where you live. If you do not know the altitude, contact your local county Extension agent. An alternative source of information would be the local district conservationist with the Soil Conservation Service.

Equipment and methods not recommended

Open-kettle canning and the processing of freshly filled jars in conventional ovens, microwave ovens, and dishwashers are not recommended, because these practices do not prevent all risks of spoilage. Steam canners are not currently recommended because processing times for use with current models are still being researched. It is not recommended that pressure processes in excess of 15 PSI be applied when using new pressure canning equipment. So-called canning powders are useless as preservatives and do not replace the need for proper heat processing. Jars with wire bails and glass caps make attractive antiques or storage containers for dry food ingredients but are not recommended for use in canning. Neither one-piece zinc porcelain-lined caps nor zinc caps that use flat rubber rings for sealing jars are recommended any longer.

Ensuring high-quality canned foods

Begin with good-quality fresh foods suitable for canning. Quality varies among varieties of fruits and vegetables. Many county Extension offices can recommend varieties best suited for canning. Examine food carefully for freshness and wholesomeness. Discard diseased and moldy food. Trim small diseased lesions or spots from food.

Can fruits and vegetables picked from your garden or purchased from nearby producers when the products are at their peak of quality-within 6 to 12 hours after harvest for most vegetables. For best quality, apricots, nectarines, peaches, pears, and plums should be ripened 1 or more days between harvest and canning. If you must delay the canning of other fresh produce, keep it in a shady, cool place.

Fresh home-slaughtered red meats and poultry should be chilled and canned without delay. Do not can meat from sickly or diseased animals. Ice fish and seafoods after harvest, eviscerate immediately, and can them within 2 days.

Maintaining color and flavor in canned food

To maintain good natural color and flavor in stored canned food, you must:
- Remove oxygen from food tissues and jars,
- Quickly destroy the food enzymes,
- Obtain high jar vacuums and airtight jar seals.

Follow these guidelines to ensure that your canned foods retain optimum colors and flavors during processing and storage:
- Use only high-quality foods which are at the proper maturity and are free of diseases and bruises.
- Use the hot-pack method, especially with acid foods to be processed in boiling water.
- Don't unnecessarily expose prepared foods to air. Can them as soon as possible.
- While preparing a canner load of jars, keep peeled, halved, quartered, sliced, or diced apples, apricots, nectarines, peaches, and pears in a solution of 3 grams (3,000 milligrams) ascorbic acid to 1 gallon of cold water. This procedure is also useful in maintaining the natural color of mushrooms and potatoes, and for preventing stem-end discoloration in cherries and grapes. You can get ascorbic acid in several forms:

   Pure powdered form—seasonally available among canners' supplies in supermarkets. One level teaspoon of pure powder weighs about 3 grams. Use 1 teaspoon per gallon of water as a treatment solution.

   Vitamin C tablets—economical and available year-round in many stores. Buy 500-milligram tablets; crush and dissolve six tablets per gallon of water as a treatment solution.

   Commercially prepared mixes of ascorbic and citric acid—seasonally available among canners' supplies in supermarkets. Sometimes citric acid powder is sold in supermarkets, but it is less effective in controlling discoloration. If you choose to use these products, follow the manufacturer's directions.

- Fill hot foods into jars and adjust headspace as specified in recipes.
- Tighten screw bands securely, but if you are especially strong, not as tightly as possible.
- Process and cool jars.
- Store the jars in a relatively cool, dark place, preferably between 50° and 70°F.
- Can no more food than you will use within a year.

Advantages of hot-packing

Many fresh foods contain from 10 percent to more than 30 percent air. How long canned food retains high quality depends on how much air is removed from food before jars are sealed.

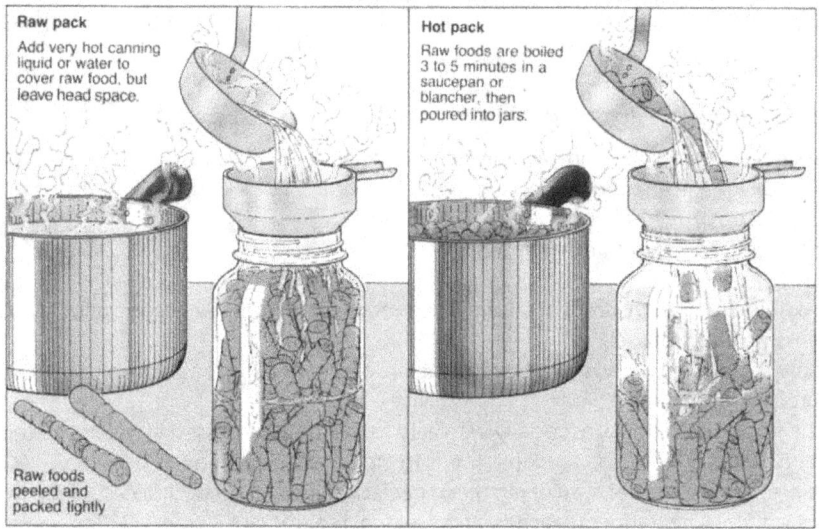

Raw-packing is the practice of filling jars tightly with freshly prepared, but unheated food. Such foods, especially fruit, will float in the jars. The entrapped air in and around the food may cause discoloration within 2 to 3 months of storage. Raw-packing is more suitable for vegetables processed in a pressure canner.

Hot-packing is the practice of heating freshly prepared food to boiling, simmering it 2 to 5 minutes, and promptly filling jars loosely with the boiled food. Whether food has been hot-packed or raw-packed, the juice, syrup, or water to be added to the foods should also be heated to boiling before adding it to the jars. This practice helps to remove air from food tissues, shrinks food, helps keep the food from floating in the jars, increases vacuum in sealed jars, and improves shelf life. Preshrinking food permits filling more food into each jar.

Hot-packing is the best way to remove air and is the preferred pack style for foods processed in a boiling-water canner. At first, the color of hot-packed foods may appear no better than that of raw-packed foods, but within a short storage period, both color and flavor of hot-packed foods will be superior.

Controlling headspace

The unfilled space above the food in a jar and below its lid is termed headspace. Directions for canning specify leaving 1/4-inch for jams and jellies, 1/2-inch for fruits and tomatoes to be processed in boiling water, and from 1- to 1-1/4-inches in low acid foods to be processed in a pressure canner. This space is needed for expansion of food as jars are processed, and for forming vacuums in cooled jars. The extent of expansion is determined by the air content in the food and by the processing temperature. Air expands greatly when heated to high temperatures; the higher the temperature, the greater the expansion. Foods expand less than air when heated.

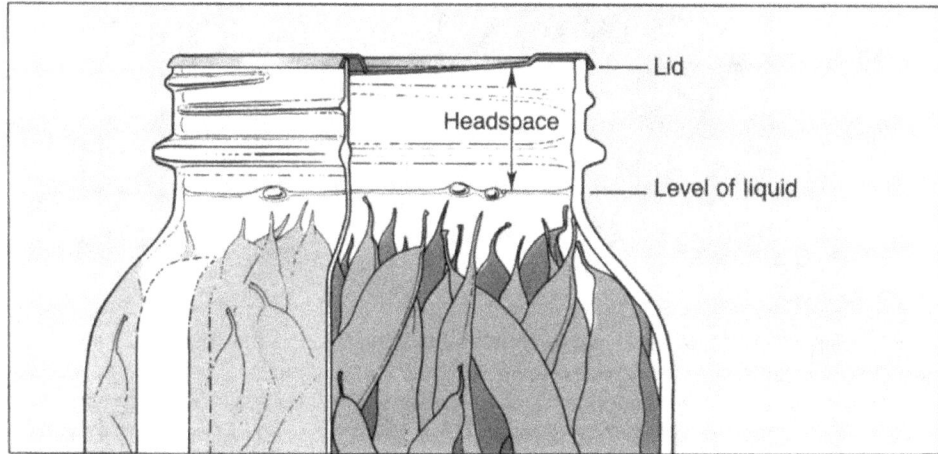

Jars and lids

Food may be canned in glass jars or metal containers. Metal containers can be used only once. They require special sealing equipment and are much more costly than jars.

Regular and wide-mouth Mason-type, threaded, home-canning jars with self-sealing lids are the best choice. They are available in 1/2 pint, pint, 1-1/2 pint, quart, and 1/2 gallon sizes. The standard jar mouth opening is about 2-3/8 inches. Wide-mouth jars have openings of about 3 inches, making them more easily filled and emptied. Half-gallon jars may be used for canning very acid juices. Regular-mouth decorator jelly jars are available in 8 and 12 ounce sizes. With careful use and handling, Mason jars may be reused many times, requiring only new lids each time. When jars and lids are used properly, jar seals and vacuums are excellent and jar breakage is rare.

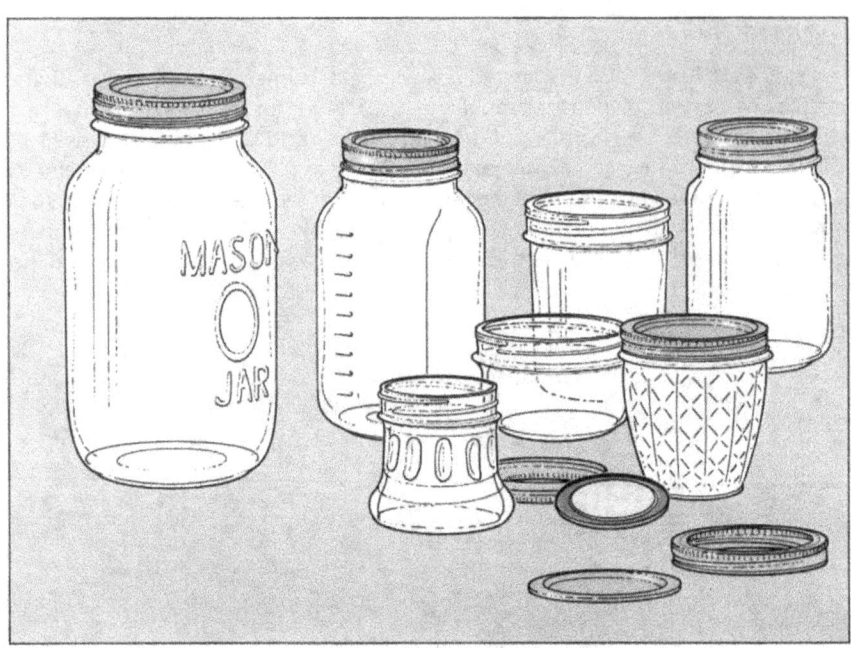

Most commercial pint- and quart-size mayonnaise or salad dressing jars may be used with new two-piece lids for canning acid foods. However, you should expect more seal failures and jar breakage. These jars have a narrower sealing surface and are tempered less than Mason jars, and may be weakened by repeated contact with metal spoons or knives used in dispensing mayonnaise or salad dressing. Seemingly insignificant scratches in glass may cause cracking and breakage while processing jars in a canner. Mayonnaise-type jars are not recommended for use with foods to be processed in a pressure canner because of excessive jar breakage. Other commercial jars with mouths that cannot be sealed with two-piece canning lids are not recommended for use in canning any food at home.

Jar cleaning and preparation

Before every use, wash empty jars in hot water with detergent and rinse well by hand, or wash in a dishwasher. Unrinsed detergent residues may cause unnatural flavors and colors. Jars should be kept hot until ready to fill with food. Submerge the clean empty jars in enough water to cover them in a large stockpot or boiling water canner. Bring the water to a simmer (180°F) and keep the jars in the simmering water until it is time to fill them with food. A dishwasher may be used for preheating jars if they are washed and dried on a complete regular cycle. Keep the jars in the closed dishwasher until needed for filling.

These washing and preheating methods do not sterilize jars. Some used jars may have a white film on the exterior surface caused by mineral deposits. This scale or hard-water film on jars is easily removed by soaking jars several hours in a solution containing 1 cup of vinegar (5 percent acidity) per gallon of water prior to washing and preheating the jars.

Sterilization of empty jars

All jams, jellies, and pickled products processed less than 10 minutes should be filled into sterile empty jars. To sterilize empty jars after washing in detergent and rinsing thoroughly, submerge them, right side up, in a boiling-water canner with the rack in the bottom. Fill the canner with enough warm water so it is 1 inch above the tops of the jars. Bring the water to a boil, and boil 10 minutes at altitudes of less than 1,000 ft. At higher elevations, boil 1 additional minute for each additional 1,000 ft elevation. Reduce the heat under the canner, and keep the jars in the hot water until it is time to fill them. Remove and drain hot sterilized jars one at a time, saving the hot water in the canner for processing filled jars. Fill the sterilized jars with food, add lids, and tighten screw bands.

Empty jars used for vegetables, meats, and fruits to be processed in a pressure canner need not be presterilized. It is also unnecessary to presterilize jars for fruits, tomatoes, and pickled or fermented foods that will be processed 10 minutes or longer in a boiling-water canner.

Lid selection, preparation, and use

The common self-sealing lid consists of a flat metal lid held in place by a metal screw band during processing. The flat lid is crimped around its bottom edge to form a trough, which is filled with a colored gasket compound. When jars are processed, the lid gasket softens and flows slightly to cover the jar-sealing surface, yet allows air to escape from the jar. The gasket then forms an airtight seal as the jar cools. Gaskets in unused lids work well for at least 5 years from date of manufacture. The gasket compound in older unused lids may fail to seal on jars.

Buy only the quantity of lids you will use in a year. To ensure a good seal, carefully follow the manufacturer's directions in preparing lids for use. Examine all metal lids carefully. Do not use old, dented, or deformed lids, or lids with gaps or other defects in the sealing gasket.

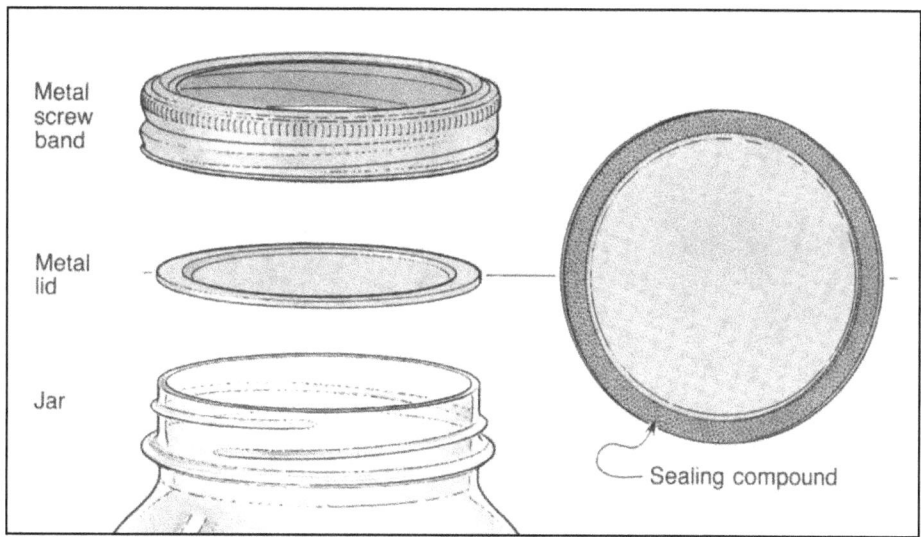

When directions say to fill jars and adjust lids, use the following procedures: After filling jars with food and adding covering liquid, release air bubbles by inserting a flat plastic (not metal) spatula between the food and the jar. Slowly turn the jar and move the spatula up and down to allow air bubbles to escape. (It is not necessary to release air bubbles when filling jams, jellies or all liquid foods such as juices.) Adjust the headspace and then clean the jar rim (sealing surface) with a dampened paper towel. Place the preheated lid, gasket down, onto the cleaned jar-sealing surface. Uncleaned jar-sealing surfaces may cause seal failures. Then fit the metal screw band over the flat lid. Follow the manufacturer's guidelines enclosed with or on the box for tightening the jar lids properly.

Do not retighten lids after processing jars. As jars cool, the contents in the jar contract, pulling the self-sealing lid firmly against the jar to form a high vacuum.

- If rings are too loose, liquid may escape from jars during processing, and seals may fail.
- If rings are too tight, air cannot vent during processing, and food will discolor during storage. Over tightening also may cause lids to buckle and jars to break, especially with raw-packed, pressure-processed food.

Screw bands are not needed on stored jars. They can be removed easily after jars are cooled. When removed, washed, dried, and stored in a dry area, screw bands may be used many times. If left on stored jars, they become difficult to remove, often rust, and may not work properly again.

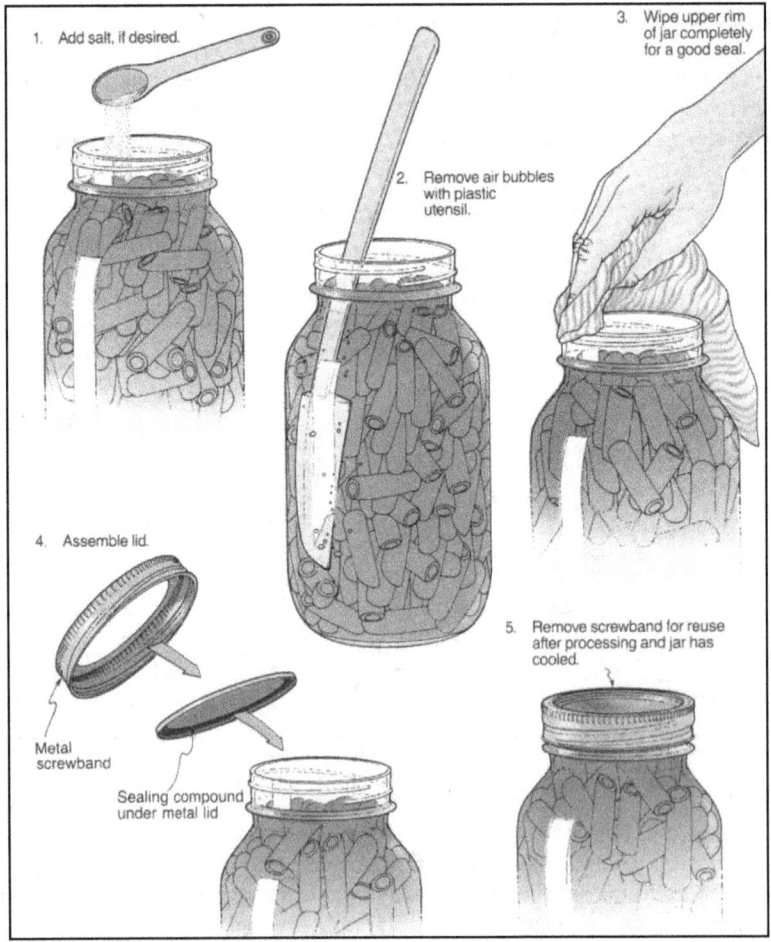

Recommended canners

Equipment for heat-processing home-canned food is of two main types—boiling water canners and pressure canners. Most are designed to hold seven quart jars or eight to nine pints. Small pressure canners hold four-quart jars; some large pressure canners hold 18 pint jars in two layers, but hold only seven quart jars. Pressure saucepans with smaller volume capacities are not recommended for use in canning. Small capacity pressure canners are treated in a similar manner as standard larger canners, and should be vented using the typical venting procedures.

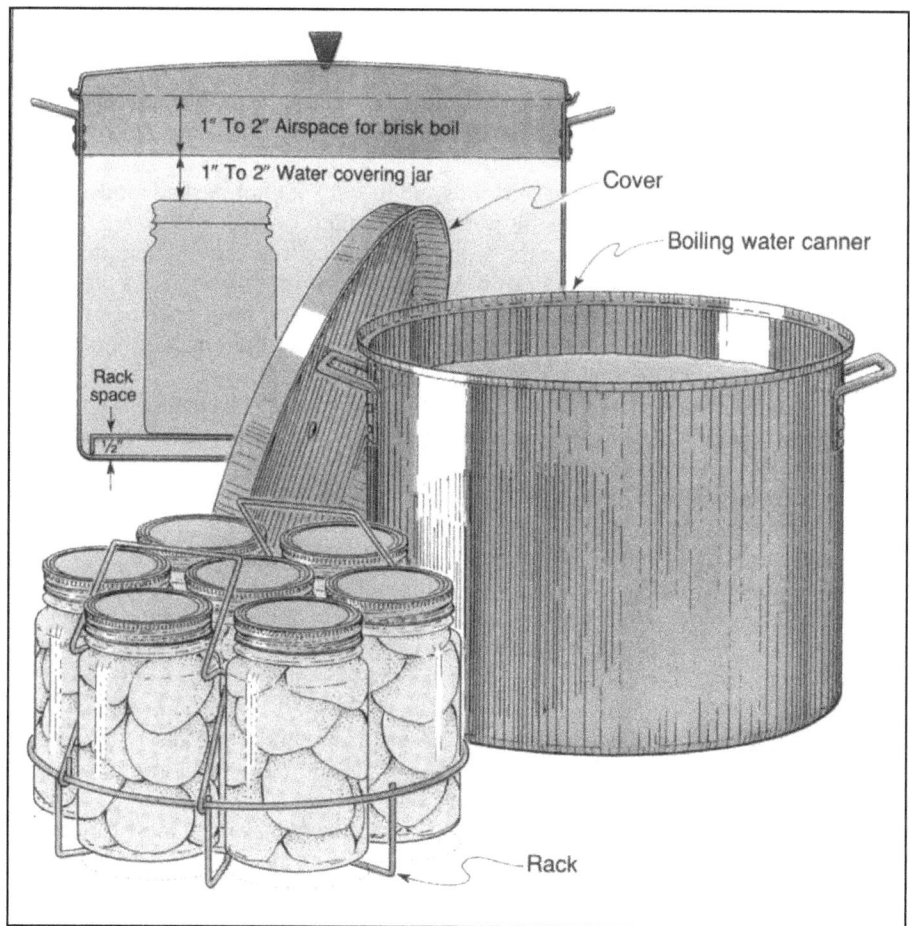

Low-acid foods must be processed in a pressure canner to be free of botulism risks. Although pressure canners may also be used for processing acid foods, boiling water canners are recommended for this purpose because they are faster. A pressure canner would require from 55 to 100 minutes to process a load of jars; while the total time for processing most acid foods in boiling water varies from 25 to 60 minutes. A boiling-water canner loaded with filled jars requires about 20 to 30 minutes of heating before its water begins to boil. A loaded pressure canner requires about 12 to 15 minutes of heating before it begins to vent; another 10 minutes to vent the canner; another 5 minutes to pressurize the canner; another 8 to 10 minutes to process the acid food; and, finally, another 20 to 60 minutes to cool the canner before removing jars.

Boiling-water canners

These canners are made of aluminum or porcelain-covered steel. They have removable perforated racks and fitted lids. The canner must be deep enough so that at least 1 inch of briskly boiling water will be over the tops of jars during processing. Some boiling-water canners do not have flat bottoms. A flat bottom must be used on an electric range. Either a flat or ridged bottom can be used on a gas burner. To ensure uniform processing of all jars with an electric range, the canner should be no more than 4 inches wider in diameter than the element on which it is heated.

Using boiling-water canners

Follow these steps for successful boiling-water canning:
1. Before you start preparing your food, fill the canner halfway with clean water. This is approximately the level needed for a canner load of pint jars. For other sizes and numbers of jars, the amount of water in the canner will need to be adjusted so it will be 1 to 2 inches over the top of the filled jars.
2. Preheat water to 140°F for raw-packed foods and to 180°F for hot-packed foods. Food preparation can begin while this water is preheating.
3. Load filled jars, fitted with lids, into the canner rack and use the handles to lower the rack into the water; or fill the canner with the rack in the bottom, one jar at a time, using a jar lifter. When using a jar lifter, make sure it is securely positioned below the neck of the jar (below the screw band of the lid). Keep the jar upright at all times. Tilting the jar could cause food to spill into the sealing area of the lid.
4. Add more boiling water, if needed, so the water level is at least 1 inch above jar tops. For process times over 30 minutes, the water level should be at least 2 inches above the tops of the jars.
5. Turn heat to its highest position, cover the canner with its lid, and heat until the water in the canner boils vigorously.
6. Set a timer for the total minutes required for processing the food.
7. Keep the canner covered and maintain a boil throughout the process schedule. The heat setting may be lowered a little as long as a complete boil is maintained for the entire process time. If the water stops boiling at any time during the process, bring the water back to a vigorous boil and begin the timing of the process over, from the beginning.
8. Add more boiling water, if needed, to keep the water level above the jars.
9. When jars have been boiled for the recommended time, turn off the heat and remove the canner lid. Wait 5 minutes before removing jars.
10. Using a jar lifter, remove the jars and place them on a towel, leaving at least 1-inch spaces between the jars during cooling. Let jars sit undisturbed to cool at room temperature for 12 to 24 hours.

Pressure canners

Pressure canners for use in the home have been extensively redesigned in recent years. Models made before the 1970's were heavy-walled kettles with clamp-on or turn-on lids. They were fitted with a dial gauge, a vent port in the form of a petcock or counterweight, and a safety fuse. Modern pressure canners are lightweight, thin walled kettles; most have turn-on lids. They have a jar rack, gasket, dial or weighted gauge, an automatic vent/cover lock, a vent port (steam vent) to be closed with a counterweight or weighted gauge, and a safety fuse.

Pressure does not destroy microorganisms, but high temperatures applied for an adequate period of time do kill microorganisms. The success of destroying all microorganisms capable of growing in canned food is based on the temperature obtained in pure steam, free of air, at sea level. At sea level, a canner operated at a gauge pressure of 10.5 lbs provides an internal temperature of 240°F.

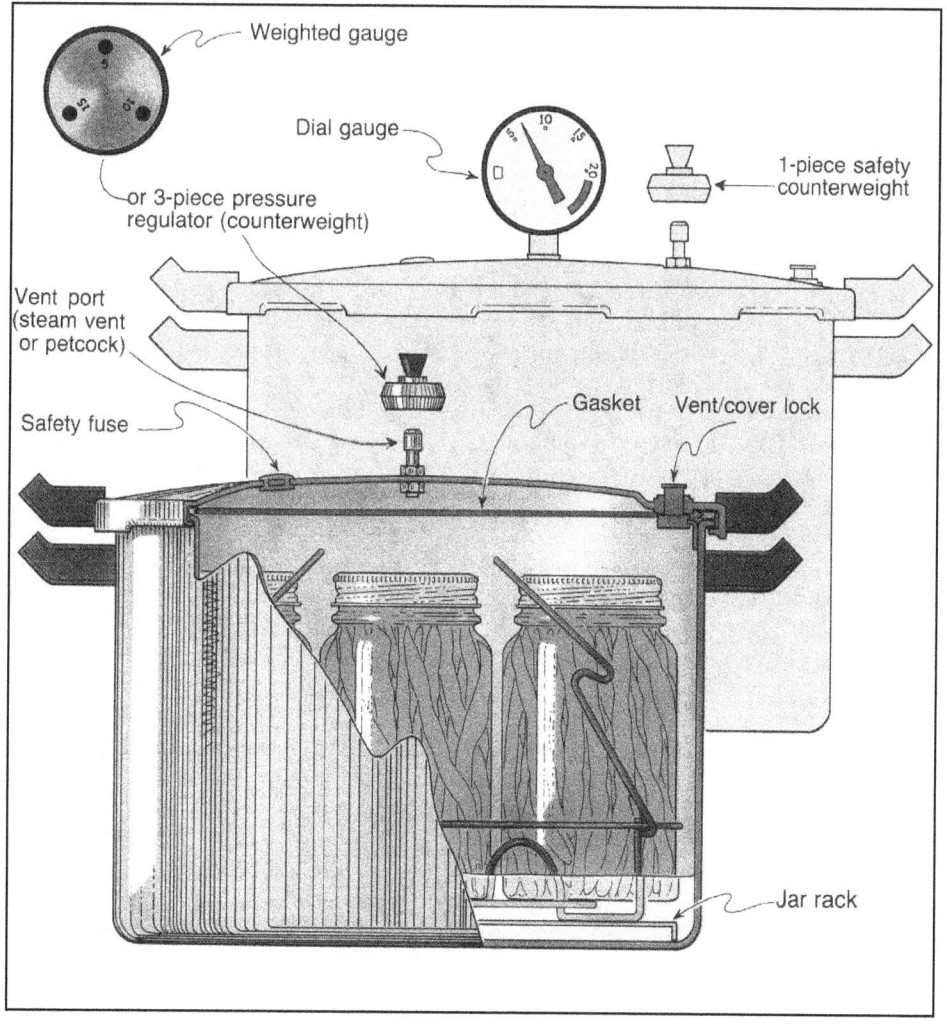

Two serious errors in temperatures obtained in pressure canners occur because:

1. **Internal canner temperatures are lower at higher altitudes.** To correct this error, canners must be operated at the increased pressures specified in this publication for appropriate altitude ranges.

2. **Air trapped in a canner lowers the temperature obtained at 5, 10, or 15 pounds of pressure and results in under processing.** The highest volume of air trapped in a canner occurs in processing raw-packed foods in dial-gauge canners. These canners do not vent air during processing. To be safe, all types of pressure canners must be vented 10 minutes before they are pressurized.

To vent a canner, leave the vent port uncovered on newer models or manually open petcocks on some older models. Heating the filled canner with its lid locked into place boils water and generates steam that escapes through the petcock or vent port. When steam first escapes, set a timer for 10 minutes. After venting 10 minutes, close the petcock or place the counterweight or weighted gauge over the vent port to pressurize the canner.

Weighted-gauge models exhaust tiny amounts of air and steam each time their gauge rocks or jiggles during processing. They control pressure precisely and need neither watching during processing nor checking for accuracy. The sound of the weight rocking or jiggling indicates that the canner is maintaining the recommended pressure. The single disadvantage of weighted-gauge canners is that they cannot correct precisely for higher altitudes. At altitudes above 1,000 feet, they must be operated at canner pressures of 10 instead of 5, or 15 instead of 10, PSI.

Check dial gauges for accuracy before use each year. Gauges that read high cause under-processing and may result in unsafe food. Low readings cause over-processing. Pressure adjustments can be made if the gauge reads up to 2 pounds high or low. Replace gauges that differ by more than 2 pounds. Every pound of pressure is very important to the temperature needed inside the canner for producing safe food, so accurate gauges and adjustments are essential when a gauge reads higher than it should. If a gauge is reading lower than it should, adjustments may be made to avoid overprocessing, but are not essential to safety. Gauges may be checked at many county Cooperative Extension offices or contact the pressure canner manufacturer for other options.

Handle canner lid gaskets carefully and clean them according to the manufacturer's directions. Nicked or dried gaskets will allow steam leaks during pressurization of canners. Keep gaskets clean between uses. Gaskets on older model canners may require a light coat of vegetable oil once per year. Gaskets on newer model canners are pre-lubricated and do not benefit from oiling. Check your canner's instructions if there is doubt that the particular gasket you use has been pre-lubricated.

Lid safety fuses are thin metal inserts or rubber plugs designed to relieve excessive pressure from the canner. Do not pick at or scratch fuses while cleaning lids. Use only canners that have the Underwriter's Laboratory (UL) approval to ensure their safety.

Replacement gauges and other parts for canners are often available at stores offering canning equipment or from canner manufacturers. When ordering parts, give your canner model number and describe the parts needed.

Using pressure canners

Follow these steps for successful pressure canning:

1. Put 2 to 3 inches of hot water in the canner. Some specific products in this Guide require that you start with even more water in the canner. Always follow the directions with USDA processes for specific foods if they require more water added to the canner. Place filled jars on the rack, using a jar lifter. When using a jar lifter, make sure it is securely positioned below the neck of the jar (below the screw band of the lid). Keep the jar upright at all times. Tilting the jar could cause food to spill into the sealing are of the lid. Fasten canner lid securely.
2. Leave weight off vent port or open petcock. Heat at the highest setting until steam flows freely from the open petcock or vent port.

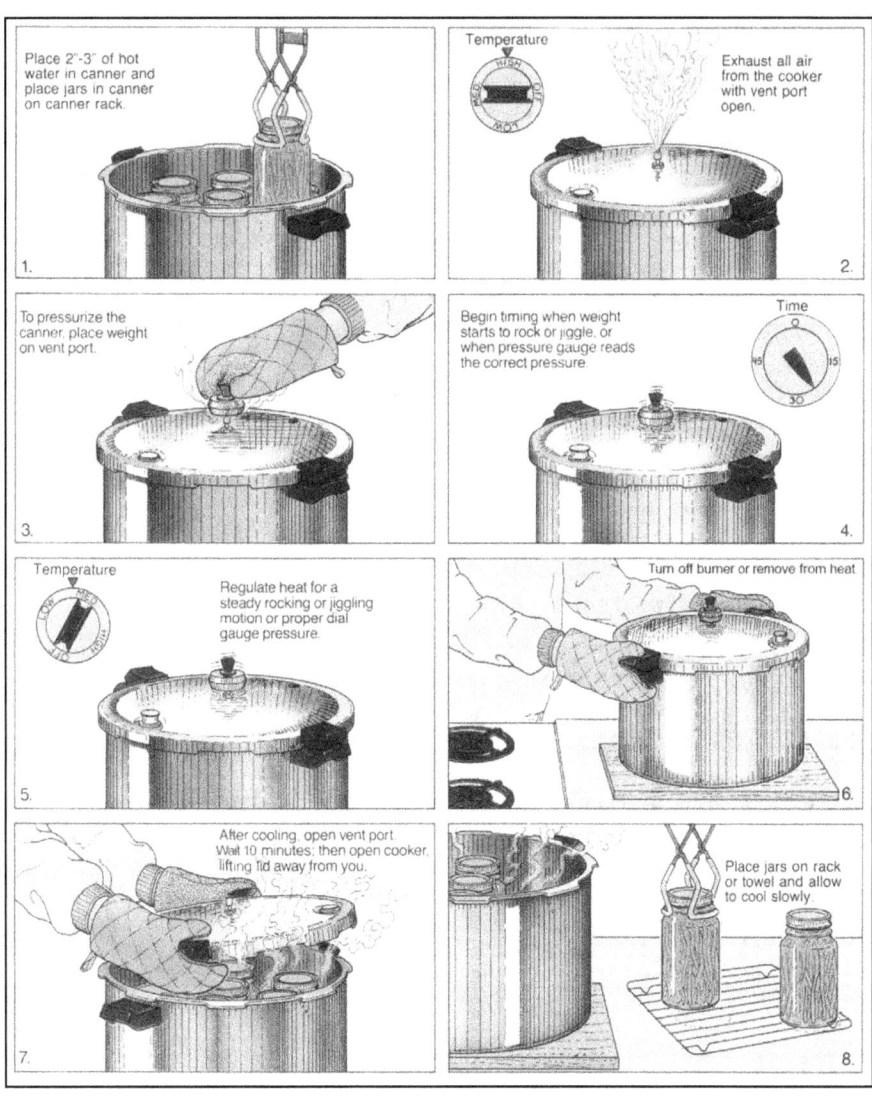

3. While maintaining the high heat setting, let the steam flow (exhaust) continuously for 10 minutes, and then place the weight on the vent port or close the petcock. The canner will pressurize during the next 3 to 5 minutes.
4. Start timing the process when the pressure reading on the dial gauge indicates that the recommended pressure has been reached, or when the weighted gauge begins to jiggle or rock as the canner manufacturer describes.
5. Regulate heat under the canner to maintain a steady pressure at or slightly above the correct gauge pressure. Quick and large pressure variations during processing may cause unnecessary liquid losses from jars. Follow the canner manufacturer's directions for how a weighted gauge should indicate it is maintaining the desired pressure.

   IMPORTANT: If at any time pressure goes below the recommended amount, bring the canner back to pressure and begin the timing of the process over, from the beginning (using the total original process time). This is important for the safety of the food.

6. When the timed process is completed, turn off the heat, remove the canner from heat if possible, and let the canner depressurize. **Do not force-cool the canner.** Forced cooling may result in unsafe food or food spoilage. Cooling the canner with cold running water or opening the vent port before the canner is fully depressurized will cause loss of liquid from jars and seal failures. Force-cooling may also warp the canner lid of older model canners, causing steam leaks. Depressurization of older models without dial gauges should be timed. Standard-size heavy-walled canners require about 30 minutes when loaded with pints and 45 minutes with quarts. Newer thin-walled canners cool more rapidly and are equipped with vent locks. These canners are depressurized when their vent lock piston drops to a normal position.
7. After the canner is depressurized, remove the weight from the vent port or open the petcock. Wait 10 minutes, unfasten the lid, and remove it carefully. Lift the lid away from you so that the steam does not burn your face.
8. Remove jars with a jar lifter, and place them on a towel, leaving at least 1-inch spaces between the jars during cooling. Let jars sit undisturbed to cool at room temperature for 12 to 24 hours.

Selecting the correct processing time

When canning in boiling water, more processing time is needed for most raw-packed foods and for quart jars than is needed for hot-packed foods and pint jars.

To destroy microorganisms in acid foods processed in a boiling-water canner, you must:

- Process jars for the correct number of minutes in boiling water.
- Cool the jars at room temperature.

The food may spoil if you fail to add process time for lower boiling-water temperatures at altitudes above 1,000 feet, process for fewer minutes than specified, or cool jars in cold water.

To destroy microorganisms in low-acid foods processed with a pressure canner, you must:

- Process the jars using the correct time and pressure specified for your altitude.
- Allow canner to cool at room temperature until it is completely depressurized.

The food may spoil if you fail to select the proper process times for specific altitudes, fail to exhaust canners properly, process at lower pressure than specified, process for fewer minutes than specified, or cool the canner with water.

Using tables for determining proper process times

This set of guides includes processing times with altitude adjustments for each product. Process times for 1/2-pint and pint jars are the same, as are times for 1-1/2 pint and quart jars. For some products, you have a choice of processing at 5, 10, or 15 PSI. In these cases, choose the canner pressure you wish to use and match it with your pack style (raw or hot) and jar size to find the correct process time. The following examples show how to select the proper process for each type of canner. Process times are given in separate tables for sterilizing jars in boiling-water, dial-gauge, and weighted-gauge pressure canners.

Example A: Boiling-water Canner

Suppose you are canning peaches as a hot-pack in quarts at 2,500 ft above sea level, using a *boiling-water canner*. First, select the process table for boiling-water canner. The example for peaches is given in **Table for Example A** below. From that table, select the process time given for (1) the style of pack (hot), (2) the jar size (quarts), and (3) the altitude where you live (2,500 ft). You should have selected a process time of 30 minutes.

Table for Example A
Recommended process time for Peaches in a boiling-water canner

Style of Pack	Jar Size	Process Time at Altitudes of			
		0–1,000 ft	1,001–3,000 ft	3,001–6,000 ft	Above 6,000 ft
Hot	Pints	20 min	25 min	30 min	35 min
	Quarts	25	30	35	40
Raw	Pints	25	30	35	40
	Quarts	30	35	40	45

Example B: Dial-gauge Pressure Canner

Suppose you are canning peaches as a hot-pack in quarts at 2,500 ft above sea level, using a *dial-gauge pressure canner*. First, select the process table for dial-gauge pressure canner. The example for peaches is given in **Table for Example B** below. From that table, select the process pressure (PSI) given for (1) the style of pack (hot), (2) the jar size (quarts), (3) the process time (10 minutes), (4) the altitude where you live (2,500 ft). You should have selected a pressure of 7 lbs for the 10 minutes process time.

Table for Example B
Recommended process time for Peaches in a dial-gauge pressure canner

Style of Pack	Jar Size	Process Time	Canner Pressure (PSI) at Altitudes of			
			0–2,000 ft	2,001–4,000 ft	4,001–6,000 ft	6,001–8,000 ft
Hot and Raw	Pints or Quarts	10 min	6 lb	7 lb	8 lb	9 lb

Example C: Weighted-gauge Pressure Canner

Suppose you are canning peaches as a hot-pack in quarts at 2,500 ft above sea level, using a *weighted-gauge pressure canner*. First, select the process table for weighted-gauge pressure canner. The example for peaches is given in **Table for Example C** below. From that table, select the process pressure (PSI) given for (1) the style of pack (hot), (2) the jar size (quarts), (3) the process time (10 minutes), and (4) the altitude where you live (2,500 ft). You should have selected a pressure of 10 lbs for the 10 minutes process time.

Table for Example C
Recommended process time for Peaches in a weighted-gauge pressure canner

Style of Pack	Jar Size	Process Time	Canner Pressure (PSI) at Altitudes of	
			0–1,000 ft	Above 1,000 ft
Hot and Raw	Pints or Quarts	10 min	5 lb	10 lb

Cooling jars

When you remove hot jars from a canner, do not retighten their jar lids. Retightening of hot lids may cut through the gasket and cause seal failures. Cool the jars at room temperature for 12 to 24 hours. Jars may be cooled on racks or towels to minimize heat damage to counters. The food level and liquid volume of raw-packed jars will be noticeably lower after cooling. Air is exhausted during processing and food shrinks. If a jar loses excessive liquid during processing, do not open it to add more liquid. Check for sealed lids as described below.

Use rack or towel during cooling period.

Testing jar seals

After cooling jars for 12 to 24 hours, remove the screw bands and test seals with one of the following options:

Option 1. Press the middle of the lid with a finger or thumb. If the lid springs up when you release your finger, the lid is unsealed.

Option 2. Tap the lid with the bottom of a teaspoon. If it makes a dull sound, the lid is not sealed. If food is in contact with the underside of the lid, it will also cause a dull sound. If the jar is sealed correctly, it will make a ringing, high-pitched sound.

Option 3. Hold the jar at eye level and look across the lid. The lid should be concave (curved down slightly in the center). If center of the lid is either flat or bulging, it may not be sealed.

Reprocessing unsealed jars

If a lid fails to seal on a jar, remove the lid and check the jar-sealing surface for tiny nicks. If necessary, change the jar, add a new, properly prepared lid, and reprocess within 24 hours using the same processing time. Headspace in unsealed jars may be adjusted to 1-1/2 inches and jars could be frozen instead of reprocessed. Foods in single unsealed jars could be stored in the refrigerator and consumed within several days.

Storing canned foods

If lids are tightly vacuum sealed on cooled jars, remove screw bands, wash the lid and jar to remove food residue; then rinse and dry jars. Label and date the jars and store them in a clean, cool, dark, dry place. Do not store jars above 95°F or near hot pipes, a range, a furnace, under a sink, in an uninsulated attic, or in direct sunlight. Under these conditions, food will lose quality in a few weeks or months and may spoil. Dampness may corrode metal lids, break seals, and allow recontamination and spoilage.

Accidental freezing of canned foods will not cause spoilage unless jars become unsealed and recontaminated. However, freezing and thawing may soften food. If jars must be stored where they may freeze, wrap them in newspapers, place them in heavy cartons, and cover with more newspapers and blankets.

Identifying and handling spoiled canned food

Do not taste food from a jar with an unsealed lid or food that shows signs of spoilage.
You can more easily detect some types of spoilage in jars stored without screw bands. Growth of spoilage bacteria and yeast produces gas which pressurizes the food, swells lids, and breaks jar seals. As each stored jar is selected for use, examine its lid for tightness and vacuum. Lids with concave centers have good seals.

Next, while holding the jar upright at eye level, rotate the jar and examine its outside surface for streaks of dried food originating at the top of the jar. Look at the contents for rising air bubbles and unnatural color.

While opening the jar, smell for unnatural odors and look for spurting liquid and cotton-like mold growth (white, blue, black, or green) on the top food surface and underside of lid.

Spoiled low-acid foods, including tomatoes, may exhibit different kinds of spoilage evidence or very little evidence. Therefore, all suspect containers of spoiled low-acid foods, including tomatoes, should be treated as having produced botulinum toxin and handled carefully in one of two ways:

- If the suspect glass jars or swollen metal cans are still sealed, place them in a heavy garbage bag. Close and place the bag in a regular trash container or dispose in a nearby landfill.
- If the suspect glass jars or cans are unsealed, open, or leaking, they should be detoxified before disposal.

Detoxification process: Wear disposable rubber or heavy plastic gloves. Carefully place the suspect containers and lids on their sides in an 8-quart volume or larger stock pot, pan, or boiling-water canner. Wash your hands with gloves thoroughly. Carefully add water to the pot and avoid splashing the water. The water should completely cover the containers with a minimum of a 1-inch level above the containers. Place a lid on the pot and heat the water to boiling. Boil 30 minutes to ensure detoxifying the food and all container components. Cool and discard the containers, their lids, and food in the trash or dispose in a nearby landfill.

Cleaning up the area: Contact with botulinum toxin can be fatal whether it is ingested or enters through the skin. Take care to avoid contact with suspect foods or liquids. Wear rubber or heavy plastic gloves when handling suspect foods or cleaning up contaminated work surfaces and equipment. A fresh solution of 1 part unscented liquid household chlorine bleach (5 to 6% sodium hypochlorite) to 5 parts clean water should be used to treat work surfaces, equipment, or other items, including can openers and clothing, that may have come in contact with suspect foods or liquids. Spray or wet contaminated surfaces with the bleach solution and let stand for 30 minutes. Wearing gloves, wipe up treated spills with paper towels being careful to minimize the spread of contamination. Dispose of these paper towels by placing them in a plastic bag before putting them in the trash. Next, apply the bleach solution to all surfaces and equipment again, and let stand for 30 minutes and rinse. As a last step, thoroughly wash all detoxified counters, containers, equipment, clothing, etc. Discard gloves when cleaning process is complete. (Note: Bleach is an irritant itself and should not be inhaled or allowed to come in contact with the skin.)

Preparing pickled and fermented foods

The many varieties of pickled and fermented foods are classified by ingredients and method of preparation.

Regular dill pickles and sauerkraut are fermented and cured for about 3 weeks. Refrigerator dills are fermented for about 1 week. During curing, colors and flavors change and acidity increases. Fresh-pack or quick-process pickles are not fermented; some are brined several hours or overnight, then drained and covered with vinegar and seasonings. Fruit pickles usually are prepared by heating fruit in a seasoned syrup acidified with either lemon juice or vinegar. Relishes are made from chopped fruits and vegetables that are cooked with seasonings and vinegar.

Be sure to remove and discard a 1/16-inch slice from the blossom end of fresh cucumbers. Blossoms may contain an enzyme which causes excessive softening of pickles.

Caution: The level of acidity in a pickled product is as important to its safety as it is to taste and texture.

- **Do not alter vinegar, food, or water proportions in a recipe or use a vinegar with unknown acidity.**
- **Use only recipes with tested proportions of ingredients.**
- **There must be a minimum, uniform level of acid throughout the mixed product to prevent the growth of botulinum bacteria.**

Ingredients

Select fresh, firm fruits or vegetables free of spoilage. Measure or weigh amounts carefully, because the proportion of fresh food to other ingredients will affect flavor and, in many instances, safety.

Use canning or pickling salt. Noncaking material added to other salts may make the brine cloudy. Since flake salt varies in density, it is not recommended for making pickled and fermented foods. White granulated and brown sugars are most often used. Corn syrup and honey, unless called for in reliable recipes, may produce undesirable flavors. White distilled and cider vinegars of 5 percent acidity (50 grain) are recommended. White vinegar is usually preferred when light color is desirable, as is the case with fruits and cauliflower.

Pickles with reduced salt content

Recipes for pickles with reduced sodium content are provided in Guide 6.

In the making of fresh-pack pickles, cucumbers are acidified quickly with vinegar. Use only tested recipes formulated to produce the proper acidity. While these pickles may be prepared safely with reduced or no salt, their quality may be noticeably lower. Both texture and flavor may be slightly, but noticeably, different than expected. You may wish to make small quantities first to determine if you like them.

However, the salt used in making fermented sauerkraut and brined pickles not only provides characteristic flavor but also is vital to safety and texture. In fermented foods, salt favors the growth of desirable bacteria while inhibiting the growth of others. **Caution: Do not attempt to make sauerkraut or fermented pickles by cutting back on the salt required.**

Firming agents

Alum may be safely used to firm fermented pickles. However, it is unnecessary and is not included in the recipes in this publication. Alum does not improve the firmness of quick-process pickles. The calcium in lime definitely improves pickle firmness. Food-grade lime may be used as a lime-water solution for soaking fresh cucumbers 12 to 24 hours before pickling them. Excess lime absorbed by the cucumbers must be removed to make safe pickles. To remove excess lime, drain the lime-water solution, rinse, and then resoak the cucumbers in fresh water for 1 hour. Repeat the rinsing and soaking steps two more times. To further improve pickle firmness, you may process cucumber pickles for 30 minutes in water at 180°F. This process also prevents spoilage, **but the water temperature should not fall below 180°F**. Use a candy or jelly thermometer to check the water temperature.

Preventing spoilage

Pickle products are subject to spoilage from microorganisms, particularly yeasts and molds, as well as enzymes that may affect flavor, color, and texture. Processing the pickles in a boiling-water canner will prevent both of these problems. Standard canning jars and self-sealing lids are recommended. Processing times and procedures will vary according to food acidity and the size of food pieces.

Preparing butters, jams, jellies, and marmalades

Sweet spreads are a class of foods with many textures, flavors, and colors. They all consist of fruits preserved mostly by means of sugar and they are thickened or jellied to some extent. Fruit jelly is a semi-solid mixture of fruit juice and sugar that is clear and firm enough to hold its shape. Other spreads are made from crushed or ground fruit.

Jam also will hold its shape, but it is less firm than jelly. Jam is made from crushed or chopped fruits and sugar. Jams made from a mixture of fruits are usually called conserves, especially when they include citrus fruits, nuts, raisins, or coconut. Preserves are made of small, whole fruits or uniform-size pieces of fruits in a clear, thick, slightly jellied syrup. Marmalades are soft fruit jellies with small pieces of fruit or citrus peel evenly suspended in a transparent jelly. Fruit butters are made from fruit pulp cooked with sugar until thickened to a spreadable consistency.

Ingredients

For proper texture, jellied fruit products require the correct combination of fruit, pectin, acid, and sugar. The fruit gives each spread its unique flavor and color. It also supplies the water to dissolve the rest of the necessary ingredients and furnishes some or all of the pectin and acid. Good-quality, flavorful fruits make the best jellied products.

Pectins are substances in fruits that form a gel if they are in the right combination with acid and sugar. All fruits contain some pectin. Apples, crab apples, gooseberries, and some plums and grapes usually contain enough natural pectin to form a gel. Other fruits, such as strawberries, cherries, and blueberries, contain little pectin and must be combined with other fruits high in pectin or with commercial pectin products to obtain gels. Because fully ripened fruit has less pectin, one-fourth of the fruit used in making jellies without added pectin should be underripe.

Caution: Commercially frozen and canned juices may be low in natural pectins and make soft textured spreads.

The proper level of acidity is critical to gel formation. If there is too little acid, the gel will never set; if there is too much acid, the gel will lose liquid (weep). For fruits low in acid, add lemon juice or other acid ingredients as directed. Commercial pectin products contain acids which help to ensure gelling.

Sugar serves as a preserving agent, contributes flavor, and aids in gelling. Cane and beet sugar are the usual sources of sugar for jelly or jam. Corn syrup and honey may be used to replace part of the sugar in recipes, but too much will mask the fruit flavor and alter the gel structure. Use tested recipes for replacing sugar with honey and corn syrup. Do not try to reduce the amount of sugar in traditional recipes. Too little sugar prevents gelling and may allow yeasts and molds to grow.

Jams and jellies with reduced sugar

Jellies and jams that contain modified pectin, gelatin, or gums may be made with noncaloric sweeteners. Jams with less sugar than usual also may be made with concentrated fruit pulp, which contains less liquid and less sugar. See Guide 7 for recipes.

Two types of modified pectin are available for home use. One gels with one-third less sugar. The other is a low-methoxyl pectin which requires a source of calcium for gelling. To prevent spoilage, jars of these products may need to be processed longer in a boiling-water canner. Recipes and processing times provided with each modified pectin product must be followed carefully. The proportions of acids and fruits should not be altered, as spoilage may result. Acceptably gelled refrigerator fruit spreads also may be made with gelatin and sugar substitutes. Such products spoil at room temperature, must be refrigerated, and should be eaten within 1 month.

Preventing spoilage

Even though sugar helps preserve jellies and jams, molds can grow on the surface of these products. Research now indicates that the mold which people usually scrape off the surface of jellies may not be as harmless as it seems. Mycotoxins have been found in some jars of jelly having surface mold growth. Mycotoxins are known to cause cancer in animals; their effects on humans are still being researched. Because of possible mold contamination, paraffin or wax seals are no longer recommended for any sweet spread, including jellies. To prevent growth of molds and loss of good flavor or color, fill products hot into sterile Mason jars, leaving 1/4-inch headspace, seal with self-sealing lids, and process 5 minutes in a boiling-water canner. Correct process time at higher elevations by adding 1 additional minute per 1,000 ft above sea level. If unsterile jars are used, the filled jars should be processed 10 minutes. Use of sterile jars is preferred, especially when fruits are low in pectin, since the added 5-minute process time may cause weak gels. To sterilize empty jars, see page 1-14.

Methods of making jams and jellies

The two basic methods of making jams and jellies are described in Guide 7. The standard method, which does not require added pectin, works best with fruits naturally high in pectin. The other method, which requires the use of commercial liquid or powdered pectin, is much quicker. The gelling ability of various pectins differs. To make uniformly gelled products, be sure to add the quantities of commercial pectins to specific fruits as instructed on each package. Overcooking may break down pectin and prevent proper gelling. When using either method, make one batch at a time, according to the recipe. Increasing the quantities often results in soft gels. Stir constantly while cooking to prevent burning. Recipes are developed for specific jar sizes. If jellies are filled into larger jars, excessively soft products may result.

Canned foods for special diets

The cost of commercially canned special diet food often prompts interest in preparing these products at home. Some low-sugar and low-salt foods may be easily and safely canned at home. However, the color, flavor, and texture of these foods may be different than expected and be less acceptable.

Canning without sugar

In canning regular fruits without sugar, it is very important to select fully ripe but firm fruits of the best quality. Prepare these as described for hot-packs in Guide 2, but use water or regular unsweetened fruit juices instead of sugar syrup. Juice made from the fruit being canned is best. Blends of unsweetened apple, pineapple, and white grape juice are also good for filling over solid fruit pieces. Adjust headspaces and lids and use the processing recommendations given for regular fruits. Splenda® is the only sugar substitute currently in the marketplace that can be added to covering liquids before canning fruits. Other sugar substitutes, if desired, should be added when serving.

Canning without salt (reduced sodium)

To can tomatoes, vegetables, meats, poultry, and seafood, use the procedures given in Guides 3 through 5, but omit the salt. In these products, salt seasons the food but is not necessary to ensure its safety. Add salt substitutes, if desired, when serving.

Canning fruit-based baby foods

You may prepare any chunk-style or pureed fruit with or without sugar, using the procedure for preparing each fruit as given in Guide 2. Pack in half-pint, preferably, or pint jars and use the following processing times.

Recommended process time for fruit-based baby foods in a boiling-water canner

Style of Pack	Jar Size	Process Time at Altitudes of		
		0–1,000 ft	1,001–6,000 ft	Above 6,000 ft
Hot	Pints	20 min	25 min	30 min

Caution: Do not attempt to can pureed vegetables, red meats, or poultry meats, because proper processing times for pureed foods have not been determined for home use. Instead, can and store these foods using the standard processing procedures; puree or blend them at serving time. Heat the blended foods to boiling, simmer for 10 minutes, cool, and serve. Store unused portions in the refrigerator and use within 2 days for best quality.

How much should you can?

The amount of food to preserve for your family, either by canning or freezing, should be based on individual choices. The following table can serve as a worksheet to plan how much food you should can for use within a year.

Suggested Preservation Plan for Canned and Frozen Foods

Kind of Food	Serving Size	Servings/week[a] Per Person		My Family[b]	My family needs Cups/Week[c]	Qts/Week[d]	Weeks served/yr[a]	Quarts/year Total[e]	Canned[a]	Frozen[a]
		Suggest	Actual							
Example: Family of 4										
Fruits	1/2 cup	12	12	48	24	6	36	216	72	144
My Plan:										
Fruits— apples, berries, peaches, plums, pears, tomatoes	1/2 cup	12								
Juices— apple, berry, grape, tomato	1 cup	7								
Vegetables— beets, beans, carrots, corn, peas, pumpkin, squash	1/2 cup	16								
Meat & Seafood— red meat, poultry, shellfish, fish	1/2 cup	14								
Soups	1 cup	2								
Pickles & Relishes— ketchup, fruit pickles, vegetable pickles, relish, etc.	—	1/2 cup								
Fruit Spreads— honey, jellies, jam, syrups, preserves, etc.	—	1/2 cup								
Sauces— tomato, etc.	1/2 cup	2								

[a] Your family should make these decisions.

[b] Servings/week for my family = actual weekly servings/person multiplied by number of family members who eat that food.

[c] Cups/week = servings/week multiplied by recommended serving size.

[d] Quarts/week = cups/week divided by 4.

[e] Total quarts/year = quarts/week multiplied by weeks served/year.

Glossary of Terms

Acid foods Foods which contain enough acid to result in a pH of 4.6 or lower. Includes all fruits except figs; most tomatoes; fermented and pickled vegetables; relishes; and jams, jellies, and marmalades. Acid foods may be processed in boiling water.

Altitude The vertical elevation of a location above sea level.

Ascorbic acid The chemical name for vitamin C. Lemon juice contains large quantities of ascorbic acid and is commonly used to prevent browning of peeled, light-colored fruits and vegetables.

Bacteria A large group of one-celled microorganisms widely distributed in nature. See microorganism.

Blancher A 6- to 8-quart lidded pot designed with a fitted perforated basket to hold food in boiling water, or with a fitted rack to steam foods. Useful for loosening skins on fruits to be peeled, or for heating foods to be hot packed.

Boiling-water canner A large standard-sized lidded kettle with jar rack, designed for heat-processing 7 quarts or 8 to 9 pints in boiling water.

Botulism An illness caused by eating toxin produced by growth of *Clostridium botulinum* bacteria in moist, low-acid food, containing less than 2 percent oxygen, and stored between 40° and 120°F. Proper heat processing destroys this bacterium in canned food. Freezer temperatures inhibit its growth in frozen food. Low moisture controls its growth in dried food. High oxygen controls its growth in fresh foods.

Canning A method of preserving food in air-tight vacuum-sealed containers and heat processing sufficiently to enable storing the food at normal home temperatures.

Canning salt Also called pickling salt. It is regular table salt without the anticaking or iodine additives.

Citric acid A form of acid that can be added to canned foods. It increases the acidity of low-acid foods and may improve the flavor and color.

Cold pack Canning procedure in which jars are filled with raw food. "Raw pack" is the preferred term for describing this practice. "Cold pack" is often used incorrectly to refer to foods that are open-kettle canned or jars that are heat-processed in boiling water.

Enzymes	Proteins in food which accelerate many flavor, color, texture, and nutritional changes, especially when food is cut, sliced, crushed, bruised, and exposed to air. Proper blanching or hot-packing practices destroy enzymes and improve food quality.
Exhausting	Removal of air from within and around food and from jars and canners. Blanching exhausts air from live food tissues. Exhausting or venting of pressure canners is necessary to prevent a risk of botulism in low-acid canned foods.
Fermentation	Changes in food caused by intentional growth of bacteria, yeast, or mold. Native bacteria ferment natural sugars to lactic acid, a major flavoring and preservative in sauerkraut and in naturally fermented dills. Alcohol, vinegar, and some dairy products are also fermented foods.
Headspace	The unfilled space above food or liquid in jars. Allows for food expansion as jars are heated, and for forming vacuums as jars cool.
Heat processing	Treatment of jars with sufficient heat to enable storing food at normal home temperatures.
Hermetic seal	An absolutely airtight container seal which prevents reentry of air or microorganisms into packaged foods.
Hot pack	Heating of raw food in boiling water or steam and filling it hot into jars.
Low-acid foods	Foods which contain very little acid and have a pH above 4.6. The acidity in these foods is insufficient to prevent the growth of the bacterium *Clostridium botulinum*. Vegetables, some tomatoes, figs, all meats, fish, seafoods, and some dairy foods are low acid. To control all risks of botulism, jars of these foods must be (1) heat processed in a pressure canner, or (2) acidified to a pH of 4.6 or lower before processing in boiling water.
Microorganisms	Independent organisms of microscopic size, including bacteria, yeast, and mold. When alive in a suitable environment, they grow rapidly and may divide or reproduce every 10 to 30 minutes. Therefore, they reach high populations very quickly. Undesirable microorganisms cause disease and food spoilage. Microorganisms are sometimes intentionally added to ferment foods, make antibiotics, and for other reasons.
Mold	A fungus-type microorganism whose growth on food is usually visible and colorful. Molds may grow on many foods, including acid foods like jams and jellies and canned fruits. Recommended heat processing and sealing practices prevent their growth on these foods.
Mycotoxins	Toxins produced by the growth of some molds on foods.

Open-kettle canning	A non-recommended canning method. Food is supposedly adequately heat processed in a covered kettle, and then filled hot and sealed in sterile jars. Foods canned this way have low vacuums or too much air, which permits rapid loss of quality in foods. Moreover, these foods often spoil because they become recontaminated while the jars are being filled.
Pasteurization	Heating of a specific food enough to destroy the most heat-resistant pathogenic or disease-causing microorganism known to be associated with that food.
pH	A measure of acidity or alkalinity. Values range from 0 to 14. A food is neutral when its pH is 7.0, lower values are increasingly more acid; higher values are increasingly more alkaline.
Pickling	The practice of adding enough vinegar or lemon juice to a low-acid food to lower its pH to 4.6 or lower. Properly pickled foods may be safely heat processed in boiling water.
Pressure Canner	A specifically designed metal kettle with a lockable lid used for heat processing low-acid food. These canners have jar racks, one or more safety devices, systems for exhausting air, and a way to measure or control pressure. Canners with 16- to 23- quart capacity are common. The minimum volume of canner that can be used is one that will hold 4 quart jars sitting upright on the rack. Use of pressure saucepans with smaller capacities is not recommended.
Raw pack	The practice of filling jars with raw, unheated food. Acceptable for canning low-acid foods, but allows more rapid quality losses in acid foods heat processed in boiling water.
Spice bag	A closeable fabric bag used to extract spice flavors in pickling solution.
Style of pack	Form of canned food, such as whole, sliced, piece, juice, or sauce. The term may also be used to reveal whether food is filled raw or hot into jars.
Vacuum	The state of negative pressure. Reflects how thoroughly air is removed from within a jar of processed food—the higher the vacuum, the less air left in the jar.
Yeasts	A group of microorganisms which reproduce by budding. They are used in fermenting some foods and in leavening breads.

Index of Foods

	Guide	Page
Apples		
Apple-pear jam	7	8
Butter	2	6
Juice	2	6
Pie filling	2	26
Salsa, peach-apple	2	25
Sauce	2	7
Spread with gelatin, refrigerated	7	12
Sliced	2	7
Spiced crab	2	9
Spiced rings	2	8
Apricots		
Halved or sliced	2	9
Puree	2	14
Asian Pears		
Halved or sliced	2	20
Asparagus		
Pickled	6	13
Spears or pieces	4	5
Beans		
Baked	4	6
Dry, with tomato or molasses sauce	4	6
Italian green, pieces	4	8
Lima	4	7
Pickled dilled	6	14
Shelled and dried	4	5
Snap green and wax, pieces	4	8
Three-bean salad	6	14
Bear		
Ground or chopped	5	6
Strips, cubes, or chunks	5	6
Beef		
Ground or chopped	5	6
Strips, cubes, or chunks	5	6
Beets		
Pickled	6	15
Pickled, no sugar added	6	32
Whole, cubed, or sliced	4	9

	Guide	Page
Berries		
Blackberries, whole	2	10
Blueberries		
pie filling	2	27
spice jam	7	9
syrup	2	10
whole	2	10
Currants, whole	2	10
Dewberries, whole	2	10
Elderberries, whole	2	10
Gooseberries, whole	2	10
Huckleberries, whole	2	10
Loganberries, whole	2	10
Mulberries, whole	2	10
Puree	2	14
Raspberries		
syrup	2	10
whole	2	10
Strawberries		
-rhubarb jelly	7	8
syrup	2	10
Broth, Meat	5	7
Brussels Sprouts		
Pickled	6	17
Cantaloupe		
Pickles	2	11
Pickles, no sugar added	2	12
Carrots		
Pickled	6	16
Pickled, baby	6	16
Sliced or diced	4	10
Cauliflower		
Pickled	6	17
Chayote		
-Pear relish	6	26
-Jicama slaw	6	17
Cherries		
Pie filling	2	27
Syrup	2	10
Whole	2	12
Chicken	5	5
Chile con carne	5	8

Index of Foods

	Guide	Page
Clams		
Whole or minced	5	9
Corn		
Cream style	4	10
Pickled corn relish	6	28
Whole kernel	4	11
Crab meat		
King or Dungeness	5	9
Cranberry		
-Orange chutney	2	13
-Spicy salsa	2	23
Figs	2	14
Fish		
Blue, mackerel, salmon, steelhead, trout, and other fatty fish, except tuna		
in pint jars	5	10
in quart jars	5	11
Smoked	5	13
Tuna	5	14
Fruit Cocktail		
Mixed	2	18
Fruit Purees	2	14
Grapefruit Sections	2	15
Grapes		
Juice	2	15
-Plum jelly	7	10
Puree	2	14
Spread with gelatin, refrigerated	7	12
Syrup	2	10
Whole	2	16
Greens	4	19
Horseradish sauce		
Pickled	6	30
Jam		
Blueberry-spice	7	9
Low-sugar peach-pineapple spread	7	11
Pear-apple	7	8
Standard or long-boil	7	6
With added pectin	7	7
Without added pectin	7	6
Jelly		
Apple spread with gelatin, refrigerated	7	12
Golden pepper	7	10
Grape-plum	7	10
Grape spread with gelatin, refrigerated	7	12
Standard or long-boil	7	5
Strawberry-rhubarb	7	8
With added pectin	7	7
Without added pectin	7	5
Jicama		
Bread-and-butter pickled	6	18
-Chayote slaw	6	17
Spicy relish	6	30
Lamb		
Ground or chopped	5	6
Strips, cubes or chunks	5	6
Mango		
Chutney	2	16
Salsa	2	24
Sauce	2	17
Meat Stock (broth)	5	7
Mincemeat		
Festive pie filling	2	28
Mushrooms		
Marinated	6	18
Whole or sliced	4	13
Nectarines		
Halved or sliced	2	18
Puree	2	14
Okra		
Pickled dilled	6	19
Whole or sliced	4	14
With tomatoes	3	12

Index of Foods

	Guide	Page
Onion		
-Pepper relish	6	30
Pickled pearl	6	20
Orange Sections	2	15
Oysters	5	12
Peaches		
-Apple salsa	2	25
Halved or sliced	2	19
Low sugar peach-pineapple spread	7	11
Pie filing	2	30
Puree	2	14
Salsa	2	24
Pears		
Asian, halved or sliced	2	20
-Apple jam	7	8
-Chayote relish	6	26
Halved	2	19
Puree	2	14
Peas		
Green or English, shelled	4	14
Shelled and dried	4	5
Peppers		
Hot or sweet	4	15
Jelly, golden pepper	7	10
Marinated	6	20
Pepper-onion relish	6	30
Piccalilli	6	27
Picked bell	6	21
Pickled hot	6	22
Pickled jalapeño rings	6	23
Pickled yellow pepper rings	6	24
Pickled Vegetables		
Asparagus	6	13
Beans, dilled	6	14
Beets	6	15
Beets, no sugar added	6	32
Brussels sprouts	6	17
Carrots	6	16
Carrots, baby	6	16
Cauliflower	6	17
Chayote and jicama slaw	6	17
Green tomatoes, sweet	6	24
Horseradish sauce	6	30
Jalapeño pepper rings	6	23

	Guide	Page
Mixed vegetables	6	25
Mushrooms, whole, marinated	6	18
Okra, dilled	6	19
Onions, pearl	6	20
Peppers, bell	6	21
Peppers, hot	6	22
Peppers, marinated	6	20
Piccalilli	6	27
Squash, bread-and-butter	6	9
Three bean salad	6	14
Yellow pepper rings	6	24
Zucchini, bread-and-butter	6	26
Pickles		
Bread-and-Butter	6	9
Dill		
fermented	6	7
fresh-pack, quick	6	10
reduced-sodium	6	34
Sweet		
14- day	6	11
cucumber slices, no sugar added	6	33
gherkin	6	10
quick	6	12
reduced-sodium	6	34
Pie Fillings		
Apple	2	26
Blueberry	2	27
Cherry	2	27
Mincemeat, festive	2	28
Tomato, green	2	29
Peach	2	30
Pineapple		
Low-sugar peach-pineapple spread	7	11
Pieces	2	21
Puree	2	14
-Zucchini	2	22
Plums		
Halved or whole	2	21
-Grape jelly	7	10
Puree	2	14
Pork		
Ground or chopped	5	6
Strips, cubes or chunks	5	6

Index of Foods

	Guide	Page
Potatoes		
Sweet, pieces or whole	4	16
White, cubed or whole	4	17
Pumpkin		
Cubed	4	18
Rabbit	5	5
Relish		
Chayote and pear	6	26
Corn	6	28
Horseradish	6	30
Jicama, spicy	6	30
Pepper-onion	6	30
Piccalilli	6	27
Pickle	6	28
Tomatillo, tangy	6	31
Tomato, green	6	29
Rhubarb		
Stewed	2	22
-Strawberry jelly	7	8
Salsa		
Chile salsa	3	21
Chile salsa II	3	22
Cranberry, spicy	2	23
Mango	2	24
Peach	2	24
Peach apple	2	25
Tomatillo green	3	22
Tomato using paste tomatoes	3	23
Tomato using slicing tomatoes	3	24
Tomato/green chile	3	24
Tomato/tomato paste	3	25
Sauerkraut	6	8
Smoked Fish	5	13
Soups		
Dried bean or pea	4	18
Meat	4	18
Poultry	4	18
Seafood	4	18
Vegetable	4	18
Spinach and other greens	4	19
Squash		
Pumpkin, cubed	4	18
Winter, cubed	4	18

	Guide	Page
Stock, Meat	5	7
Strawberry		
Puree	2	14
-Rhubarb jelly	7	8
Syrup	2	10
Succotash	4	20
Sweet Potatoes		
Pieces or whole	4	16
Syrup		
Blueberry	2	10
Cherry	2	10
Grape	2	10
Raspberry	2	10
Strawberry	2	10
Tomatillos		
-Green salsa	3	22
Tangy tomatillo relish	6	31
Whole	3	13
Tomatoes		
Chile salsa	3	21
Chile salsa II	3	22
Crushed	3	7
-Green chile salsa	3	24
Green tomato pie filling	2	29
Green tomato relish	6	29
Hot sauce, easy	3	16
Juice	3	5
Ketchup		
blender	3	18
country western	3	18
tomato	3	17
Pepper sauce, cayenne	3	17
Piccalilli	6	27
Pickled, sweet green	6	24
Salsa using paste tomatoes	3	23
Salsa using slicing tomatoes	3	24
Sauce, Mexican	3	15
Sauce, spaghetti		
with meat	3	14
without meat	3	13
Sauce, standard	3	8
Sauce, taco	3	26
-Tomato paste salsa	3	25
Vegetable juice blend	3	6

Index of Foods

	Guide	Page
Whole or halved		
packed in juice	3	10
packed in water	3	9
packed raw without added liquid	3	11
With okra or zucchini	3	12

Tuna   5   14

Veal

	Guide	Page
Ground or chopped	5	6
Strips, cubes or chunks	5	6

Vegetables, Mixed

	Guide	Page
Regular	4	12
Quick pickled	6	25

Venison

	Guide	Page
Ground or chopped	5	6
Strips, cubes or chunks	5	6

Winter Squash

	Guide	Page
Cubed	4	18

Zucchini

	Guide	Page
Bread-and-butter pickles	6	26
-Pineapple	2	22
With tomatoes	3	12

Complete Guide to
Home Canning

Guide 2
Selecting, Preparing, and Canning Fruit and Fruit Products

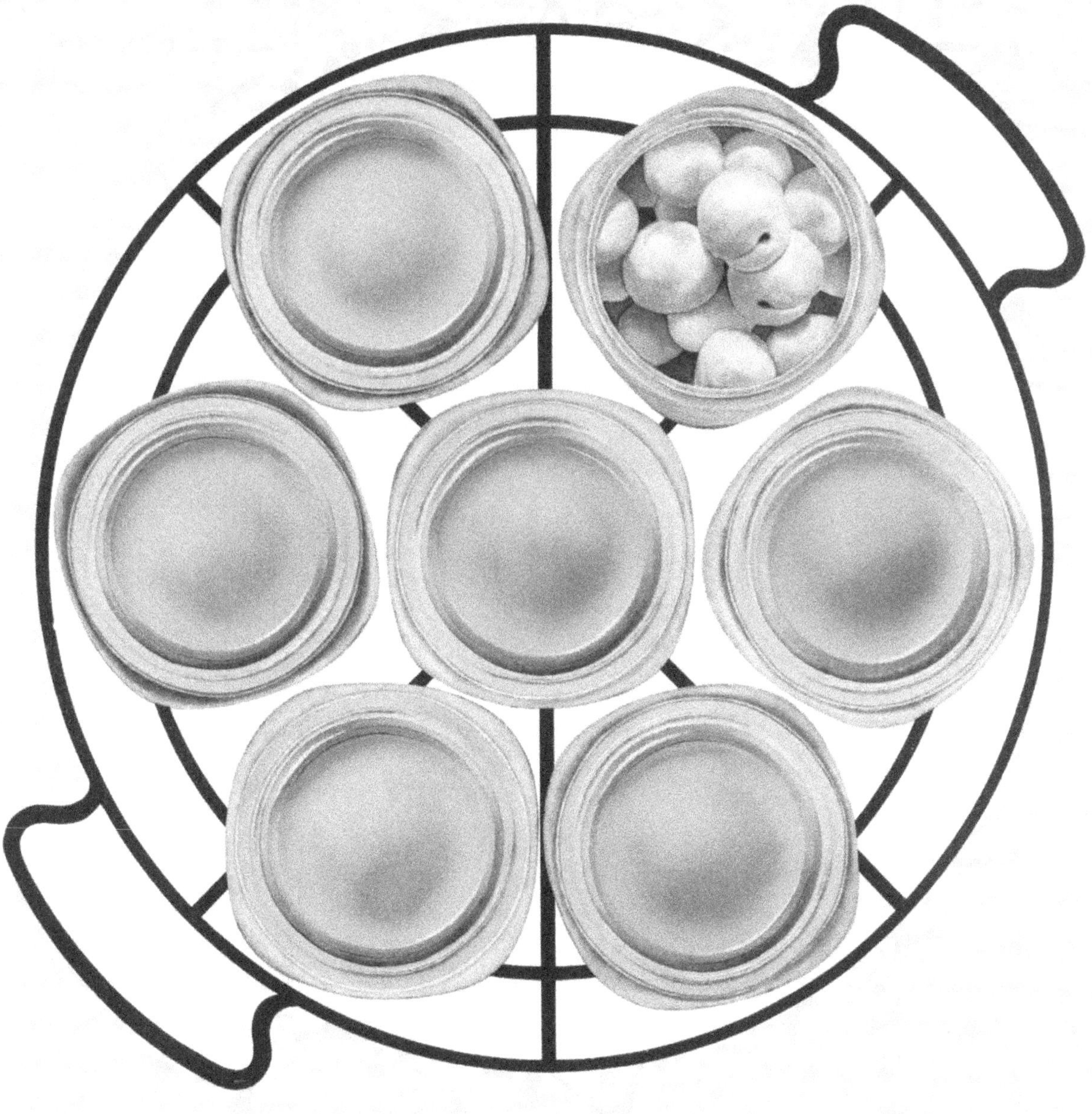

United States Department of Agriculture

National Institute of Food and Agriculture

Guide 2
Selecting, Preparing, and Canning Fruit and Fruit Products

Table of Contents

Section	Page
General	2-5
Preparing and using syrups	2-5
Apple butter	2-6
Apple juice	2-6
Apples—sliced	2-7
Applesauce	2-7
Spiced apple rings	2-8
Spiced crab apples	2-9
Apricots—halved or sliced	2-9
Berries—whole	2-10
Berry syrup	2-10
Cantaloupe pickles	2-11
Cantaloupe pickles, no sugar added	2-12
Cherries—whole	2-12
Cranberry orange chutney	2-13
Figs	2-14
Fruit purees	2-14
Grapefruit and orange sections	2-15
Grape juice	2-15
Grapes—whole	2-16
Mango chutney	2-16
Mango sauce	2-17
Mixed fruit cocktail	2-18
Nectarines—halved or sliced	2-18
Peaches—halved or sliced	2-19
Pears—halved	2-19
Pears, Asian–halved or sliced	2-20
Pineapple	2-21
Plums—halved or whole	2-21
Rhubarb—stewed	2-22
Zucchini-pineapple	2-22
Fruit salsas	**2-23**
Spicy cranberry salsa	2-23
Mango salsa	2-24
Peach salsa	2-24
Peach apple salsa	2-25
Pie fillings	**2-25**
Apple pie filling	2-26
Blueberry pie filling	2-27
Cherry pie filling	2-27
Festive mincemeat pie filling	2-28
Green tomato pie filling	2-29
Peach pie filling	2-30
Process times for some acid foods in a dial-gauge pressure canner	2-31
Process times for some acid foods in a weighted-gauge pressure canner	2-32

General

Adding syrup to canned fruit helps to retain its flavor, color, and shape. It does not prevent spoilage of these foods. The following guidelines for preparing and using syrups offer a new "very light" syrup, which approximates the natural sugar content of many fruits. The sugar content in each of the five syrups is increased by about 10 percent. Quantities of water and sugar to make enough syrup for a canner load of pints or quarts are provided for each syrup type.

Preparing and using syrups

Syrup Type	Approx. % Sugar	Measures of Water and Sugar				Fruits commonly packed in syrup**
		For 9-Pt Load*		For 7-Qt Load		
		Cups Water	Cups Sugar	Cups Water	Cups Sugar	
Very Light	10	6-1/2	3/4	10-1/2	1-1/4	Approximates natural sugar level in most fruits and adds the fewest calories.
Light	20	5-3/4	1-1/2	9	2-1/4	Very sweet fruit. Try a small amount the first time to see if your family likes it.
Medium	30	5-1/4	2-1/4	8-1/4	3-3/4	Sweet apples, sweet cherries, berries, grapes.
Heavy	40	5	3-1/4	7-3/4	5-1/4	Tart apples, apricots, sour cherries, gooseberries, nectarines, peaches, pears, plums.
Very Heavy	50	4-1/4	4-1/4	6-1/2	6-3/4	Very sour fruit. Try a small amount the first time to see if your family likes it.

* This amount is also adequate for a 4-quart load.

** Many fruits that are typically packed in heavy syrup are excellent and tasteful products when packed in lighter syrups. It is recommended that lighter syrups be tried, since they contain fewer calories from added sugar.

Procedure: Heat water and sugar together. Bring to a boil and pour over raw fruits in jars. For hot packs, bring water and sugar to boil, add fruit, reheat to boil, and fill into jars immediately.

Other sweeteners: Light corn syrups or mild-flavored honey may be used to replace up to half the table sugar called for in syrups. See the section, "Canned foods for special diets," page 1-31 for further discussion.

APPLE BUTTER

Use Jonathan, Winesap, Stayman, Golden Delicious, MacIntosh, or other tasty apple varieties for good results.

8 lbs apples
2 cups cider
2 cups vinegar
2-1/4 cups white sugar
2-1/4 cups packed brown sugar
2 tbsp ground cinnamon
1 tbsp ground cloves

Yield: About 8 to 9 pints

Procedure: Wash, remove stems, quarter, and core fruit. Cook slowly in cider and vinegar until soft. Press fruit through a colander, food mill, or strainer. Cook fruit pulp with sugar and spices, stirring frequently. To test for doneness, remove a spoonful and hold it away from steam for 2 minutes. It is done if the butter remains mounded on the spoon. Another way to determine when the butter is cooked adequately is to spoon a small quantity onto a plate. When a rim of liquid does not separate around the edge of the butter, it is ready for canning. Fill hot into sterile half-pint or pint jars, leaving 1/4-inch headspace. Quart jars need not be presterilized but should be clean and kept hot until filling. To presterilize jars, see page 1-14. Remove air bubbles and adjust headspace if needed. Wipe rims of jars with a dampened clean paper towel. Adjust lids and process.

Recommended process time for Apple Butter in a boiling-water canner				
		Process Time at Altitudes of		
Style of Pack	Jar Size	0–1,000 ft	1,001–6,000 ft	Above 6,000 ft
Hot	Half-pints or Pints	5 min	10	15
	Quarts	10	15	20

APPLE JUICE

Quality: Good quality apple juice is made from a blend of varieties. For best results, buy fresh juice from a local cider maker within 24 hours after it has been pressed.

Procedure: Refrigerate juice for 24 to 48 hours. Without mixing, carefully pour off clear liquid and discard sediment. Strain clear liquid through a paper coffee filter or double layers of damp cheesecloth. Heat quickly, stirring occasionally, until juice begins to boil. Fill immediately into sterile pint or quart jars (see page 1-14 to sterilize jars), or fill into clean hot half-gallon jars, leaving 1/4-inch headspace. Wipe rims of jars with a dampened clean paper towel. Adjust lids and process.

Recommended process time for Apple Juice in a boiling-water canner

Style of Pack	Jar Size	Process Time at Altitudes of		
		0–1,000 ft	1,001–6,000 ft	Above 6,000 ft
Hot	Pints or Quarts	5 min	10	15
	Half-gallons	10	15	20

APPLES—SLICED

Quantity: An average of 19 pounds is needed per canner load of 7 quarts; an average of 12-1/4 pounds is needed per canner load of 9 pints. A bushel weighs 48 pounds and yields 16 to 19 quarts—an average of 2-3/4 pounds per quart.

Quality: Select apples that are juicy, crispy, and preferably both sweet and tart.

Procedure: Wash, peel, and core apples. To prevent discoloration, slice apples into water containing ascorbic acid (see page 1-11). Raw packs make poor quality products. Place drained slices in large saucepan and add 1 pint water or very light, light, or medium syrup (see page 2-5) per 5 pounds of sliced apples. Boil 5 minutes, stirring occasionally to prevent burning. Fill hot jars with hot slices and hot syrup or water, leaving 1/2-inch headspace. Remove air bubbles and adjust headspace if needed. Wipe rims of jars with a dampened clean paper towel. Adjust lids and process.

Processing directions for canning sliced apples in a dial- or weighted-gauge canner are given on pages 2-31 and 2-32.

Recommended process time for Apples, sliced in a boiling-water canner

Style of Pack	Jar Size	Process Time at Altitudes of			
		0–1,000 ft	1,001–3,000 ft	3,001–6,000 ft	Above 6,000 ft
Hot	Pints or Quarts	20 min	25	30	35

APPLESAUCE

Quantity: An average of 21 pounds is needed per canner load of 7 quarts; an average of 13-1/2 pounds is needed per canner load of 9 pints. A bushel weighs 48 pounds and yields 14 to 19 quarts of sauce—an average of 3 pounds per quart.

Quality: Select apples that are sweet, juicy, and crisp. For a tart flavor, add 1 to 2 pounds of tart apples to each 3 pounds of sweeter fruit.

Procedure: Wash, peel, and core apples. If desired, slice apples into water containing ascorbic acid (see page 1-11) to prevent browning. Placed drained slices in an 8 to 10-quart pot. Add 1/2 cup water. Stirring occasionally to prevent burning, heat quickly until tender (5 to 20 minutes, depending on maturity and variety). Press through a sieve or food mill, or skip the pressing step if you prefer chunk-style sauce. Sauce may be packed without sugar. If desired, add 1/8 cup sugar per quart of sauce. Taste and add more, if preferred. Reheat sauce to a rolling boil. Fill hot jars with hot sauce, leaving 1/2-inch headspace. Remove air bubbles and adjust headspace if needed. Wipe rims of jars with a dampened clean paper towel. Adjust lids and process.

Recommended process time for Applesauce in a boiling-water canner

Style of Pack	Jar Size	Process Time at Altitudes of			
		0–1,000 ft	1,001–3,000 ft	3,001–6,000 ft	Above 6,000 ft
Hot	Pints	15 min	20	20	25
	Quarts	20	25	30	35

SPICED APPLE RINGS

12 lbs firm tart apples (maximum diameter, 2-1/2 inches)
12 cups sugar
6 cups water
1-1/4 cups white vinegar (5%)
3 tbsp whole cloves
3/4 cup red hot cinnamon candies or
    8 cinnamon sticks and
    1 tsp red food coloring (optional)

Yield: About 8 to 9 pints

Procedure: Wash apples. To prevent discoloration, peel and slice one apple at a time. Immediately cut crosswise into 1/2-inch slices, remove core area with a melon baller, and immerse in ascorbic acid solution (see page 1-11). To make flavored syrup, combine sugar, water, vinegar, cloves, cinnamon candies, or cinnamon sticks and food coloring in a 6-qt saucepan. Stir, heat to boil, and simmer 3 minutes. Drain apples, add to hot syrup, and cook 5 minutes. Fill hot jars (preferably wide-mouth) with apple rings and hot flavored syrup, leaving 1/2-inch headspace. Remove air bubbles and adjust headspace if needed. Wipe rims of jars with a dampened clean paper towel. Adjust lids and process.

Recommended process time for Spiced Apple Rings in a boiling-water canner

Style of Pack	Jar Size	Process Time at Altitudes of		
		0–1,000 ft	1,001–6,000 ft	Above 6,000 ft
Hot	Half-pints or Pints	10 min	15	20

SPICED CRAB APPLES

5 lbs crab apples
4-1/2 cups apple cider vinegar (5%)
3-3/4 cups water
7-1/2 cups sugar
4 tsp whole cloves
4 sticks cinnamon
Six 1/2-inch cubes of fresh ginger root

Yield: About 9 pints

Procedure: Remove blossom petals and wash apples, but leave stems attached. Puncture the skin of each apple four times with an ice pick or toothpick. Mix vinegar, water, and sugar and bring to a boil. Add spices tied in a spice bag or cheesecloth. Using a blancher basket or sieve, immerse 1/3 of the apples at a time in the boiling vinegar/syrup solution for 2 minutes. Place cooked apples and spice bag in a clean 1- or 2-gallon crock and add hot syrup. Cover and let stand overnight. Remove spice bag, drain syrup into a large saucepan, and reheat to boiling. Fill hot pint jars with apples and hot syrup, leaving 1/2-inch headspace. Remove air bubbles and adjust headspace if needed. Wipe rims of jars with a dampened clean paper towel. Adjust lids and process.

Recommended process time for Spiced Crab Apples in a boiling-water canner

Style of Pack	Jar Size	0–1,000 ft	1,001–3,000 ft	3,001–6,000 ft	Above 6,000 ft
Hot	Pints	20 min	25	30	35

APRICOTS—HALVED OR SLICED

Quantity: An average of 16 pounds is needed per canner load of 7 quarts; an average of 10 pounds is needed per canner load of 9 pints. A bushel weighs 50 pounds and yields 20 to 25 quarts—an average of 2-1/4 pounds per quart.

Quality: Select firm, well-colored mature fruit of ideal quality for eating fresh.

Procedure: Follow directions for peaches. The boiling water dip and removal of skin process is optional. Wash fruit well if skins are not removed; use either hot or raw pack, and use the same process time. (See page 2-19)

BERRIES—WHOLE

Blackberries, blueberries, currants, dewberries, elderberries, gooseberries, huckleberries, loganberries, mulberries, raspberries.

Quantity: An average of 12 pounds is needed per canner load of 7 quarts; an average of 8 pounds is needed per canner load of 9 pints. A 24-quart crate weighs 36 pounds and yields 18 to 24 quarts—an average of 1-3/4 pounds per quart.

Quality: Choose ripe, sweet berries with uniform color.

Procedure: Wash 1 or 2 quarts of berries at a time. Drain, cap, and stem if necessary. For gooseberries, snip off heads and tails with scissors. Prepare and boil preferred syrup (see page 2-5), if desired. Add 1/2 cup syrup, juice, or water to each clean jar.

Hot pack—For blueberries, currants, elderberries, gooseberries, and huckleberries. Heat berries in boiling water for 30 seconds and drain. Fill hot jars and cover with hot juice, leaving 1/2-inch headspace.

Raw pack—Fill hot jars with any of the raw berries, shaking down gently while filling. Cover with hot syrup, juice, or water, leaving 1/2-inch headspace.

Remove air bubbles and adjust headspace if needed. Wipe rims of jars with a dampened clean paper towel. Adjust lids and process.

Recommended process time for Berries, whole in a boiling-water canner					
		Process Time at Altitudes of			
Style of Pack	Jar Size	0–1,000 ft	1,001–3,000 ft	3,001–6,000 ft	Above 6,000 ft
Hot	Pints or Quarts	15 min	20	20	25
Raw	Pints	15	20	20	25
	Quarts	20	25	30	35

Processing directions for canning berries in a dial- or weighted-gauge canner are given on pages 2-31 and 2-32.

BERRY SYRUP

Juices from fresh or frozen blueberries, cherries, grapes, raspberries (black or red), and strawberries are easily made into toppings for use on ice cream and pastries.

Yield: About 9 half-pints.

Procedure: Select 6-1/2 cups of fresh or frozen fruit of your choice. Wash, cap, and stem fresh fruit and crush in a saucepan. Heat to boiling and simmer until soft (5 to 10 minutes). Strain hot through a colander and drain until cool enough to handle. Strain the collected juice through a double layer of cheesecloth or jelly bag. Discard the dry pulp. The yield of the pressed juice should be about 4-1/2 to 5 cups. Combine the juice with 6-3/4 cups of sugar in a large saucepan, bring to boil, and simmer 1 minute. To make a syrup with whole fruit pieces, save 1 or 2 cups of the fresh or frozen fruit, combine these with the sugar, and simmer as in making regular syrup. Remove from heat, skim off foam, and fill into hot half-pint or pint jars, leaving 1/2-inch headspace. Remove air bubbles and adjust headspace if needed. Wipe rims of jars with a dampened clean paper towel. Adjust lids and process.

Recommended process time for Berry Syrup in a boiling-water canner

Style of Pack	Jar Size	Process Time at Altitudes of		
		0–1,000 ft	1,001–6,000 ft	Above 6,000 ft
Hot	Half-pints or Pints	10 min	15	20

CANTALOUPE PICKLES

5 lbs of 1-inch cantaloupe cubes (about 2 medium underripe* cantaloupe)
1 tsp crushed red pepper flakes
2 one-inch cinnamon sticks
2 tsp ground cloves
1 tsp ground ginger
4-1/2 cups cider vinegar (5%)
2 cups water
1-1/2 cups white sugar
1-1/2 cups packed light brown sugar

*Select cantaloupe that are full size but almost fully green and firm to the touch in all areas including the stem area.

Yield: About 4 pint jars

Procedure: Day One: Wash cantaloupe and cut into halves; remove seeds. Cut into 1 inch slices and peel. Cut strips of flesh into 1 inch cubes. Weigh out 5 pounds of pieces and place in large glass bowl. Place red pepper flakes, cinnamon sticks, cloves and ginger in a spice bag and tie the ends firmly. Combine vinegar and water in a 4-quart stockpot. Bring to a boil, then turn heat off. Add spice bag to the vinegar-water mixture, and let steep for 5 minutes, stirring occasionally. Pour hot vinegar solution and spice bag over melon pieces in the bowl. Cover with a food-grade plastic lid or wrap and let stand overnight in the refrigerator (about 18 hours).
Day Two: Carefully pour off vinegar solution into a large 8- to 10-quart saucepan and bring to a boil. Add sugar; stir to dissolve. Add cantaloupe and bring back to a boil. Lower heat and simmer until cantaloupe pieces turn translucent (about 1 to 1-1/4 hours). Remove cantaloupe pieces into a medium-sized stockpot, cover and set aside. Bring remaining liquid to a boil and boil an additional 5 minutes. Return cantaloupe to the liquid syrup, and bring back to a boil. With a slotted spoon, fill hot cantaloupe pieces into hot pint jars, leaving 1-inch headspace. Cover with boiling hot syrup, leaving 1/2-inch headspace. Remove air bubbles and adjust headspace if needed. Wipe rims of jars with a dampened clean paper towel. Adjust lids and process.

		Process Time at Altitudes of		
Style of Pack	Jar Size	0– 1,000 ft	1,001– 6,000 ft	Above 6,000 ft
Hot	Pints	15 min	20	25

Recommended process time for Cantaloupe Pickles in a boiling-water canner

CANTALOUPE PICKLES, NO SUGAR ADDED

6 lbs of one-inch cantaloupe cubes (about 3 medium underripe* cantaloupe)
1 tsp crushed red pepper flakes
2 one-inch cinnamon sticks
2 tsp ground cloves
1 tsp ground ginger
4-1/2 cups cider vinegar (5%)
2 cups water
3 cups Splenda®

*Select cantaloupe that are full size but almost fully green and firm to the touch in all areas including the stem area.

Yield: About 4 pint jars

Procedure: Follow the directions for Cantaloupe Pickles, weighing out 6 pounds of prepared cantaloupe cubes instead and substituting Splenda® when sugar would be added.

CHERRIES—WHOLE

Sweet or Sour

Quantity: An average of 17-1/2 pounds is needed per canner load of 7 quarts; an average of 11 pounds is needed per canner load of 9 pints. A lug weighs 25 pounds and yields 8 to 12 quarts—an average of 2-1/2 pounds per quart.

Quality: Select bright, uniformly colored cherries that are mature (of ideal quality for eating fresh or cooking).

Procedure: Stem and wash cherries. Remove pits if desired. If pitted, place cherries in water containing ascorbic acid (see page 1-11) to prevent stem-end discoloration. If canned unpitted, prick skins on opposite sides with a clean needle to prevent splitting. Cherries may be canned in water, apple juice, white grape juice, or syrup. If syrup is desired, select and prepare preferred type as directed on page 2-5.

Hot pack—In a large saucepan add 1/2 cup water, juice, or syrup for each quart of drained fruit and bring to boil. Fill hot jars with cherries and cooking liquid, leaving 1/2-inch headspace.

Raw pack—Add 1/2 cup hot water, juice, or syrup to each jar. Fill hot jars with drained cherries, shaking down gently as you fill. Add more hot liquid, leaving 1/2-inch headspace.

Remove air bubbles and adjust headspace if needed. Wipe rims of jars with a dampened clean paper towel. Adjust lids and process.

Recommended process time for Cherries, whole in a boiling-water canner

Style of Pack	Jar Size	Process Time at Altitudes of			
		0–1,000 ft	1,001–3,000 ft	3,001–6,000 ft	Above 6,000 ft
Hot	Pints	15 min	20	20	25
	Quarts	20	25	30	35
Raw	Pints or Quarts	25	30	35	40

Processing directions for canning cherries in a dial- or weighted-gauge canner are given on pages 2-31 and 2-32.

CRANBERRY ORANGE CHUTNEY

24 ounces fresh whole cranberries
2 cups chopped white onion
2 cups golden raisins
1-1/2 cups white sugar
1-1/2 cups packed brown sugar
2 cups white distilled vinegar (5%)
1 cup orange juice
4 tsp peeled, grated fresh ginger
3 sticks cinnamon

Yield: About 8 half-pint jars

Procedure: Rinse cranberries well. Combine all ingredients in a large Dutch oven. Bring to a boil over high heat; reduce heat and simmer gently for 15 minutes or until cranberries are tender. Stir often to prevent scorching. Remove cinnamon sticks and discard. Fill the hot chutney into hot half-pint jars, leaving 1/2-inch headspace. Remove air bubbles and adjust headspace if needed. Wipe rims of jars with a dampened clean paper towel. Adjust lids and process.

Recommended process time for Cranberry-Orange Chutney in a boiling-water canner

Style of Pack	Jar Size	Process Time at Altitudes of		
		0–1,000 ft	1,001–6,000 ft	Above 6,000 ft
Hot	Half-pints	10 min	15	20

Note: Other dried spices can be added to taste (for example, cloves, dry mustard, or cayenne pepper). Add or adjust spices during the simmering period.

FIGS

Important: All home-canned Figs must be acidified before canning in a boiling water canner to make them safe from the microorganism that causes botulism.

Quantity: An average of 16 pounds is needed per canner load of 7 quarts; an average of 11 pounds is needed per canner load of 9 pints—an average of 2-1/2 pounds yields 1 quart.

Quality: Select firm, ripe, uncracked figs. The mature color depends on the variety. Avoid overripe figs with very soft flesh.

Procedure: Wash figs thoroughly in clean water. Drain. Do not peel or remove stems. Cover figs with water and boil 2 minutes. Drain. Gently boil figs in light syrup (see page 2-5) for 5 minutes. **Add 2 tablespoons bottled lemon juice per quart or 1 tablespoon per pint to the jars; or add 1/2 teaspoon citric acid per quart or 1/4 teaspoon per pint to the jars.** Fill hot jars with hot figs and cooking syrup, leaving 1/2-inch headspace. Remove air bubbles and adjust headspace if needed. Wipe rims of jars with a dampened clean paper towel. Adjust lids and process.

Recommended process time for Figs in a boiling-water canner					
		Process Time at Altitudes of			
Style of Pack	Jar Size	0–1,000 ft	1,001–3,000 ft	3,001–6,000 ft	Above 6,000 ft
Hot	Pints	45 min	50	55	60
	Quarts	50	55	60	65

FRUIT PUREES

Important: These recommendations should not be used with bananas, Asian pears, figs, tomatoes, cantaloupe and other melons, papaya, ripe mango or coconut. There are no home canning recommendations available for purees of these products.

Procedure: Stem, wash, drain, peel, and remove pits if necessary. Measure fruit into large saucepan, crushing slightly if desired. Add 1 cup hot water for each quart of fruit. Cook slowly until fruit is soft, stirring frequently. Press through sieve or food mill. If desired for flavor, add sugar to taste. Reheat pulp to boil, or until sugar dissolves if added. Fill hot into hot jars, leaving 1/4-inch headspace. Remove air bubbles and adjust headspace if needed. Wipe rims of jars with a dampened clean paper towel. Adjust lids and process.

Recommended process time for Fruit Purees in a boiling-water canner				
		Process Time at Altitudes of		
Style of Pack	Jar Size	0–1,000 ft	1,001–6,000 ft	Above 6,000 ft
Hot	Pints or Quarts	15 min	20	25

Processing directions for canning purees in a dial- or weighted-gauge canner are given on pages 2-31 and 2-32.

GRAPEFRUIT AND ORANGE SECTIONS

Quantity: An average of 15 pounds is needed per canner load of 7 quarts; an average of 13 pounds is needed per canner load of 9 pints—an average of about 2 pounds yields 1 quart.

Quality: Select firm, mature, sweet fruit of ideal quality for eating fresh. The flavor of orange sections is best if the sections are canned with equal parts of grapefruit. Grapefruit may be canned without oranges. Sections may be packed in your choice of water, citrus juice or syrup.

Procedure: Wash and peel fruit and remove white tissue to prevent a bitter taste. If you use syrup, prepare a very light, light, or medium syrup (see page 2-5) and bring to boil. Fill hot jars with sections and water, juice or hot syrup, leaving 1/2-inch headspace. Remove air bubbles and adjust headspace if needed. Wipe rims of jars with a dampened clean paper towel. Adjust lids and process.

Recommended process time for Grapefruit and Orange Sections in a boiling-water canner

Style of Pack	Jar Size	Process Time at Altitudes of		
		0–1,000 ft	1,001–6,000 ft	Above 6,000 ft
Raw	Pints or Quarts	10 min	15	20

Processing directions for canning citrus sections in a dial- or weighted-gauge canner are given on pages 2-31 and 2-32.

GRAPE JUICE

Quantity: An average of 24-1/2 pounds is needed per canner load of 7 quarts; an average of 16 pounds per canner load of 9 pints. A lug weighs 26 pounds and yields 7 to 9 quarts of juice—an average of 3-1/2 pounds per quart.

Quality: Select sweet, well-colored, firm, mature fruit of ideal quality for eating fresh or cooking.

Procedure: Wash and stem grapes. Place grapes in saucepan, crush and add just enough boiling water to cover grapes. Heat to simmering and simmer slowly until skin is soft about 10 minutes. Strain through a damp jelly bag or double layers of cheesecloth. Refrigerate juice for 24 to 48 hours. Without mixing, carefully pour off clear liquid and save; discard sediment. If desired, strain through a paper coffee filter for a clearer juice. Add juice to a saucepan and sweeten to taste. Heat and stir until sugar is dissolved. Continue heating with occasional stirring until juice begins to boil. Fill into hot or presterilized jars immediately, leaving 1/4-inch headspace. (To sterilize empty pint and quart jars, see page 1-14.) Wipe rims of jars with a dampened clean paper towel. Adjust lids and process.

Recommended process time for Grape Juice in a boiling-water canner

Style of Pack	Jar Size	Process Time at Altitudes of		
		0–1,000 ft	1,001–6,000 ft	Above 6,000 ft
Hot	Pints or Quarts	5 min	10	15
	Half-gallons	10	15	20

GRAPES—WHOLE

Quantity: An average of 14 pounds is needed per canner load of 7 quarts; an average of 9 pounds is needed per canner load of 9 pints. A lug weighs 26 pounds and yields 12 to 14 quarts of whole grapes—an average of 2 pounds per quart.

Quality: Choose unripe, tight-skinned, preferably green seedless grapes harvested 2 weeks before they reach optimum eating quality.

Procedure: Stem, wash, and drain grapes. Prepare very light, or light syrup (see page 2-5).

Hot pack—Blanch grapes in boiling water for 30 seconds. Drain, and proceed as for raw pack.

Raw pack—Fill hot jars with grapes and hot syrup, leaving 1-inch headspace.

Remove air bubbles and adjust headspace if needed. Wipe rims of jars with a dampened clean paper towel. Adjust lids and process.

Recommended process time for Grapes, whole in a boiling-water canner

Style of Pack	Jar Size	Process Time at Altitudes of			
		0–1,000 ft	1,001–3,000 ft	3,001–6,000 ft	Above 6,000 ft
Hot	Pints or Quarts	10 min	15	15	20
Raw	Pints	15	20	20	25
	Quarts	20	25	30	35

MANGO CHUTNEY

11 cups or 4 lbs chopped unripe (hard) mango, either Tommy Atkins or Kent varieties
2-1/2 cups or 3/4 lb finely chopped yellow onion
2-1/2 tbsp grated fresh ginger
1-1/2 tbsp finely chopped fresh garlic
4-1/2 cups sugar
3 cups white distilled vinegar (5%)
2-1/2 cups golden raisins
1-1 tsp canning salt
4 tsp chili powder

Caution: Handling green mangoes may irritate the skin of some people in the same way as poison ivy. (They belong to the same plant family.) To avoid this reaction, wear plastic or rubber gloves while working with raw green mango. Do not touch your face, lips or eyes after touching or cutting raw green mangoes until all traces are washed away.

Yield: About 6 pint jars

Procedure: Wash all produce well. Peel, core and chop mangoes into 3/4-inch cubes. Chop mango cubes in food processor, using 6 one-second pulses per food processor batch. (Do not puree or chop too finely.) By hand, peel and dice onion, finely chop garlic, and grate ginger. Mix sugar and vinegar in an 8- to 10-quart stockpot. Bring to a boil, and boil 5 minutes. Add all other ingredients and bring back to a boil. Reduce heat and simmer 25 minutes, stirring occasionally. Fill hot chutney into hot pint or half-pint jars, leaving 1/2-inch headspace. Remove air bubbles and adjust headspace if needed. Wipe rims of jars with a dampened clean paper towel. Adjust lids and process.

Recommended process time for Mango Chutney in a boiling-water canner

Style of Pack	Jar Size	Process Time at Altitudes of		
		0–1,000 ft	1,001–6,000 ft	Above 6,000 ft
Hot	Half-pints or Pints	10 min	15	20

MANGO SAUCE

5-1/2 cups or 3-1/4 lbs mango puree (use slightly underripe to just-ripe mango)
6 tbsp honey
4 tbsp bottled lemon juice
3/4 cup sugar
2-1/2 tsp (7500 milligrams) ascorbic acid
1/8 tsp ground cinnamon
1/8 tsp ground nutmeg

Caution: Handling green mangoes may irritate the skin of some people in the same way as poison ivy. (They belong to the same plant family.) To avoid this reaction, wear plastic or rubber gloves while working with raw green mango. Do not touch your face, lips or eyes after touching or cutting raw green mangoes until all traces are washed away.

Yield: About 6 half-pint jars

Storage Notes: Store in a dark place, away from direct light, to preserve the color of the canned sauce. This sauce is best used within 4 to 6 months; otherwise, discoloration may occur.

Procedure: Wash, peel, and separate mango flesh from seed. Chop mango flesh into chunks and purée in blender or food processor until smooth. Combine all ingredients in a 6- to 8-quart Dutch oven or stockpot and heat on medium-high heat, with continuous stirring, until the mixture reaches

200°F. The mixture will sputter as it is being heated, so be sure to wear gloves or oven mitts to avoid burning skin. Fill hot sauce into hot half-pint jars, leaving 1/4-inch headspace. Remove air bubbles and adjust headspace if needed. Wipe rims of jars with a dampened clean paper towel. Adjust lids and process.

Recommended process time for Mango Sauce in a boiling-water canner				
		Process Time at Altitudes of		
Style of Pack	Jar Size	0–1,000 ft	1,001–6,000 ft	Above 6,000 ft
Hot	Half-pints	15 min	20	25

MIXED FRUIT COCKTAIL

3 lbs peaches
3 lbs pears
1-1/2 lbs slightly underripe seedless green grapes
10-oz jar of maraschino cherries
3 cups sugar
4 cups water

Yield: About 6 pints

Procedure: Stem and wash grapes, and keep in ascorbic acid solution (see page 1-11). Dip ripe but firm peaches, a few at a time, in boiling water for 1 to 1-1/2 minutes to loosen skins. Dip in cold water and slip off skins. Cut in half, remove pits, cut into 1/2-inch cubes and keep in solution with grapes. Peel, halve, and core pears. Cut into 1/2-inch cubes, and keep in solution with grapes and peaches. Combine sugar and water in a saucepan and bring to boil. Drain mixed fruit. Add 1/2 cup of hot syrup to each hot jar. Then add a few cherries and gently fill the jar with mixed fruit and more hot syrup, leaving 1/2-inch headspace. Remove air bubbles and adjust headspace if needed. Wipe rims of jars with a dampened clean paper towel. Adjust lids and process.

Recommended process time for Mixed Fruit Cocktail in a boiling-water canner					
		Process Time at Altitudes of			
Style of Pack	Jar Size	0–1,000 ft	1,001–3,000 ft	3,001–6,000 ft	Above 6,000 ft
Raw	Half-pints or Pints	20 min	25	30	35

NECTARINES—HALVED OR SLICED

Quantity: An average of 17-1/2 pounds is needed per canner load of 7 quarts; an average of 11 pounds is needed per canner load of 9 pints. A bushel weighs 48 pounds and yields 16 to 24 quarts—an average of 2-1/2 pounds per quart.

Quality: Choose ripe, mature fruit of ideal quality for eating fresh or cooking.

Procedure: Follow directions for peaches except do not dip in hot water or remove skins. Wash fruit and use either hot or raw pack, and use the same process time.

PEACHES—HALVED OR SLICED

Quantity: An average of 17-1/2 pounds is needed per canner load of 7 quarts; an average of 11 pounds is needed per canner load of 9 pints. A bushel weighs 48 pounds and yields 16 to 24 quarts—an average of 2-1/2 pounds per quart.

Quality: Choose ripe, mature fruit of ideal quality for eating fresh or cooking.

Procedure: Dip fruit in boiling water for 30 to 60 seconds until skins loosen. Dip quickly in cold water and slip off skins. Cut in half, remove pits and slice if desired. To prevent darkening, keep peeled fruit in ascorbic acid solution (see page 1-11). Prepare and boil a very light, light, or medium syrup (see page 2-5) or pack peaches in water, apple juice, or white grape juice. Raw packs make poor quality peaches.

Hot pack—In a large saucepan place drained fruit in syrup, water, or juice and bring to boil. Fill hot jars with hot fruit and cooking liquid, leaving 1/2-inch headspace. Place halves in layers, cut side down.

Raw pack—Fill hot jars with raw fruit, cut side down, and add hot water, juice, or syrup, leaving 1/2-inch headspace.

Remove air bubbles and adjust headspace if needed. Wipe rims of jars with a dampened clean paper towel. Adjust lids and process.

Recommended process time for Peaches, halved or sliced in a boiling-water canner

Style of Pack	Jar Size	Process Time at Altitudes of			
		0–1,000 ft	1,001–3,000 ft	3,001–6,000 ft	Above 6,000 ft
Hot	Pints	20 min	25	30	35
	Quarts	25	30	35	40
Raw	Pints	25	30	35	40
	Quarts	30	35	40	45

Processing directions for canning peaches in a dial- or weighted-gauge canner are given on pages 2-31 and 2-32.

PEARS—HALVED

Quantity: An average of 17-1/2 pounds is needed per canner load of 7 quarts; an average of 11 pounds is needed per canner load of 9 pints. A bushel weighs 50 pounds and yields 16 to 25 quarts—an average of 2-1/2 pounds per quart.

Quality: Choose ripe, mature fruit of ideal quality for eating fresh or cooking.

Procedure: Wash and peel pears. Cut lengthwise in halves and remove core. A melon baller or metal measuring spoon is suitable for coring pears. To prevent discoloration, keep pears in an ascorbic acid solution (see page 1-11). Prepare a very light, light, or medium syrup (see page 2-5) or pack pears in apple juice, white grape juice, or water. Raw packs make poor quality pears. Boil drained pears 5 minutes in syrup, juice, or water. Fill hot jars with hot fruit and cooking liquid, leaving 1/2-inch headspace. Remove air bubbles and adjust headspace if needed. Wipe rims of jars with a dampened clean paper towel. Adjust lids and process.

Recommended process time for Pears, halved in a boiling-water canner					
		Process Time at Altitudes of			
Style of Pack	Jar Size	0–1,000 ft	1,001–3,000 ft	3,001–6,000 ft	Above 6,000 ft
Hot	Pints	20 min	25	30	35
	Quarts	25	30	35	40

Processing directions for canning pears in a dial- or weighted-gauge canner are given on pages 2-31 and 2-32.

PEARS, ASIAN —HALVED OR SLICED

Important: All home-canned Asian Pears must be acidified before canning in a boiling water canner to make them safe from the microorganism that causes botulism.

Quantity: An average of 17-19 pounds is needed per canner load of 7 quarts; an average of 11-13 pounds is needed per canner load of 9 pints.

Quality: Choose ripe, mature fruit of ideal quality for eating fresh or cooking.

Procedure: Wash and peel pears. Cut lengthwise in halves and remove cores. Slice, if desired. To prevent discoloration, keep pears in an ascorbic acid solution (see page 1-11). Prepare a very light, light, or medium syrup (see page 2-5) or pack pears in apple juice, white grape juice, or water.

Hot pack – Boil drained pears 5 minutes in syrup, juice or water. Fill hot jars with hot fruit and cover with boiling cooking liquid, leaving 1/2-inch headspace. **Add 1 tablespoon bottled lemon juice per pint jar or 2 tablespoons per quart jar.** Remove air bubbles and adjust headspace if needed. Wipe rims of jars with a dampened clean paper towel. Adjust lids and process.

Recommended process time for Asian Pears, halved or sliced in a boiling-water canner					
		Process Time at Altitudes of			
Style of Pack	Jar Size	0–1,000 ft	1,001–3,000 ft	3,001–6,000 ft	Above 6,000 ft
Hot	Pints	20 min	25	30	35
	Quarts	25	30	35	40

PINEAPPLE

Quantity: An average of 21 pounds is needed per canner load of 7 quarts; an average of 13 pounds is needed per canner load of 9 pints—an average of 3 pounds per quart.

Quality: Select firm, ripe pineapples.

Procedure: Wash pineapple. Peel and remove eyes and tough fiber. Slice or cube. Pineapple may be packed in water, apple juice, white grape juice, or in very light, light, or medium syrup (see page 2-5). In a large saucepan, add pineapple to syrup, water, or juice, and simmer 10 minutes. Fill hot jars with hot pieces and cooking liquid, leaving 1/2-inch headspace. Remove air bubbles and adjust headspace if needed. Wipe rims of jars with a dampened clean paper towel. Adjust lids and process.

Recommended process time for Pineapple in a boiling-water canner					
		Process Time at Altitudes of			
Style of Pack	Jar Size	0–1,000 ft	1,001–3,000 ft	3,001–6,000 ft	Above 6,000 ft
Hot	Pints	15 min	20	20	25
	Quarts	20	25	30	35

PLUMS—HALVED OR WHOLE

Quantity: An average of 14 pounds is needed per canner load of 7 quarts; an average of 9 pounds is needed per canner load of 9 pints. A bushel weighs 56 pounds and yields 22 to 36 quarts—an average of 2 pounds per quart.

Quality: Select deep-colored, mature fruit of ideal quality for eating fresh or cooking. Plums may be packed in water or syrup.

Procedure: Stem and wash plums. Plums may be packed in water or syrup. To can whole, prick skins on two sides of plums with fork to prevent splitting. Freestone varieties may be halved and pitted. If you use syrup, prepare very light, light, or medium syrup according to directions on page 2-5.

Hot pack—Add plums to hot water or hot syrup and boil 2 minutes. Cover saucepan and let stand 20 to 30 minutes. Fill hot jars with hot plums and cooking liquid or syrup, leaving 1/2-inch headspace.

Raw pack—Fill hot jars with raw plums, packing firmly. Add hot water or syrup, leaving 1/2-inch headspace.

Remove air bubbles and adjust headspace if needed. Wipe rims of jars with a dampened clean paper towel. Adjust lids and process.

Recommended process time for Plums, halved or whole in a boiling-water canner

Style of Pack	Jar Size	Process Time at Altitudes of			
		0–1,000 ft	1,001–3,000 ft	3,001–6,000 ft	Above 6,000 ft
Hot and Raw	Pints	20 min	25	30	35
	Quarts	25	30	35	40

Processing directions for canning plums in a dial- or weighted-gauge canner are given on pages 2-31 and 2-32.

RHUBARB—STEWED

Quantity: An average of 10-1/2 pounds is needed per canner load of 7 quarts; an average of 7 pounds is needed per canner load of 9 pints. A lug weighs 28 pounds and yields 14 to 28 quarts—an average of 1-1/2 pounds per quart.

Quality: Select young, tender, well-colored stalks from the spring or late fall crop.

Procedure: Trim off leaves. Wash stalks and cut into 1/2-inch to 1-inch pieces. In a large saucepan add 1/2 cup sugar for each quart of fruit. Let stand until juice appears. Heat gently to boiling. Fill hot jars without delay, leaving 1/2-inch headspace. Remove air bubbles and adjust headspace if needed. Wipe rims of jars with a dampened clean paper towel. Adjust lids and process.

Recommended process time for Rhubarb, stewed in a boiling-water canner

Style of Pack	Jar Size	Process Time at Altitudes of		
		0–1,000 ft	1,001–6,000 ft	Above 6,000 ft
Hot	Pints or Quarts	15 min	20	25

Process directions for canning rhubarb in a dial- or weighted-gauge canner are given on pages 2-31 and 2-32.

ZUCCHINI-PINEAPPLE

4 qts cubed or shredded zucchini
46 oz canned unsweetened pineapple juice
1-1/2 cups bottled lemon juice
3 cups sugar

Yield: About 8 to 9 pints

Procedure: Peel zucchini and either cut into 1/2-inch cubes or shred. Mix zucchini with other ingredients in a large saucepan and bring to a boil. Simmer 20 minutes. Fill hot jars with hot mixture and cooking liquid, leaving 1/2-inch headspace. Remove air bubbles and adjust headspace if needed. Wipe rims of jars with a dampened clean paper towel. Adjust lids and process.

Recommended process time for Zucchini-Pineapple in a boiling-water canner

Style of Pack	Jar Size	Process Time at Altitudes of		
		0–1,000 ft	1,001–6,000 ft	Above 6,000 ft
Hot	Half-pints or Pints	15 min	20	25

FRUIT SALSAS

SPICY CRANBERRY SALSA

6 cups chopped red onion
4 finely chopped large Serrano peppers*
1-1/2 cups water
1-1/2 cups cider vinegar (5%)
1 tbsp canning salt
1-1/3 cups sugar
6 tbsp clover honey
12 cups (2-3/4 lbs) rinsed, fresh whole cranberries

*Caution: Wear plastic or rubber gloves when handling and cutting hot peppers or wash hands thoroughly with soap and water before touching your face or eyes.

Yield: About 6 pint jars

Procedure: Combine all ingredients except cranberries in a large Dutch oven. Bring to a boil over high heat; reduce heat slightly and boil gently for 5 minutes. Add cranberries, reduce heat slightly and simmer mixture for 20 minutes, stirring occasionally to prevent scorching. Fill the hot mixture into hot pint jars, leaving 1/4-inch headspace. Leave saucepot over low heat while filling jars. Remove air bubbles and adjust headspace if needed. Wipe rims of jars with a dampened clean paper towel. Adjust lids and process.

Recommended process time for Spicy Cranberry Salsa in a boiling-water canner

Style of Pack	Jar Size	Process Time at Altitudes of		
		0–1,000 ft	1,001–6,000 ft	Above 6,000 ft
Hot	Half-pints or Pints	10 min	15	20

MANGO SALSA

6 cups diced unripe mango (about 3 to 4 large, hard green mangoes)
1-1/2 cups diced red bell pepper
1/2 cup finely chopped yellow onion
1/2 tsp crushed red pepper flakes
2 tsp finely chopped garlic
2 tsp finely chopped ginger
1 cup light brown sugar
1-1/4 cups cider vinegar (5%)
1/2 cup water

Caution: Handling green mangoes may irritate the skin of some people in the same way as poison ivy. (They belong to the same plant family.) To avoid this reaction, wear plastic or rubber gloves while working with raw green mango. Do not touch your face, lips or eyes after touching or cutting raw green mangoes until all traces are washed away.

Yield: About 6 half-pint jars

Procedure: Wash all produce well. Peel and chop mango into 1/2-inch cubes. Dice bell pepper into 1/2-inch pieces. Finely chop yellow onions. Combine all ingredients in an 8-quart Dutch oven or stockpot. Bring to a boil over high heat, stirring to dissolve sugar. Reduce to simmering, and simmer 5 minutes. Fill hot solids into hot half-pint jars, leaving 1/2-inch headspace. Cover with hot liquid, leaving 1/2-inch headspace. Remove air bubbles and adjust headspace if needed. Wipe rims of jars with a dampened clean paper towel. Adjust lids and process.

Recommended process time for Mango Salsa in a boiling-water canner				
		Process Time at Altitudes of		
Style of Pack	Jar Size	0–1,000 ft	1,001–6,000 ft	Above 6,000 ft
Hot	Half-pints	10 min	15	20

PEACH SALSA

Procedure: Follow directions for Mango Salsa using diced hard, underripe but yellow peaches in place of the mango.

PEACH APPLE SALSA

6 cups chopped Roma tomatoes
2-1/2 cups diced yellow onions
2 cups chopped green bell peppers
10 cups chopped hard, unripe peaches
2 cups chopped Granny Smith apples
4 tbsp mixed pickling spice
1 tbsp canning salt
2 tsp crushed red pepper flakes
3-3/4 cups (1-1/4 pounds) packed light brown sugar
2-1/4 cups cider vinegar (5%)

Yield: About 7 pint jars

Procedure: Place pickling spice on a clean, double-layered, 6-inch-square piece of 100% cheesecloth. Bring corners together and tie with a clean string. (Or use a purchased muslin spice bag). Wash and peel tomatoes (place washed tomatoes in boiling water for 1 minute, immediately place in cold water, and slip off skins). Chop into 1/2-inch pieces. Peel, wash and dice onions into 1/4-inch pieces. Wash, core, and seed bell peppers; chop into 1/4-inch pieces. Combine chopped tomatoes, onions and peppers in an 8- or 10- quart Dutch oven or saucepot. Wash, peel and pit peaches; cut into halves and soak for 10 minutes in an ascorbic acid solution (1500 mg in half gallon water). Wash, peel and core apples; cut into halves and soak for 10 minutes in ascorbic acid solution. Quickly chop peaches and apples into 1/2-inch cubes to prevent browning. Add chopped peaches and apples to the saucepot with the vegetables. Add the pickling spice bag to the saucepot; stir in the salt, red pepper flakes, brown sugar and vinegar. Bring to boiling, stirring gently to mix ingredients. Reduce heat and simmer 30 minutes, stirring occasionally. Remove spice bag from pan and discard. With a slotted spoon, fill salsa solids into hot pint jars, leaving 1-1/4-inch headspace (about 3/4 pound solids in each jar). Cover with cooking liquid, leaving 1/2-inch headspace. Remove air bubbles and adjust headspace if needed. Wipe rims of jars with a dampened clean paper towel. Adjust lids and process.

Recommended process time for Peach-Apple Salsa in a boiling-water canner

Style of Pack	Jar Size	Process Time at Altitudes of		
		0–1,000 ft	1,001–6,000 ft	Above 6,000 ft
Hot	Pints	15 min	20	25

PIE FILLINGS

General: The following fruit fillings are excellent and safe products. Each canned quart makes one 8-inch to 9-inch pie. The filling may be used as toppings on dessert or pastries. "Clear Jel®" is a chemically modified corn starch that produces excellent sauce consistency even after fillings are canned and baked. Other available starches break down when used in these pie fillings, causing a runny sauce consistency. Clear Jel® is available only through a few supply outlets and is not currently available in grocery stores. Find out about its availability prior to gathering other ingredients to make these pie fillings. If you cannot find it, ask your county Extension family and consumer sciences educator about sources for Clear Jel®.

Because the variety of fruit may alter the flavor of the fruit pie, it is suggested that you first make a single quart, make a pie with it, and serve. Then adjust the sugar and spices in the recipe to suit your personal preferences. The amount of lemon juice should not be altered, as it aids in controlling the safety and storage stability of the fillings.

When using frozen cherries and blueberries, select unsweetened fruit. If sugar has been added, rinse it off while fruit is frozen. Thaw fruit, then collect, measure, and use juice from fruit to partially replace the water specified in the recipe. Use only 1/4 cup Clear Jel® per quart, or 1-3/4 cups for 7 quarts. Use fresh fruit in the apple and peach pie filling recipes.

APPLE PIE FILLING

	Quantities of Ingredients Needed for:	
	1 Quart	**7 Quarts**
Blanched, sliced fresh apples	3-1/2 cups	6 quarts
Granulated sugar	3/4 cups + 2 tbsp	5-1/2 cups
Clear Jel®	1/4 cup	1-1/2 cups
Cinnamon	1/2 tsp	1 tbsp
Cold water	1/2 cup	2-1/2 cups
Apple juice	3/4 cups	5 cups
Bottled lemon juice	2 tbsp	3/4 cup
Nutmeg (optional)	1/8 tsp	1 tsp
Yellow food coloring (optional)	1 drop	7 drops

Quality: Use firm, crisp apples. Stayman, Golden Delicious, Rome, and other varieties of similar quality are suitable. If apples lack tartness, use an additional 1/4 cup of lemon juice for each 6 quarts of slices.

Yield: 1 quart or 7 quarts

Procedure: Wash, peel, and core apples. Prepare slices 1/2-inch wide and place in water containing ascorbic acid to prevent browning (see page 1-11). For fresh fruit, place 6 cups at a time in 1 gallon of boiling water. Boil each batch 1 minute after the water returns to a boil. Drain but keep heated fruit in a covered bowl or pot. Combine sugar, Clear Jel® and cinnamon in a large kettle with water and apple juice. If desired, food coloring and nutmeg may be added. Stir and cook on medium high heat until mixture thickens and begins to bubble. Add lemon juice and boil 1 minute, stirring constantly. Fold in drained apple slices immediately and fill hot jars with mixture without delay, leaving 1-inch headspace. Remove air bubbles and adjust headspace if needed. Wipe rims of jars with a dampened clean paper towel. Adjust lids and process immediately.

Recommended process time for Apple Pie Filling in a boiling-water canner					
		Process Time at Altitudes of			
Style of Pack	Jar Size	0– 1,000 ft	1,001– 3,000 ft	3,001– 6,000 ft	Above 6,000 ft
Hot	Pints or Quarts	25 min	30	35	40

BLUEBERRY PIE FILLING

	Quantities of Ingredients Needed for:	
	1 Quart	**7 Quarts**
Fresh or thawed blueberries	3-1/2 cups	6 quarts
Granulated sugar	3/4 cup + 2 tbsp	6 cups
Clear Jel®	1/4 cup + 1 tbsp	2-1/4 cups
Cold water	1 cup	7 cups
Bottled lemon juice	3 tbsp	1/2 cup
Blue food coloring (optional)	3 drops	20 drops
Red food coloring (optional)	1 drop	7 drops

Quality: Select fresh, ripe, and firm blueberries. Unsweetened frozen blueberries may be used. If sugar has been added, rinse it off while fruit is still frozen.

Yield: 1 quart or 7 quarts

Procedure: Wash and drain fresh blueberries. For fresh fruit, place 6 cups at a time in 1 gallon boiling water. Boil each batch 1 minute after the water returns to a boil. Drain but keep heated fruit in a covered bowl or pot. Combine sugar and Clear Jel® in a large kettle. Stir. Add water and, if desired, food coloring. Cook on medium high heat until mixture thickens and begins to bubble. Add lemon juice and boil 1 minute, stirring constantly. Fold in drained berries immediately and fill hot jars with mixture without delay, leaving 1-inch headspace. Remove air bubbles and adjust headspace if needed. Wipe rims of jars with a dampened clean paper towel. Adjust lids and process immediately.

Recommended process time for Blueberry Pie Filling in a boiling-water canner

Style of Pack	Jar Size	Process Time at Altitudes of			
		0–1,000 ft	1,001–3,000 ft	3,001–6,000 ft	Above 6,000 ft
Hot	Pints or Quarts	30 min	35	40	45

CHERRY PIE FILLING

	Quantities of Ingredients Needed for:	
	1 Quart	**7 Quarts**
Fresh or thawed sour cherries	3-1/3 cups	6 quarts
Granulated sugar	1 cup	7 cups
Clear Jel®	1/4 cup + 1 tbsp	1-3/4 cups
Cold water	1-1/3 cups	9-1/3 cups
Bottled lemon juice	1 tbsp + 1 tsp	1/2 cups
Cinnamon (optional)	1/8 tsp	1 tsp
Almond extract (optional)	1/4 tsp	2 tsp
Red food coloring (optional)	6 drops	1/4 tsp

Quality: Select fresh, very ripe, and firm cherries. Unsweetened frozen cherries may be used. If sugar has been added, rinse it off while the fruit is still frozen.

Yield: 1 quart or 7 quarts

Procedure: Rinse and pit fresh cherries, and hold in cold water. To prevent stem end browning, use ascorbic acid solution (see page 1-11). For fresh fruit, place 6 cups at a time in 1 gallon boiling water. Boil each batch 1 minute after the water returns to a boil. Drain but keep heated in a covered bowl or pot. Combine sugar and Clear Jel® in a large saucepan and add water. If desired, add cinnamon, almond extract, and food coloring. Stir mixture and cook over medium high heat until mixture thickens and begins to bubble. Add lemon juice and boil 1 minute, stirring constantly. Fold in drained cherries immediately and fill hot jars with mixture without delay, leaving 1-inch headspace. Remove air bubbles and adjust headspace if needed. Wipe rims of jars with a dampened clean paper towel. Adjust lids and process immediately.

Recommended process time for Cherry Pie Filling in a boiling-water canner					
		Process Time at Altitudes of			
Style of Pack	Jar Size	0–1,000 ft	1,001–3,000 ft	3,001–6,000 ft	Above 6,000 ft
Hot	Pints or Quarts	30 min	35	40	45

FESTIVE MINCEMEAT PIE FILLING

2 cups finely chopped suet
4 lbs ground beef or 4 lb ground venison and 1 lb sausage
5 qts chopped apples
2 lbs dark seedless raisins
1 lb white raisins
2 qts apple cider
2 tbsp ground cinnamon
2 tsp ground nutmeg
5 cups sugar
2 tbsp salt

Yield: About 7 quarts

Procedure: Cook meat and suet in water to avoid browning. Peel, core, and quarter apples. Put meat, suet, and apples through food grinder using a medium blade. Combine all ingredients in a large saucepan, and simmer 1 hour or until slightly thickened. Stir often. Fill hot jars with mixture without delay, leaving 1-inch headspace. Remove air bubbles and adjust headspace if needed. Wipe rims of jars with a dampened clean paper towel. Adjust lids and process.

Recommended process time for Festive Mincemeat Pie Filling in a dial-gauge pressure canner						
			Canner Pressure (PSI) at Altitudes of			
Style of Pack	Jar Size	Process Time	0–2,000 ft	2,001–4,000 ft	4,001–6,000 ft	6,001–8,000 ft
Hot	Quarts	90 min	11 lb	12 lb	13 lb	14 lb

Recommended process time for **Festive Mincemeat Pie Filling** in a weighted-gauge pressure canner

Style of Pack	Jar Size	Process Time	Canner Pressure (PSI) at Altitudes of	
			0–1,000 ft	Above 1,000 ft
Hot	Quarts	90 min	10 lb	15 lb

GREEN TOMATO PIE FILLING

4 qts chopped green tomatoes
3 qts peeled and chopped tart apples
1 lb dark seedless raisins
1 lb white raisins
1/4 cup minced citron, lemon, or orange peel
2 cups water
2-1/2 cups brown sugar
2-1/2 cups white sugar
1/2 cup vinegar (5%)
1 cup bottled lemon juice
2 tbsp ground cinnamon
1 tsp ground nutmeg
1 tsp ground cloves

Yield: About 7 quarts

Procedure: Combine all ingredients in a large saucepan. Cook slowly, stirring often, until tender and slightly thickened (about 35 to 40 minutes). Fill hot jars with hot mixture, leaving 1/2-inch headspace. Remove air bubbles and adjust headspace if needed. Wipe rims of jars with a dampened clean paper towel. Adjust lids and process.

Recommended process time for **Green Tomato Pie Filling** in a boiling-water canner

Style of Pack	Jar Size	Process Time at Altitudes of		
		0–1,000 ft	1,001–6,000 ft	Above 6,000 ft
Hot	Quarts	15 min	20	25

PEACH PIE FILLING

	Quantities of Ingredients Needed for:	
	1 Quart	**7 Quarts**
Sliced fresh peaches	3-1/2 cups	6 quarts
Granulated sugar	1 cup	7 cups
Clear Jel®	1/4 cup + 1 tbsp	2 cups + 3 tbsp
Cold water	3/4 cup	5-1/4 cups
Cinnamon (optional)	1/8 tsp	1 tsp
Almond extract (optional)	1/8 tsp	1 tsp
Bottled lemon juice	1/4 cup	1-3/4 cups

Quality: Select ripe, but firm fresh peaches. Red Haven, Redskin, Sun High, and other varieties of similar quality are suitable.

Yield: 1 quart or 7 quarts.

Procedure: Peel peaches. To loosen skins, submerge peaches in boiling water for approximately 30-60 seconds, and then place in cold water for 20 seconds. Slip off skins and prepare slices 1/2-inch thick. Place slices in water containing 1/2 tsp of ascorbic acid crystals or six 500-milligram vitamin C tablets in 1 gallon of water to prevent browning. For fresh fruit, place 6 cups at a time in 1 gallon boiling water. Boil each batch 1 minute after the water returns to a boil. Drain but keep heated fruit in a covered bowl or pot. Combine water, sugar, Clear Jel®, and, if desired, cinnamon and/or almond extract in a large kettle. Stir and cook over medium high heat until mixture thickens and begins to bubble. Add lemon juice and boil sauce 1 minute more, stirring constantly. Fold in drained peach slices and continue to heat mixture for 3 minutes. Fill hot jars without delay, leaving 1-inch headspace. Remove air bubbles and adjust headspace if needed. Wipe rims of jars with a dampened clean paper towel. Adjust lids and process immediately.

Recommended process time for Peach Pie Filling in a boiling-water canner					
		Process Time at Altitudes of			
Style of Pack	Jar Size	0– 1,000 ft	1,001– 3,000 ft	3,001– 6,000 ft	Above 6,000 ft
Hot	Pints or Quarts	30 min	35	40	45

Process times for some acid foods in a dial-gauge pressure canner

Type of Fruit	Style of Pack	Jar Size	Process Time (Min)	Canner Pressure (PSI) at Altitudes of			
				0–2,000 ft	2,001–4,000 ft	4,001–6,000 ft	6,001–8,000 ft
Applesauce	Hot	Pints	8	6 lb	7 lb	8 lb	9 lb
	Hot	Quarts	10	6	7	8	9
Apples, sliced	Hot	Pints or Quarts	8	6	7	8	9
Berries, whole	Hot	Pints or Quarts	8	6	7	8	9
	Raw	Pints	8	6	7	8	9
	Raw	Quarts	10	6	7	8	9
Cherries, sour or sweet	Hot	Pints	8	6	7	8	9
	Hot	Quarts	10	6	7	8	9
	Raw	Pints or Quarts	10	6	7	8	9
Fruit Purees	Hot	Pints or Quarts	8	6	7	8	9
Grapefruit and Orange Sections	Hot	Pints or Quarts	8	6	7	8	9
	Raw	Pints	8	6	7	8	9
	Raw	Quarts	10	6	7	8	9
Peaches, Apricots, and Nectarines	Hot and Raw	Pints or Quarts	10	6	7	8	9
Pears	Hot	Pints or Quarts	10	6	7	8	9
Plums	Hot and Raw	Pints or Quarts	10	6	7	8	9
Rhubarb	Hot	Pints or Quarts	8	6	7	8	9

Process times for some acid foods in a weighted-gauge pressure canner

Type of Fruit	Style of Pack	Jar Size	Process Time (Min)	Canner Pressure (PSI) at Altitudes of	
				0–1,000 ft	Above 1,000 ft
Applesauce	Hot	Pints	8	5 lb	10 lb
	Hot	Quarts	10	5	10
Apples, sliced	Hot	Pints or Quarts	8	5	10
Berries, whole	Hot	Pints or Quarts	8	5	10
	Raw	Pints	8	5	10
	Raw	Quarts	10	5	10
Cherries, sour or sweet	Hot	Pints	8	5	10
	Hot	Quarts	10	5	10
	Raw	Pints or Quarts	10	5	10
Fruit Purees	Hot	Pints or Quarts	8	5	10
Grapefruit and Orange Sections	Hot	Pints or Quarts	8	5	10
	Raw	Pints	8	5	10
	Raw	Quarts	10	5	10
Peaches, Apricots, and Nectarines	Hot and Raw	Pints or Quarts	10	5	10
Pears	Hot	Pints or Quarts	10	5	10
Plums	Hot and Raw	Pints or Quarts	10	5	10
Rhubarb	Hot	Pints or Quarts	8	5	10

Complete Guide to
Home Canning

Guide 3
Selecting, Preparing, and Canning Tomatoes and Tomato Products

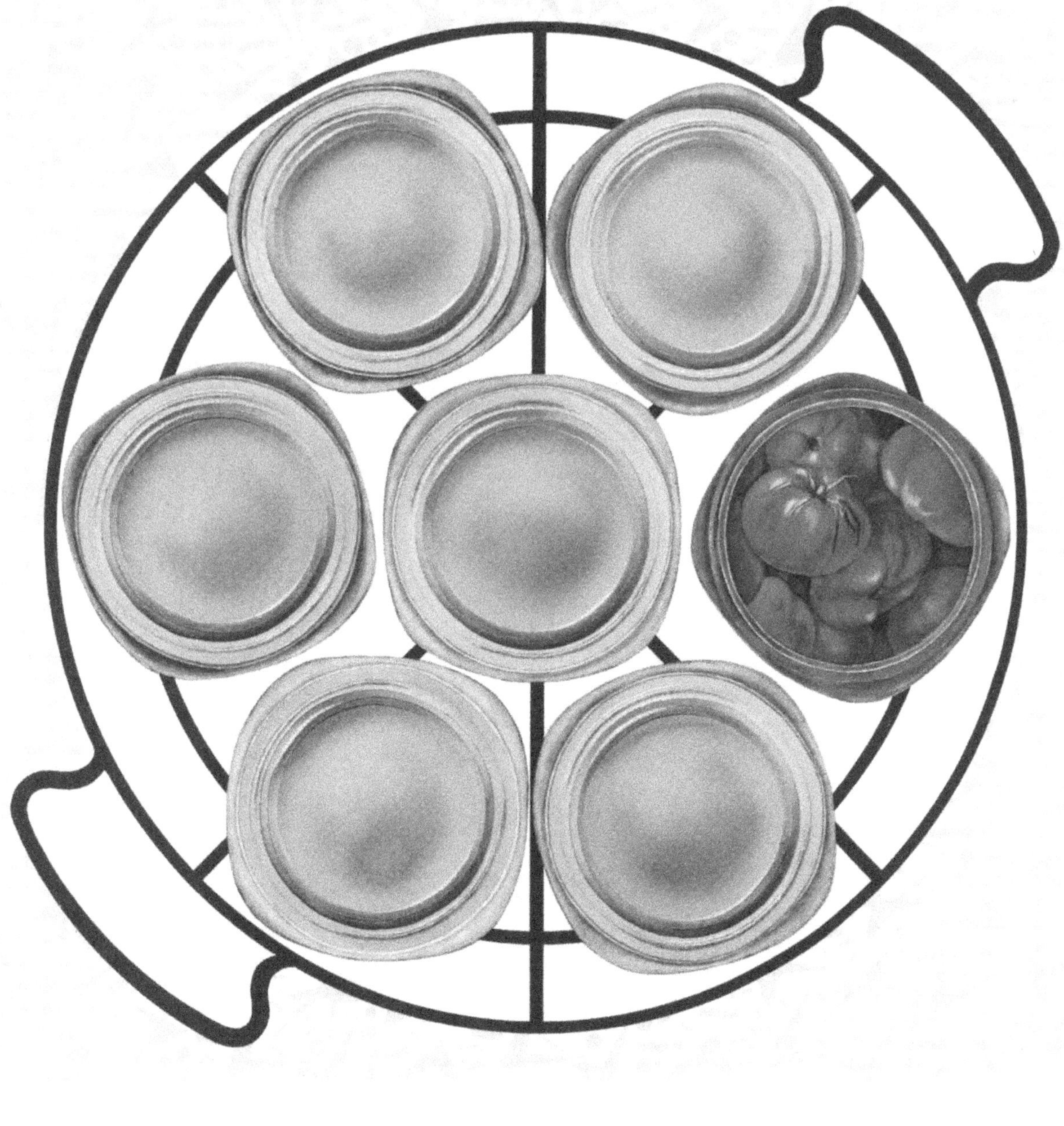

United States Department of Agriculture

National Institute of Food and Agriculture

Guide 3
Selecting, Preparing, and Canning Tomatoes and Tomato Products

Table of Contents

Section	Page
General	3-5
Tomato juice	3-5
Tomato and vegetable juice blend	3-6
Tomatoes—crushed	3-7
Standard tomato sauce	3-8
Tomatoes—whole or halved (packed in water)	3-9
Tomatoes—whole or halved (packed in tomato juice)	3-10
Tomatoes—whole or halved (packed raw without added liquid)	3-11
Tomatoes with okra or zucchini	3-12
Tomatillos	3-13
Spaghetti sauce without meat	3-13
Spaghetti sauce with meat	3-14
Mexican tomato sauce	3-15
Easy hot sauce	3-16
Cayenne pepper sauce	3-17
Tomato ketchup	3-17
Country western ketchup	3-18
Blender ketchup	3-18
Salsa Recipes	**3-19**
Selection and preparation of ingredients	3-19
Chile salsa (hot tomato-pepper sauce)	3-21
Chile salsa II	3-22
Tomatillo green salsa	3-22
Tomato salsa using paste tomatoes	3-23
Tomato salsa using slicing tomatoes	3-24
Tomato/green chile salsa	3-24
Tomato/tomato paste salsa	3-25
Tomato taco sauce	3-26

General

Quality: Select only disease-free, preferably vine-ripened, firm fruit for canning.

Caution: Do not can tomatoes from dead or frost-killed vines. Green tomatoes are more acidic than ripened fruit and can be canned safely with any of the following recommendations.

Acidification: To ensure safe acidity in whole, crushed, or juiced tomatoes, add 2 tablespoons of bottled lemon juice or 1/2 teaspoon of citric acid per quart of tomatoes. For pints, use 1 tablespoon bottled lemon juice or 1/4 teaspoon citric acid. Acid can be added directly to the jars before filling with product. Add sugar to offset acid taste, if desired. Four tablespoons of a 5 percent acidity vinegar per quart may be used instead of lemon juice or citric acid. However, vinegar may cause undesirable flavor changes.

When a procedure in this Guide for canning tomatoes offers both boiling water and pressure canning options, all steps in the preparation ("Procedure") are still required even if the pressure processing option is chosen. This includes acidification. The boiling water and pressure alternatives are equal processes with different time/temperature combinations calculated for these products.

Recommendation: Use of a pressure canner will result in higher quality and more nutritious canned tomato products. If your pressure canner cannot be operated above 15 PSI, select a process time at a lower pressure.

TOMATO JUICE

Quantity: An average of 23 pounds is needed per canner load of 7 quarts, or an average of 14 pounds per canner load of 9 pints. A bushel weighs 53 pounds and yields 15 to 18 quarts of juice—an average of 3-1/4 pounds per quart.

Procedure: Wash, remove stems, and trim off bruised or discolored portions. To prevent juice from separating, quickly cut about 1 pound of fruit into quarters and put directly into saucepan. Heat immediately to boiling while crushing. Continue to slowly add and crush freshly cut tomato quarters to the boiling mixture. Make sure the mixture boils constantly and vigorously while you add the remaining tomatoes. Simmer 5 minutes after you add all pieces.

If you are not concerned about juice separation, simply slice or quarter tomatoes into a large saucepan. Crush, heat, and simmer for 5 minutes before juicing.

Press both types of heated juice through a sieve or food mill to remove skins and seeds. **Add bottled lemon juice or citric acid to jars.** See acidification instructions on page 3-5. Heat juice again to boiling. Add 1 teaspoon of salt per quart to the jars, if desired. Fill hot jars with hot tomato juice, leaving 1/2-inch headspace. Wipe rims of jars with a dampened clean paper towel. Adjust lids and process. (Acidification is still required for the pressure canning options; follow all steps in the Procedures above for any of the processing options.)

Recommended process time for Tomato Juice in a boiling-water canner

Style of Pack	Jar Size	Process Time at Altitudes of			
		0–1,000 ft	1,001–3,000 ft	3,001–6,000 ft	Above 6,000 ft
Hot	Pints	35 min	40	45	50
	Quarts	40	45	50	55

Recommended process time for Tomato Juice in a dial-gauge pressure canner

Style of Pack	Jar Size	Process Time	Canner Pressure (PSI) at Altitudes of			
			0–2,000 ft	2,001–4,000 ft	4,001–6,000 ft	6,001–8,000 ft
Hot	Pints or Quarts	20 min	6 lb	7 lb	8 lb	9 lb
		15	11	12	13	14

Recommended process time for Tomato Juice in a weighted-gauge pressure canner

Style of Pack	Jar Size	Process Time	Canner Pressure (PSI) at Altitudes of	
			0–1,000 ft	Above 1,000 ft
Hot	Pints or Quarts	20 min	5 lb	10 lb
		15	10	15
		10	15	Not recommended

TOMATO AND VEGETABLE JUICE BLEND

Quantity: An average of 22 pounds of tomatoes is needed per canner load of 7 quarts. No more than 3 cups of other vegetables may be added for each 22 pounds of tomatoes.

Procedure: Crush and simmer tomatoes as for making tomato juice (see page 3-5). Add no more than 3 cups of any combination of finely chopped celery, onions, carrots, and peppers for each 22 lbs of tomatoes. Simmer mixture 20 minutes. Press hot cooked tomatoes and vegetables through a sieve or food mill to remove skins and seeds. **Add bottled lemon juice or citric acid to jars.** See acidification directions on page 3-5. Add 1 teaspoon of salt per quart to the jars, if desired. Reheat tomato-vegetable juice blend to boiling and fill immediately into hot jars, leaving 1/2-inch headspace. Wipe rims of jars with a dampened clean paper towel. Adjust lids and process. (Acidification is still required for the pressure canning options; follow all steps in the Procedures above for any of the processing options.)

Recommended process time for Tomato-Vegetable Blend in a boiling-water canner

Style of Pack	Jar Size	Process Time at Altitudes of			
		0–1,000 ft	1,001–3,000 ft	3,001–6,000 ft	Above 6,000 ft
Hot	Pints	35 min	40	45	50
	Quarts	40	45	50	55

Recommended process time for Tomato-Vegetable Blend in a dial-gauge pressure canner

Style of Pack	Jar Size	Process Time	Canner Pressure (PSI) at Altitudes of			
			0–2,000 ft	2,001–4,000 ft	4,001–6,000 ft	6,001–8,000 ft
Hot	Pints or Quarts	20 min	6 lb	7 lb	8 lb	9 lb
		15	11	12	13	14

Recommended process time for Tomato-Vegetable Blend in a weighted-gauge pressure canner

Style of Pack	Jar Size	Process Time	Canner Pressure (PSI) at Altitudes of	
			0–1,000 ft	Above 1,000 ft
Hot	Pints or Quarts	20 min	5 lb	10 lb
		15	10	15
		10	15	Not recommended

TOMATOES-CRUSHED (with no added liquid)

A high-quality product, ideally suited for use in soups, stews, and casseroles. This recipe is similar to that formerly referred to as "Quartered Tomatoes."

Quantity: An average of 22 pounds is needed per canner load of 7 quarts; an average of 14 fresh pounds is needed per canner load of 9 pints. A bushel weighs 53 pounds and yields 17 to 20 quarts of crushed tomatoes—an average of 2-3/4 pounds per quart.

Procedure: Wash tomatoes and dip in boiling water for 30 to 60 seconds or until skins split. Then dip in cold water, slip off skins, and remove cores. Trim off any bruised or discolored portions and quarter. Heat one-sixth of the quarters quickly in a large pot, crushing them with a wooden mallet or spoon as they are added to the pot. This will exude juice. Continue heating the tomatoes, stirring to prevent burning. Once the tomatoes are boiling, gradually add remaining quartered tomatoes, stirring constantly. These remaining tomatoes do not need to be crushed. They will soften with heating and stirring. Continue until all tomatoes are added. Then boil gently 5 minutes. **Add bottled lemon juice or citric acid to jars.** See acidification directions on page 3-5. Add 1 teaspoon of salt per quart to the jars, if desired. Fill hot jars immediately with hot tomatoes, leaving 1/2-inch headspace. Remove air bubbles and adjust headspace if needed. Wipe rims of jars with a dampened clean paper towel. Adjust lids and process. (Acidification is still required for the pressure canning options; follow all steps in the Procedures above for any of the processing options.)

Recommended process time for Crushed Tomatoes in a boiling-water canner					
		Process Time at Altitudes of			
Style of Pack	Jar Size	0–1,000 ft	1,001–3,000 ft	3,001–6,000 ft	Above 6,000 ft
Hot	Pints	35 min	40	45	50
	Quarts	45	50	55	60

Recommended process time for Crushed Tomatoes in a dial-gauge pressure canner						
			Canner Pressure (PSI) at Altitudes of			
Style of Pack	Jar Size	Process Time	0–2,000 ft	2,001–4,000 ft	4,001–6,000 ft	6,001–8,000 ft
Hot	Pints or Quarts	20 min	6 lb	7 lb	8 lb	9 lb
		15	11	12	13	14

Recommended process time for Crushed Tomatoes in a weighted-gauge pressure canner				
			Canner Pressure (PSI) at Altitudes of	
Style of Pack	Jar Size	Process Time	0–1,000 ft	Above 1,000 ft
Hot	Pints or Quarts	20 min	5 lb	10 lb
		15	10	15
		10	15	Not recommended

STANDARD TOMATO SAUCE

Quantity: For thin sauce—an average of 35 pounds is needed per canner load of 7 quarts; an average of 21 pounds is needed per canner load of 9 pints. A bushel weighs 53 pounds and yields 10 to 12 quarts of sauce—an average of 5 pounds per quart. For thick sauce—an average of 46 pounds is needed per canner load of 7 quarts; an average of 28 pounds is needed per canner load of 9 pints. A bushel weighs 53 pounds and yields 7 to 9 quarts of thick sauce—an average of 6-1/2 pounds per quart.

Procedure: Prepare and press as for making tomato juice, see page 3-5. Simmer in large-diameter saucepan until sauce reaches desired consistency. Boil until volume is reduced by about one-third for thin sauce, or by one-half for thick sauce. **Add bottled lemon juice or citric acid to jars.** See acidification directions on page 3-5. Add 1 teaspoon of salt per quart to the jars, if desired. Fill hot jars, leaving 1/4-inch headspace. Remove air bubbles and adjust headspace if needed. Wipe rims of jars with a dampened clean paper towel. Adjust lids and process. (Acidification is still required for the pressure canning options; follow all steps in the Procedures above for any of the processing options.)

Recommended process time for Standard Tomato Sauce in a boiling-water canner

Style of Pack	Jar Size	Process Time at Altitudes of			
		0–1,000 ft	1,001–3,000 ft	3,001–6,000 ft	Above 6,000 ft
Hot	Pints	35 min	40	45	50
	Quarts	40	45	50	55

Recommended process time for Standard Tomato Sauce in a dial-gauge pressure canner

Style of Pack	Jar Size	Process Time	Canner Pressure (PSI) at Altitudes of			
			0–2,000 ft	2,001–4,000 ft	4,001–6,000 ft	6,001–8,000 ft
Hot	Pints or Quarts	20 min	6 lb	7 lb	8 lb	9 lb
		15	11	12	13	14

Recommended process time for Standard Tomato Sauce in a weighted-gauge pressure canner

Style of Pack	Jar Size	Process Time	Canner Pressure (PSI) at Altitudes of	
			0–1,000 ft	Above 1,000 ft
Hot	Pints or Quarts	20 min	5 lb	10 lb
		15	10	15
		10	15	Not recommended

TOMATOES—WHOLE OR HALVED (packed in water)

Quantity: An average of 21 pounds is needed per canner load of 7 quarts; an average of 13 pounds is needed per canner load of 9 pints. A bushel weighs 53 pounds and yields 15 to 21 quarts—an average of 3 pounds per quart.

Procedure for hot or raw tomatoes filled with water in jars: Wash tomatoes. Dip in boiling water for 30 to 60 seconds or until skins split; then dip in cold water. Slip off skins and remove cores. Leave whole or halve. **Add bottled lemon juice or citric acid to jars.** See acidification directions on page 3-5. Add 1 teaspoon of salt per quart to the jars, if desired. For hot pack products, add enough water to cover the tomatoes and boil them gently for 5 minutes. Fill hot jars with hot tomatoes or with raw peeled tomatoes. Add the hot cooking liquid to the hot pack, or hot water for raw pack to cover, leaving 1/2-inch headspace. Remove air bubbles and adjust headspace if needed. Wipe rims of jars with a dampened clean paper towel. Adjust lids and process. (Acidification is still required for the pressure canning options; follow all steps in the Procedures above for any of the processing options.)

Recommended process time for Water-Packed Whole Tomatoes in a boiling-water canner					
		Process Time at Altitudes of			
Style of Pack	Jar Size	0–1,000 ft	1,001–3,000 ft	3,001–6,000 ft	Above 6,000 ft
Hot and Raw	Pints	40 min	45	50	55
	Quarts	45	50	55	60

Recommended process time for Water-Packed Whole Tomatoes in a dial-gauge pressure canner						
			Canner Pressure (PSI) at Altitudes of			
Style of Pack	Jar Size	Process Time	0–2,000 ft	2,001–4,000 ft	4,001–6,000 ft	6,001–8,000 ft
Hot and Raw	Pints or Quarts	15 min	6 lb	7 lb	8 lb	9 lb
		10	11	12	13	14

Recommended process time for Water-Packed Whole Tomatoes in a weighted-gauge pressure canner				
			Canner Pressure (PSI) at Altitudes of	
Style of Pack	Jar Size	Process Time	0–1,000 ft	Above 1,000 ft
Hot and Raw	Pints or Quarts	15 min	5 lb	10 lb
		10	10	15
		1	15	Not recommended

TOMATOES—WHOLE OR HALVED (packed in tomato juice)

Quantity: See whole tomatoes packed in water (page 3-9).

Procedure: Wash tomatoes. Dip in boiling water for 30 to 60 seconds or until skins split, then dip in cold water. Slip off skins and remove cores. Leave whole or halve. **Add bottled lemon juice or citric acid to the jars.** See acidification instructions on page 3-5. Add 1 teaspoon of salt per quart to the jars, if desired.

Raw pack—Heat tomato juice in a saucepan. Fill hot jars with raw tomatoes, leaving 1/2-inch headspace. Cover tomatoes in the jars with hot tomato juice, leaving 1/2-inch headspace.

Hot pack—Put tomatoes in a large saucepan and add enough tomato juice to completely cover them. Boil tomatoes and juice gently for 5 minutes. Fill hot jars with hot tomatoes, leaving 1/2-inch headspace. Add hot tomato juice to the jars to cover the tomatoes, leaving 1/2-inch headspace.

Remove air bubbles and adjust headspace if needed. Wipe rims of jars with a dampened clean paper towel. Adjust lids and process. (Acidification is still required for the pressure canning options; follow all steps in the Procedures above for any of the processing options.)

Recommended process time for Tomato Juice-Packed Whole Tomatoes in a boiling-water canner

Style of Pack	Jar Size	Process Time at Altitudes of			
		0–1,000 ft	1,001–3,000 ft	3,001–6,000 ft	Above 6,000 ft
Hot and Raw	Pints or Quarts	85 min	90	95	100

Recommended process time for Tomato Juice-Packed Whole Tomatoes in a dial-gauge pressure canner

Style of Pack	Jar Size	Process Time	Canner Pressure (PSI) at Altitudes of			
			0–2,000 ft	2,001–4,000 ft	4,001–6,000 ft	6,001–8,000 ft
Hot and Raw	Pints or Quarts	40 min	6 lb	7 lb	8 lb	9 lb
		25	11	12	13	14

Recommended process time for Tomato Juice-Packed Whole Tomatoes in a weighted-gauge pressure canner

Style of Pack	Jar Size	Process Time	Canner Pressure (PSI) at Altitudes of	
			0–1,000 ft	Above 1,000 ft
Hot and Raw	Pints or Quarts	40 min	5 lb	10 lb
		25	10	15
		15	15	Not recommended

TOMATOES—WHOLE OR HALVED (packed raw without added liquid)

Quantity: See whole tomatoes packed in water (page 3-9).

Procedure: Wash tomatoes. Dip in boiling water for 30 to 60 seconds or until skins split, then dip in cold water. Slip off skins and remove cores. Leave whole or halve. **Add bottled lemon juice or citric acid to the jars.** See acidification instructions on page 3-5. Add 1 teaspoon of salt per quart to the jars, if desired.

Fill hot jars with raw tomatoes, leaving 1/2-inch headspace. Press tomatoes in the jars until spaces between them fill with juice. Leave 1/2-inch headspace. Remove air bubbles and adjust headspace if needed. Wipe rims of jars with a dampened clean paper towel. Adjust lids and process. (Acidification is still required for the pressure canning options; follow all steps in the Procedures above for any of the processing options.)

Recommended process time for Raw Whole Tomatoes Without Added Liquid in a boiling-water canner					
		Process Time at Altitudes of			
Style of Pack	Jar Size	0–1,000 ft	1,001–3,000 ft	3,001–6,000 ft	Above 6,000 ft
Raw	Pints or Quarts	85 min	90	95	100

Recommended process time for Raw Whole Tomatoes Without Added Liquid in a dial-gauge pressure canner						
			Canner Pressure (PSI) at Altitudes of			
Style of Pack	Jar Size	Process Time	0–2,000 ft	2,001–4,000 ft	4,001–6,000 ft	6,001–8,000 ft
Raw	Pints or Quarts	40 min	6 lb	7 lb	8 lb	9 lb
		25	11	12	13	14

Recommended process time for Raw Whole Tomatoes Without Added Liquid in a weighted-gauge pressure canner				
			Canner Pressure (PSI) at Altitudes of	
Style of Pack	Jar Size	Process Time	0–1,000 ft	Above 1,000 ft
Raw	Pints or Quarts	40 min	5 lb	10 lb
		25	10	15
		15	15	Not recommended

TOMATOES WITH OKRA OR ZUCCHINI

Quantity: An average of 12 pounds of tomatoes and 4 pounds of okra or zucchini is needed per canner load of 7 quarts. An average of 7 pounds of tomatoes and 2-1/2 pounds of okra or zucchini is needed per canner load of 9 pints. (Use about 3 pounds tomatoes to 1 pound vegetable.)

Procedure: Wash tomatoes and okra or zucchini. Dip tomatoes in boiling water 30 to 60 seconds or until skins split. Then dip in cold water, slip off skins and remove cores, and quarter. Trim stems from okra and slice into 1-inch pieces or leave whole. Slice or cube zucchini if used. Bring tomatoes to a boil and simmer 10 minutes. Add okra or zucchini and boil gently 5 minutes. Add 1 teaspoon of salt for each quart to the jars, if desired. Fill hot jars with mixture, leaving 1-inch headspace. Remove air bubbles and adjust headspace if needed. Wipe rims of jars with a dampened clean paper towel. Adjust lids and process.

Variation: You may add four or five pearl onions or two onion slices to each jar.

Recommended process time for **Tomatoes with Okra or Zucchini** in a dial-gauge pressure canner

Style of Pack	Jar Size	Process Time	Canner Pressure (PSI) at Altitudes of			
			0–2,000 ft	2,001–4,000 ft	4,001–6,000 ft	6,001–8,000 ft
Hot	Pints	30 min	11 lb	12 lb	13 lb	14 lb
	Quarts	35	11	12	13	14

Recommended process time for **Tomatoes with Okra or Zucchini** in a weighted-gauge pressure canner

Style of Pack	Jar Size	Process Time	Canner Pressure (PSI) at Altitudes of	
			0–1,000 ft	Above 1,000 ft
Hot	Pints	30 min	10 lb	15 lb
	Quarts	35	10	15

TOMATILLOS

Quantity: An average of 14 pounds is needed per canner load of 7 quarts; an average of 9 pounds is needed per canner load of 9 pints. A bushel weighs 32 pounds and yields 14 to 16 quarts—an average of 2 pounds per quart.

Quality: Select unblemished firm, deep bright green tomatillos with a dry papery husk.

Procedure: Remove the dry outer husks entirely from the tomatillos and wash the fruit well. Leave whole; do not peel or remove seeds. **Add bottled lemon juice or citric acid to jars**. Follow the acidification amounts for tomatoes on page 3-5. Add enough water to cover the tomatillos in a large saucepan and boil them gently until tender, about 5 to 10 minutes. Drain and fill hot tomatillos loosely into hot jars, leaving 1/2-inch headspace. Fill hot jars with boiling water, leaving 1/2-inch headspace. Remove air bubbles and adjust headspace if needed. Wipe rims of jars with a dampened clean paper towel. Adjust lids and process.

Process the same as Water-Packed Whole Tomatoes, hot pack, on page 3-10.

SPAGHETTI SAUCE WITHOUT MEAT

30 lbs tomatoes
1 cup chopped onions
5 cloves garlic, minced
1 cup chopped celery or green peppers
1 lb fresh mushrooms, sliced (optional)
4-1/2 tsp salt
2 tbsp oregano
4 tbsp minced parsley
2 tsp black pepper
1/4 cup brown sugar
1/4 cup vegetable oil

Yield: About 9 pints

Procedure: Caution: Do not increase the proportion of onions, peppers, or mushrooms.
Wash tomatoes and dip in boiling water for 30 to 60 seconds or until skins split. Dip in cold water and slip off skins. Remove cores and quarter tomatoes. Boil 20 minutes, uncovered, in large saucepan. Put through food mill or sieve. Saute onions, garlic, celery or peppers, and mushrooms (if desired) in vegetable oil until tender. Combine sauteed vegetables and tomatoes and add remainder of spices, salt, and sugar. Bring to a boil. Simmer, uncovered, until thick enough for serving. At this time the initial volume will have been reduced by nearly one-half. Stir frequently to avoid burning. Fill hot jars, leaving 1-inch headspace. Remove air bubbles and adjust headspace if needed. Wipe rims of jars with a dampened clean paper towel. Adjust lids and process.

Recommended process time for Spaghetti Sauce Without Meat in a dial-gauge pressure canner

Style of Pack	Jar Size	Process Time	Canner Pressure (PSI) at Altitudes of			
			0–2,000 ft	2,001–4,000 ft	4,001–6,000 ft	6,001–8,000 ft
Hot	Pints	20 min	11 lb	12 lb	13 lb	14 lb
	Quarts	25	11	12	13	14

Recommended process time for Spaghetti Sauce Without Meat in a weighted-gauge pressure canner

Style of Pack	Jar Size	Process Time	Canner Pressure (PSI) at Altitudes of	
			0–1,000 ft	Above 1,000 ft
Hot	Pints	20 min	10 lb	15 lb
	Quarts	25	10	15

SPAGHETTI SAUCE WITH MEAT

30 lbs tomatoes
2-1/2 lbs ground beef or sausage
5 cloves garlic, minced
1 cup chopped onions
1 cup chopped celery or green peppers
1 lb fresh mushrooms, sliced (optional)
4-1/2 tsp salt
2 tbsp oregano
4 tbsp minced parsley
2 tsp black pepper
1/4 cup brown sugar

Yield: About 9 pints

Procedure: To prepare tomatoes, follow directions for Spaghetti Sauce Without Meat, page 3-13. Saute beef or sausage until brown. Add garlic, onion, celery or green pepper, and mushrooms, if desired. Cook until vegetables are tender. Combine with tomato pulp in large saucepan. Add spices, salt, and sugar. Bring to a boil. Simmer, uncovered, until thick enough for serving. At this time initial volume will have been reduced by nearly one-half. Stir frequently to avoid burning. Fill hot jars, leaving 1-inch headspace. Remove air bubbles and adjust headspace if needed. Wipe rims of jars with a dampened clean paper towel. Adjust lids and process.

Recommended process time for Spaghetti Sauce With Meat in a dial-gauge pressure canner

Style of Pack	Jar Size	Process Time	Canner Pressure (PSI) at Altitudes of			
			0–2,000 ft	2,001–4,000 ft	4,001–6,000 ft	6,001–8,000 ft
Hot	Pints	60 min	11 lb	12 lb	13 lb	14 lb
	Quarts	70	11	12	13	14

Recommended process time for Spaghetti Sauce With Meat in a weighted-gauge pressure canner

Style of Pack	Jar Size	Process Time	Canner Pressure (PSI) at Altitudes of	
			0–1,000 ft	Above 1,000 ft
Hot	Pints	60 min	10 lb	15 lb
	Quarts	70	10	15

MEXICAN TOMATO SAUCE

2-1/2 to 3 lbs chile peppers
18 lbs tomatoes
3 cups chopped onions
1 tbsp salt
1 tbsp oregano
1/2 cup vinegar

Yield: About 7 quarts

Procedure: Caution: Wear plastic or rubber gloves and do not touch your face while handling or cutting hot peppers. If you do not wear gloves, wash hands thoroughly with soap and water before touching your face or eyes. Wash and dry chiles. Slit each pepper along the side to allow steam to escape. Blister skins using one of these two methods:

Oven or broiler method to blister skins – Place peppers in a hot oven (400°F) or under a broiler for 6 to 8 minutes until skins blister.
Range-top method to blister skins – Cover hot burner (either gas or electric) with heavy wire mesh. Place peppers on burner for several minutes until skins blister.

After blistering skins, place peppers in a pan and cover with a damp cloth. (This will make peeling the peppers easier.) Cool several minutes; peel off skins. Discard seeds and chop peppers. Wash tomatoes and dip in boiling water for 30 to 60 seconds or until skins split. Dip in cold water, slip off skins, and remove cores. Coarsely chop tomatoes and combine chopped peppers and remaining ingredients in large saucepan. Bring to a boil. Cover. Reduce heat and simmer 10 minutes.

Fill hot jars, leaving 1-inch headspace. Remove air bubbles and adjust headspace if needed. Wipe rims of jars with a dampened clean paper towel. Adjust lids and process.

Recommended process time for Mexican Tomato Sauce in a dial-gauge pressure canner						
			Canner Pressure (PSI) at Altitudes of			
Style of Pack	Jar Size	Process Time	0–2,000 ft	2,001–4,000 ft	4,001–6,000 ft	6,001–8,000 ft
Hot	Pints	20 min	11 lb	12 lb	13 lb	14 lb
	Quarts	25	11	12	13	14

Recommended process time for Mexican Tomato Sauce in a weighted-gauge pressure canner				
			Canner Pressure (PSI) at Altitudes of	
Style of Pack	Jar Size	Process Time	0–1,000 ft	Above 1,000 ft
Hot	Pints	20 min	10 lb	15 lb
	Quarts	25	10	15

EASY HOT SAUCE

8 cups (64 ounces) canned, diced tomatoes, undrained
1-1/2 cups seeded, chopped Serrano peppers
4 cups distilled white vinegar (5%)
2 tsp canning salt
2 tbsp whole mixed pickling spices

Yield: About 4 half-pints

Procedure: Caution: Wear plastic or rubber gloves and do not touch your face while handling or cutting hot peppers. If you do not wear gloves, wash hands thoroughly with soap and water before touching your face or eyes. Place mixed pickling spices in a spice bag and tie the ends firmly. Mix all ingredients in a Dutch oven or large saucepot. Bring to a boil, stirring occasionally. Simmer another 20 minutes, until tomatoes are soft. Press mixture through a food mill. Return the liquid to the stockpot, heat to boiling and boil for another 15 minutes. Fill hot sauce into hot half-pint jars, leaving 1/4-inch headspace. Remove air bubbles and adjust headspace if needed. Wipe rims of jars with a dampened clean paper towel. Adjust lids and process.

Recommended process time for Easy Hot Sauce in a boiling-water canner				
		Process Time at Altitudes of		
Style of Pack	Jar Size	0–1,000 ft	1,001–6,000 ft	Above 6,000 ft
Hot	Half-pints	10 min	15	20

CAYENNE PEPPER SAUCE

3 lbs hot peppers (for example, Anaheim, Hungarian, Jalapeños)
1/3 cup minced garlic
4 cups sliced onion
1/3 cup stemmed, chopped cilantro
3 cans (28 ounces each) diced tomatoes
3 cups cider vinegar (5%)
2-1/2 cups water

Yield: About 5 pints

Procedure: Caution: Wear plastic or rubber gloves and do not touch your face while handling or cutting hot peppers. If you do not wear gloves, wash hands thoroughly with soap and water before touching your face or eyes. Wash, trim and slice peppers and onions into rings, using a mandolin slicer or a food processor. In a 10-quart Dutch oven or stockpot, mix together all ingredients. Bring to a boil and boil 1 hour. Reduce heat slightly and simmer 1 additional hour. Turn heat off, and cool mixture slightly. Puree vegetables in a blender about 2 minutes per blender batch. Return pureed mixture to stockpot and bring carefully just to a boil. (The mixture will start to spatter as it gets close to boiling; heat slowly while stirring constantly, being careful not to get burned by splashing sauce.) Turn off heat. Fill hot sauce into hot pint jars, leaving 1/2-inch headspace. Remove air bubbles and adjust headspace if needed. Wipe rims of jars with a dampened clean paper towel. Adjust lids and process.

Recommended process time for Cayenne Pepper Sauce in a boiling-water canner				
		Process Time at Altitudes of		
Style of Pack	Jar Size	0–1,000 ft	1,001–6,000 ft	Above 6,000 ft
Hot	Pints	10 min	15	20

TOMATO KETCHUP

24 lbs ripe tomatoes
3 cups chopped onions
3/4 tsp ground red pepper (cayenne)
3 cups cider vinegar (5%)
4 tsp whole cloves
3 sticks cinnamon, crushed
1-1/2 tsp whole allspice
3 tbsp celery seeds
1-1/2 cups sugar
1/4 cup salt

Yield: 6 to 7 pints

Procedure: Wash tomatoes. Dip in boiling water for 30 to 60 seconds or until skins split. Dip in cold water. Slip off skins and remove cores. Quarter tomatoes into 4-gallon stockpot or a large kettle. Add onions and red pepper. Bring to boil and simmer 20 minutes, uncovered. Cover, turn off heat and let stand for 20 minutes. Combine spices in a spice bag and add to vinegar in a

2-quart saucepan. Bring to boil. Remove spice bag and combine vinegar and tomato mixture. Boil about 30 minutes. Put boiled mixture through a food mill or sieve. Return to pot. Add sugar and salt, boil gently, and stir frequently until volume is reduced by one-half or until mixture rounds up on spoon without separation. Fill hot pint jars, leaving 1/8-inch headspace. Remove air bubbles and adjust headspace if needed. Wipe rims of jars with a dampened clean paper towel. Adjust lids and process.

Recommended process time for Tomato Ketchup in a boiling-water canner

Style of Pack	Jar Size	Process Time at Altitudes of		
		0–1,000 ft	1,001–6,000 ft	Above 6,000 ft
Hot	Pints	15 min	20	25

COUNTRY WESTERN KETCHUP

24 lbs ripe tomatoes
5 chile peppers, sliced and seeded
1/4 cup salt
2-2/3 cups vinegar (5%)
1-1/4 cups sugar
1/2 tsp ground red pepper (cayenne)
4 tsp paprika
4 tsp whole allspice
4 tsp dry mustard
1 tbsp whole peppercorns
1 tsp mustard seeds
1 tbsp bay leaves

Yield: 6 to 7 pints

Procedure: Follow procedure and process time for regular tomato ketchup (page 3-17).

BLENDER KETCHUP

Use electric blender and eliminate need for pressing or sieving.

24 lbs ripe tomatoes
2 lbs onions
1 lb sweet red peppers
1 lb sweet green peppers
9 cups vinegar (5%)
9 cups sugar
1/4 cup canning or pickling salt
3 tbsp dry mustard
1-1/2 tbsp ground red pepper
1-1/2 tsp whole allspice
1-1/2 tbsp whole cloves
3 sticks cinnamon

Yield: About 9 pints

Procedure: Wash tomatoes and dip in boiling water for 30 to 60 seconds or until skins split. Then dip in cold water, slip off skins, core, and quarter. Remove seeds from peppers and slice into strips. Peel and quarter onions. Blend tomatoes, peppers, and onions at high speed for 5 seconds in electric blender. Pour into a 3- to 4-gallon stock pot or large kettle and heat. Boil gently 60 minutes, stirring frequently. Add vinegar, sugar, salt, and a spice bag containing dry mustard, red pepper, and other spices. Continue boiling and stirring until volume is reduced one-half and ketchup rounds up on a spoon with no separation of liquid and solids. Remove spice bag and fill hot jars, leaving 1/8-inch headspace. Remove air bubbles and adjust headspace if needed. Wipe rims of jars with a dampened clean paper towel. Adjust lids and follow process times for regular ketchup (see page 3-18).

SALSA RECIPES

The salsas in this Guide, as well as most salsas, are mixtures of low-acid foods, such as onions and peppers, with acid foods, such as tomatoes. It is important that ingredients be carefully measured and that the salsas be made as described to be processed safely in a boiling water canner.

SELECTION AND PREPARATION OF INGREDIENTS

ACIDS

The acid ingredients help preserve canned salsas. You must add the acid to these salsas processed in a boiling water canner because the natural acidity of the mixture without it may not be high enough. The acids are usually commercially bottled lemon juice or vinegar so the acidity level will be standardized. Use only vinegar that is at least 5% acidity; do not use homemade vinegar or fresh squeezed lemon juice because the acidity can vary and will be unknown.

The amounts of vinegar or lemon juice in these recipes cannot be reduced for safe boiling water canning. Sugar can be used to offset the tartness of the acid. An equal amount of bottled lemon juice may be substituted for vinegar in recipes, but do not substitute vinegar for lemon juice. This substitution will result in a less acid and potentially unsafe canned salsa.

TOMATOES

The type of tomato will affect the consistency of salsa. Paste tomatoes, such as Roma, have more, and usually firmer, flesh than slicing tomatoes. They will produce thicker salsas than large slicing tomatoes which usually yield a thinner, more watery salsa.

Canning is not a way to use overripe or spoiling tomatoes. Use only high quality, disease-free, preferably vine-ripened, firm tomatoes for canning salsa or any other tomato product. **Do not use tomatoes from dead or frost-killed vines.** Poor quality or overripe tomatoes will yield a thin salsa and one that may spoil. Green tomatoes or tomatillos may be used for ripe tomatoes in these recipes, but the flavor of the recipe will change.

When recipes call for peeled tomatoes, remove the skin by dipping washed tomatoes into boiling water for 30 to 60 seconds or until skins split. Dip immediately into cold water, then slip skins off and core the tomato.

TOMATILLOS

Tomatillos are also known as Mexican husk tomatoes. The dry outer husk must be removed, but they do not need to be peeled or have the seeds removed. They will need to be washed well after the husk is removed.

PEPPERS

Peppers range from mild to scorching in taste. It is this "heat" factor that makes many salsa fans want to experiment with recipes. Use only high quality peppers, unblemished and free of decay. You may substitute one type of pepper for another, including bell peppers (mild) for some or all of the chiles. Canned chiles may be used in place of fresh. **However, do not increase the total amount (pounds or cups) of peppers in any recipe.** Do not substitute the same number of whole peppers of a large size for the number of peppers of a smaller size (for example, do not use 6 bell peppers or long chiles in place of 6 jalapeños or serranos). This will result in changing the final acidity of the mixture and potentially unsafe canned salsa.

Milder varieties of peppers include Anaheim, Ancho, College, Colorado and Hungarian Yellow Wax. When the recipe calls for "long green chiles" choose a mild pepper. Jalapeño is a very popular hot pepper. Other hot varieties include Cayenne, Habanero, Serrano and Tabasco. Do not touch your face, particularly the area around your eyes, when you are handling or cutting hot chiles. **Caution: Wear plastic or rubber gloves and do not touch your face while handling or cutting hot peppers. If you do not wear gloves, wash hands thoroughly with soap and water before touching your face or eyes.**

Usually when peppers are finely chopped in a salsa, they do not need to be peeled. However, many recipes say to peel the recipes, and the skin of long green chiles in particular may be tough after canning. If you choose to peel chiles, or procedures with a recipe direct you to peel the peppers, use the following.

Peeling peppers: Wash and dry peppers; slit each pepper along the side to allow steam to escape. Blister skins using one of these two methods :

Oven or broiler method to blister skins – Place peppers in a hot oven (400°F) or under a broiler for 6 to 8 minutes until skins blister.

Range-top method to blister skins – Cover hot burner (either gas or electric) with heavy wire mesh. Place peppers on burner for several minutes until skins blister.

To peel, after blistering skins, place peppers in a pan and cover with a damp cloth. (This will make peeling the peppers easier.) Cool several minutes; peel off skins. Discard seeds and chop.

SPICES AND HERBS

Spices and herbs add unique flavoring to salsas. The amounts of dried spices and herbs in the following recipes (black pepper, salt, dried oregano leaves, and ground cumin) may be altered or left out. For a stronger cilantro flavor in recipes that list cilantro, it is best to add fresh cilantro just before serving instead of adding more before canning.

OTHER

Red, yellow or white onions may be substituted for each other. **Do not increase the total amount of onions in any recipe.**

IMPORTANT: You may change the amount of spices, if desired. Do not can salsas that do not follow these or other research tested recipes. (They may be frozen or stored in the refrigerator.)

RECIPES

IMPORTANT: Follow the directions carefully for each recipe. Use the amounts of each vegetable (peppers, onions, tomatoes, tomatillos, etc.) listed in the recipe. If the procedures call for chopped tomatoes, use the whole tomato after peeling and coring. Do not drain the tomato, or remove all the liquid and juices. Add the amount of vinegar or lemon juice as listed. The only changes you can safely make in these salsa recipes are to substitute bottled lemon juice for vinegar and to change the amount of dried spices and herbs. Do not alter the proportions of vegetables to acid and tomatoes because it might make the salsa unsafe. Do not thicken salsas with flour, cornstarch or other starches before canning. If a thicker salsa is desired, you can pour off some of the liquid or add these thickening ingredients after opening.

CHILE SALSA (Hot Tomato-Pepper Sauce)

5 lbs tomatoes
2 lbs chile peppers
1 lb onions
1 cup vinegar (5%)
3 tsp salt
1/2 tsp pepper

Yield: About 6 to 8 pints

Procedure: Caution: Wear plastic or rubber gloves and do not touch your face while handling or cutting hot peppers. If you do not wear gloves, wash hands thoroughly with soap and water before touching your face or eyes. Peel and prepare chile peppers as described on page 3-20. Wash tomatoes and dip in boiling water for 30 to 60 seconds or until skins split. Dip in cold water, slip off skins, and remove cores. Coarsely chop tomatoes and combine them with chopped peppers, onions, and remaining ingredients in a large saucepan. Heat to boil, reduce heat and simmer 10 minutes. Fill hot jars, leaving 1/2-inch headspace. Remove air bubbles and adjust headspace if needed. Wipe rims of jars with a dampened clean paper towel. Adjust lids and process.

Recommended process time for Chile Salsa in a boiling-water canner

Style of Pack	Jar Size	Process Time at Altitudes of		
		0–1,000 ft	1,001–6,000 ft	Above 6,000 ft
Hot	Pints	15 min	20	25

CHILE SALSA II

10 cups peeled, cored, chopped tomatoes
6 cups seeded, chopped chile peppers (use mixture of mild and hot peppers)
4 cups chopped onions
1 cup vinegar (5%)
3 tsp salt
1/2 tsp pepper

Yield: About 7 to 9 pints

Procedure: Caution: Wear plastic or rubber gloves and do not touch your face while handling or cutting hot peppers. If you do not wear gloves, wash hands thoroughly with soap and water before touching your face or eyes. Peel and prepare chile peppers as described on page 3-20, if desired. Wash tomatoes and dip in boiling water for 30 to 60 seconds or until skins split. Dip in cold water, slip off skins, and remove cores. Combine ingredients in a large saucepan. Heat to a boil and simmer 10 minutes. Fill hot salsa into hot pint jars, leaving 1/2-inch headspace. Remove air bubbles and adjust headspace if needed. Wipe rims of jars with a dampened clean paper towel. Adjust lids and process.

Recommended process time for Chile Salsa II in a boiling-water canner				
		Process Time at Altitudes of		
Style of Pack	Jar Size	0–1,000 ft	1,001–6,000 ft	Above 6,000 ft
Hot	Pints	15 min	20	25

TOMATILLO GREEN SALSA

5 cups chopped tomatillos (or green tomatoes may be used)
1-1/2 cups seeded, chopped long green chiles
1/2 cup seeded, finely chopped jalapeño peppers
4 cups chopped onions
1 cup bottled lemon juice
6 cloves garlic, finely chopped
1 tbsp ground cumin (optional)
3 tbsp oregano leaves (optional)
1 tbsp salt
1 tsp black pepper

Yield: About 5 pints

Procedure: Caution: Wear plastic or rubber gloves and do not touch your face while handling or cutting hot peppers. If you do not wear gloves, wash hands thoroughly with soap and water before touching your face or eyes. Peel and prepare chile peppers as described on page 3-20, if desired. Combine all ingredients in a large saucepan and stir frequently over high heat until mixture begins to boil, then reduce heat and simmer for 20 minutes, stirring occasionally. Ladle hot salsa into hot pint jars, leaving 1/2-inch headspace. Remove air bubbles and adjust headspace if needed. Wipe rims of jars with a dampened clean paper towel. Adjust lids and process.

Recommended process time for Tomatillo Green Salsa in a boiling-water canner

Style of Pack	Jar Size	Process Time at Altitudes of		
		0–1,000 ft	1,001–6,000 ft	Above 6,000 ft
Hot	Pints	15 min	20	25

TOMATO SALSA (USING PASTE TOMATOES)

7 qts peeled, cored, chopped tomatoes*
4 cups seeded, chopped long green chiles
5 cups chopped onion
1/2 cup seeded, finely chopped jalapeño peppers
6 cloves garlic, finely chopped
2 cups bottled lemon or lime juice
2 tbsp salt
1 tbsp black pepper
2 tbsp ground cumin (optional)
3 tbsp oregano leaves (optional)
2 tbsp fresh cilantro (optional)

*This recipe works best with paste tomatoes. Slicing tomatoes require a much longer cooking time to achieve a desirable consistency.

Yield: About 16 to 18 pints

Procedure: Caution: Wear plastic or rubber gloves and do not touch your face while handling or cutting hot peppers. If you do not wear gloves, wash hands thoroughly with soap and water before touching your face or eyes. Peel and prepare chile peppers as described on page 3-20, if desired. Wash tomatoes and dip in boiling water for 30 to 60 seconds or until skins split. Dip in cold water, slip off skins, and remove cores. Combine all ingredients except cumin, oregano and cilantro in a large pot and bring to a boil, stirring frequently, then reduce heat and simmer 10 minutes. Add spices and simmer for another 20 minutes, stirring occasionally. Fill hot salsa into hot pint jars, leaving 1/2-inch headspace. Remove air bubbles and adjust headspace if needed. Wipe rims of jars with a dampened clean paper towel. Adjust lids and process.

Recommended process time for Tomato Salsa Using Paste Tomatoes in a boiling-water canner

Style of Pack	Jar Size	Process Time at Altitudes of		
		0–1,000 ft	1,001–6,000 ft	Above 6,000 ft
Hot	Pints	15 min	20	25

TOMATO SALSA (USING SLICING TOMATOES)

4 cups peeled, cored, chopped tomatoes
2 cups seeded, chopped long green chiles
1/2 cup seeded, chopped jalapeño peppers
3/4 cup chopped onion
4 cloves garlic, finely chopped
2 cups vinegar (5%)
1 tsp ground cumin (optional)
1 tbsp oregano leaves (optional)
1 tbsp fresh cilantro (optional)
1-1/2 tsp salt

Yield: About 4 pints

Procedure: Caution: Wear plastic or rubber gloves and do not touch your face while handling or cutting hot peppers. If you do not wear gloves, wash hands thoroughly with soap and water before touching your face or eyes. Peel and prepare chile peppers as described on page 3-20, if desired. Wash tomatoes and dip in boiling water for 30 to 60 seconds or until skins split. Dip in cold water, slip off skins, and remove cores. Combine all ingredients in a large pot and bring to a boil, stirring frequently. Reduce heat and simmer 20 minutes, stirring occasionally. Fill hot salsa into hot pint jars, leaving 1/2-inch headspace. Remove air bubbles and adjust headspace if needed. Wipe rims of jars with a dampened clean paper towel. Adjust lids and process.

Recommended process time for Tomato Salsa Using Slicing Tomatoes in a boiling-water canner				
		Process Time at Altitudes of		
Style of Pack	Jar Size	0–1,000 ft	1,001–6,000 ft	Above 6,000 ft
Hot	Pints	15 min	20	25

TOMATO/GREEN CHILE SALSA

3 cups peeled, cored, chopped tomatoes
3 cups seeded, chopped long green chiles
3/4 cup chopped onions
1 jalapeño pepper, seeded, finely chopped
6 cloves garlic, finely chopped
1-1/2 cups vinegar (5%)
1/2 tsp ground cumin (optional)
2 tsp oregano leaves (optional)
1-1/2 tsp salt

Yield: About 3 pints

Procedure: Caution: Wear plastic or rubber gloves and do not touch your face while handling or cutting hot peppers. If you do not wear gloves, wash hands thoroughly with soap and

water before touching your face or eyes. Peel and prepare chile peppers as described on page 3-20, if desired. Wash tomatoes and dip in boiling water for 30 to 60 seconds or until skins split. Dip in cold water, slip off skins, and remove cores. Combine all ingredients in a large saucepan and heat, stirring frequently, until mixture boils. Reduce heat and simmer for 20 minutes, stirring occasionally. Fill hot salsa into hot pint jars, leaving 1/2-inch headspace. Remove air bubbles and adjust headspace if needed. Wipe rims of jars with a dampened clean paper towel. Adjust lids and process.

Recommended process time for Tomato Green Chile Salsa in a boiling-water canner

Style of Pack	Jar Size	Process Time at Altitudes of		
		0–1,000 ft	1,001–6,000 ft	Above 6,000 ft
Hot	Pints	15 min	20	25

TOMATO/TOMATO PASTE SALSA

3 qts peeled, cored, chopped slicing tomatoes
3 cups chopped onions
6 jalapeño peppers, seeded, finely chopped
4 long green chiles, seeded, chopped
4 cloves garlic, finely chopped
2 12-ounce cans tomato paste
2 cups bottled lemon or lime juice
1 tbsp salt
1 tbsp sugar
1 tbsp ground cumin (optional)
2 tbsp oregano leaves (optional)
1 tsp black pepper

Yield: About 7 to 9 pints

Procedure: Caution: Wear plastic or rubber gloves and do not touch your face while handling or cutting hot peppers. If you do not wear gloves, wash hands thoroughly with soap and water before touching your face or eyes. Peel and prepare chile peppers as described on page 3-20, if desired. Wash tomatoes and dip in boiling water for 30 to 60 seconds or until skins split. Dip in cold water, slip off skins, and remove cores. Combine all ingredients in a large saucepan. Bring to a boil. Reduce heat and simmer for 30 minutes, stirring occasionally. Fill hot salsa into hot pint jars, leaving 1/2-inch headspace. Remove air bubbles and adjust headspace if needed. Wipe rims of jars with a dampened clean paper towel. Adjust lids and process.

Recommended process time for Tomato/Tomato Paste Salsa in a boiling-water canner

Style of Pack	Jar Size	Process Time at Altitudes of		
		0–1,000 ft	1,001–6,000 ft	Above 6,000 ft
Hot	Pints	15 min	20	25

TOMATO TACO SAUCE

8 qts peeled, cored, finely chopped paste tomatoes*
2 cloves garlic, crushed
5 cups chopped onions
4 jalapeño peppers, seeded, chopped
4 long green chiles, seeded, chopped
2-1/2 cups vinegar
2 tbsp salt
1-1/2 tbsp black pepper
1 tbsp sugar
2 tbsp oregano leaves (optional)
1 tsp ground cumin (optional)

*This recipe works best with paste tomatoes, as slicing tomatoes will yield a thin watery salsa. If you only have slicing tomatoes available, use the Tomato/Tomato Paste Salsa recipe.

Yield: About 16 to 18 pints

Procedure: Caution: Wear plastic or rubber gloves and do not touch your face while handling or cutting hot peppers. If you do not wear gloves, wash hands thoroughly with soap and water before touching your face or eyes. Peel and prepare chile peppers as described on page 3-20, if desired. Wash tomatoes and dip in boiling water for 30 to 60 seconds or until skins split. Dip in cold water, slip off skins, and remove cores. Combine ingredients in a large saucepan. Bring to a boil, then reduce heat and simmer, stirring frequently until thick (about 1 hour). Fill hot sauce into hot pint jars, leaving 1/2- inch headspace. Remove air bubbles and adjust headspace if needed. Wipe rims of jars with a dampened clean paper towel. Adjust lids and process.

Recommended process time for Tomato Taco Sauce in a boiling-water canner				
		Process Time at Altitudes of		
Style of Pack	Jar Size	0–1,000 ft	1,001–6,000 ft	Above 6,000 ft
Hot	Pints	15 min	20	25

Complete Guide to
Home Canning

United States Department of Agriculture

National Institute of Food and Agriculture

Guide 4
Selecting, Preparing, and Canning Vegetables and Vegetable Products

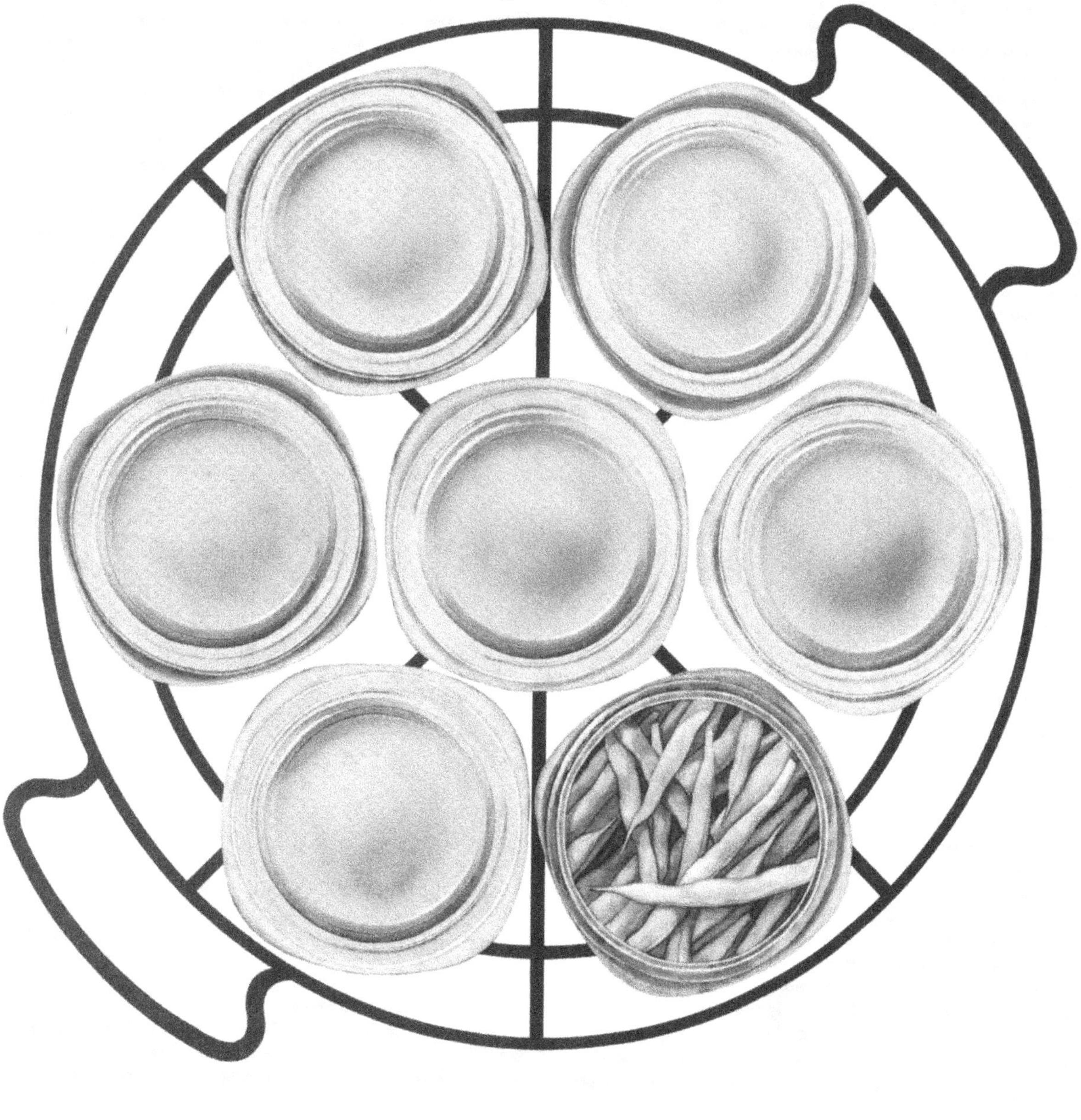

Guide 4
Selecting, Preparing, and Canning Vegetables and Vegetable Products

Table of Contents

Section	Page
Asparagus—spears or pieces	4-5
Beans or peas—shelled, dried	4-5
Beans, baked	4-6
Beans, dry, with tomato or molasses sauce	4-6
Beans, fresh lima—shelled	4-7
Beans, snap and Italian—pieces	4-8
Beets—whole, cubed, or sliced	4-9
Carrots—sliced or diced	4-10
Corn—cream style	4-10
Corn—whole kernel	4-11
Mixed vegetables	4-12
Mushrooms—whole or sliced	4-13
Okra	4-14
Peas, green or English—shelled	4-14
Peppers	4-15
Potatoes, sweet—pieces or whole	4-16
Potatoes, white—cubed or whole	4-17
Pumpkins and winter squash—cubed	4-18
Soups	4-18
Spinach and other greens	4-19
Squash, winter—cubed	4-20
Succotash	4-20

ASPARAGUS—SPEARS OR PIECES

Quantity: An average of 24-1/2 pounds is needed per canner load of 7 quarts; an average of 16 pounds is needed per canner load of 9 pints. A crate weighs 31 pounds and yields 7 to 12 quarts—an average of 3-1/2 pounds per quart.

Quality: Use tender, tight-tipped spears, 4 to 6 inches long.

Procedure: Wash asparagus and trim off tough scales. Break off tough stems and wash again. Cut into 1-inch pieces or can whole.

Hot pack—Cover asparagus with boiling water. Boil 2 or 3 minutes. Loosely fill hot jars with hot asparagus, leaving 1-inch headspace.

Raw pack—Fill hot jars with raw asparagus, packing as tightly as possible without crushing, leaving 1-inch headspace.

Add 1 teaspoon of salt per quart to the jars, if desired. Add boiling water, leaving 1-inch headspace. Remove air bubbles and adjust headspace if needed. Wipe rims of jars with a dampened clean paper towel. Adjust lids and process.

Recommended process time for Asparagus in a dial-gauge pressure canner

Style of Pack	Jar Size	Process Time	Canner Pressure (PSI) at Altitudes of			
			0–2,000 ft	2,001–4,000 ft	4,001–6,000 ft	6,001–8,000 ft
Hot and Raw	Pints	30 min	11 lb	12 lb	13 lb	14 lb
	Quarts	40	11	12	13	14

Recommended process time for Asparagus in a weighted-gauge pressure canner

Style of Pack	Jar Size	Process Time	Canner Pressure (PSI) at Altitudes of	
			0–1,000 ft	Above 1,000 ft
Hot and Raw	Pints	30 min	10 lb	15 lb
	Quarts	40	10	15

BEANS OR PEAS—SHELLED, DRIED

All varieties

Quantity: An average of 5 pounds is needed per canner load of 7 quarts; an average of 3-1/4 pounds is needed per canner load of 9 pints—an average of 3/4 pound per quart.

Quality: Select mature, dry seeds. Sort out and discard discolored seeds.

Procedure: Place dried beans or peas in a large pot and cover with water. Soak 12 to 18 hours in a cool place. Drain water. To quickly hydrate beans, you may cover sorted and washed beans with boiling water in a saucepan. Boil 2 minutes, remove from heat, soak 1 hour and drain. Cover beans soaked by either method with fresh water and boil 30 minutes. Add 1/2 teaspoon of salt per pint or 1 teaspoon per quart to the jar, if desired. Fill hot jars with beans or peas and cooking water, leaving 1-inch headspace. Remove air bubbles and adjust headspace if needed. Wipe rims of jars with a dampened clean paper towel. Adjust lids and process.

Recommended process time for Beans or Peas in a dial-gauge pressure canner

Style of Pack	Jar Size	Process Time	Canner Pressure (PSI) at Altitudes of			
			0–2,000 ft	2,001–4,000 ft	4,001–6,000 ft	6,001–8,000 ft
Hot	Pints	75 min	11 lb	12 lb	13 lb	14 lb
	Quarts	90	11	12	13	14

Recommended process time for Beans or Peas in a weighted-gauge pressure canner

Style of Pack	Jar Size	Process Time	Canner Pressure (PSI) at Altitudes of	
			0–1,000 ft	Above 1,000 ft
Hot	Pints	75 min	10 lb	15 lb
	Quarts	90	10	15

BEANS, BAKED

Procedure: Soak and boil beans and prepare molasses sauce according to directions for beans with sauce on page 4-6. Place seven 3/4-inch pieces of pork, ham, or bacon in an earthenware crock, a large casserole, or a pan. Add beans and enough molasses sauce to cover beans. Cover and bake 4 to 5 hours at 350°F Add water as needed-about every hour. Fill hot jars, leaving 1-inch headspace. Remove air bubbles and adjust headspace if needed. Wipe rims of jars with a dampened clean paper towel. Adjust lids and process as for beans with sauce on page 4-7.

BEANS, DRY, WITH TOMATO OR MOLASSES SAUCE

Quantity: An average of 5 pounds of beans is needed per canner load of 7 quarts; an average of 3-1/4 pounds is needed per canner load of 9 pints—an average of 3/4 pound per quart.

Quality: Select mature, dry seeds. Sort out and discard discolored seeds.

Procedure: Sort and wash dry beans. Add 3 cups of water for each cup of dried beans or peas. Boil 2 minutes, remove from heat and soak 1 hour and drain. Heat to boiling in fresh water, and save liquid for making sauce. Make your choice of the following sauces:

Tomato Sauce—Either mix 1 quart tomato juice, 3 tablespoons sugar, 2 teaspoons salt, 1 tablespoon chopped onion, and 1/4 teaspoon each of ground cloves, allspice, mace, and cayenne pepper; or, mix 1 cup tomato ketchup with 3 cups of cooking liquid from beans. Heat to boiling.

Molasses Sauce—Mix 4 cups water or cooking liquid from beans, 3 tablespoons dark molasses, 1 tablespoon vinegar, 2 teaspoons salt, and 3/4 teaspoon powered dry mustard. Heat to boiling.

Fill hot jars three-fourths full with hot beans. Add a 3/4-inch cube of pork, ham, or bacon to each jar, if desired. Fill jars with heated sauce, leaving 1-inch headspace. Remove air bubbles and adjust headspace if needed. Wipe rims of jars with a dampened clean paper towel. Adjust lids and process.

Recommended process time for Beans, Dry, with Tomato or Molasses Sauce in a dial-gauge pressure canner

Style of Pack	Jar Size	Process Time	Canner Pressure (PSI) at Altitudes of			
			0–2,000 ft	2,001–4,000 ft	4,001–6,000 ft	6,001–8,000 ft
Hot	Pints	65 min	11 lb	12 lb	13 lb	14 lb
	Quarts	75	11	12	13	14

Recommended process time for Beans, Dry, with Tomato or Molasses Sauce in a weighted-gauge pressure canner

Style of Pack	Jar Size	Process Time	Canner Pressure (PSI) at Altitudes of	
			0–1,000 ft	Above 1,000 ft
Hot	Pints	65 min	10 lb	15 lb
	Quarts	75	10	15

BEANS, FRESH LIMA—SHELLED

Quantity: An average of 28 pounds is needed per canner load of 7 quarts; an average of 18 pounds is needed per canner load of 9 pints. A bushel weighs 32 pounds and yields 6 to 10 quarts—an average of 4 pounds per quart.

Quality: Select well-filled pods with green seeds. Discard insect-damaged and diseased seeds.

Procedure: Shell beans and wash thoroughly.

Hot pack—Cover beans with boiling water and heat to boil. Fill hot jars loosely, leaving 1-inch headspace.

Raw pack—Fill hot jars with raw beans. Do not press or shake down.
    Small beans—leave 1-inch of headspace for pints and 1-1/2 inches for quarts.
    Large beans—leave 1-inch of headspace for pints and 1-1/4 inches for quarts.

Add 1 teaspoon of salt per quart to the jar, if desired. Add boiling water, leaving the same headspaces listed above. Remove air bubbles and adjust headspace if needed. Wipe rims of jars with a dampened clean paper towel. Adjust lids and process.

Recommended process time for Lima Beans in a dial-gauge pressure canner						
			Canner Pressure (PSI) at Altitudes of			
Style of Pack	Jar Size	Process Time	0–2,000 ft	2,001–4,000 ft	4,001–6,000 ft	6,001–8,000 ft
Hot and Raw	Pints	40 min	11 lb	12 lb	13 lb	14 lb
	Quarts	50	11	12	13	14

Recommended process time for Lima Beans in a weighted-gauge pressure canner				
			Canner Pressure (PSI) at Altitudes of	
Style of Pack	Jar Size	Process Time	0–1,000 ft	Above 1,000 ft
Hot and Raw	Pints	40 min	10 lb	15 lb
	Quarts	50	10	15

BEANS, SNAP AND ITALIAN—PIECES

Green and wax

Quantity: An average of 14 pounds is needed per canner load of 7 quarts; an average of 9 pounds is needed per canner load of 9 pints. A bushel weighs 30 pounds and yields 12 to 20 quarts—an average of 2 pounds per quart.

Quality: Select filled but tender, crisp pods. Remove and discard diseased and rusty pods.

Procedure: Wash beans and trim ends. Leave whole or cut or snap into 1-inch pieces.

Hot pack—Cover with boiling water; boil 5 minutes. Fill hot jars, loosely leaving 1-inch headspace.

Raw pack—Fill hot jars tightly with raw beans, leaving 1-inch headspace.

Add 1 teaspoon of canning salt per quart to the jar, if desired. Add boiling water, leaving 1-inch headspace. Remove air bubbles and adjust headspace if needed. Wipe rims of jars with a dampened clean paper towel. Adjust lids and process.

Recommended process time for Snap and Italian Beans in a dial-gauge pressure canner

Style of Pack	Jar Size	Process Time	Canner Pressure (PSI) at Altitudes of			
			0–2,000 ft	2,001–4,000 ft	4,001–6,000 ft	6,001–8,000 ft
Hot and Raw	Pints	20 min	11 lb	12 lb	13 lb	14 lb
	Quarts	25	11	12	13	14

Recommended process time for Snap and Italian Beans in a weighted-gauge pressure canner

Style of Pack	Jar Size	Process Time	Canner Pressure (PSI) at Altitudes of	
			0–1,000 ft	Above 1,000 ft
Hot and Raw	Pints	20 min	10 lb	15 lb
	Quarts	25	10	15

BEETS—WHOLE, CUBED, OR SLICED

Quantity: An average of 21 pounds (without tops) is needed per canner load of 7 quarts; an average of 13-1/2 pounds is needed per canner load of 9 pints. A bushel (without tops) weighs 52 pounds and yields 15 to 20 quarts—an average of 3 pounds per quart.

Quality: Beets with a diameter of 1 to 2 inches are preferred for whole packs. Beets larger than 3 inches in diameter are often fibrous.

Procedure: Trim off beet tops, leaving an inch of stem and roots to reduce bleeding of color. Scrub well. Cover with boiling water. Boil until skins slip off easily; about 15 to 25 minutes depending on size. Cool, remove skins, and trim off stems and roots. Leave baby beets whole. Cut medium or large beets into 1/2-inch cubes or slices. Halve or quarter very large slices. Add 1 teaspoon of salt per quart to the jar, if desired. Fill hot jars with hot beets and fresh hot water, leaving 1-inch headspace. Remove air bubbles and adjust headspace if needed. Wipe rims of jars with a dampened clean paper towel. Adjust lids and process.

Recommended process time for Beets in a dial-gauge pressure canner

Style of Pack	Jar Size	Process Time	Canner Pressure (PSI) at Altitudes of			
			0–2,000 ft	2,001–4,000 ft	4,001–6,000 ft	6,001–8,000 ft
Hot	Pints	30 min	11 lb	12 lb	13 lb	14 lb
	Quarts	35	11	12	13	14

Recommended process time for Beets in a weighted-gauge pressure canner

Style of Pack	Jar Size	Process Time	Canner Pressure (PSI) at Altitudes of	
			0–1,000 ft	Above 1,000 ft
Hot	Pints	30 min	10 lb	15 lb
	Quarts	35	10	15

CARROTS—SLICED OR DICED

Quantity: An average of 17-1/2 pounds (without tops) is needed per canner load of 7 quarts; an average of 11 pounds is needed per canner load of 9 pints. A bushel (without tops) weighs 50 pounds and yields 17 to 25 quarts—an average of 2-1/2 pounds per quart.

Quality: Select small carrots, preferably 1 to 1-1/4 inches in diameter. Larger carrots are often too fibrous.

Procedure: Wash, peel, and rewash carrots. Slice or dice.

Hot pack—Cover with boiling water; bring to boil and simmer for 5 minutes. Fill hot jars, leaving 1-inch of headspace.

Raw pack—Fill hot jars tightly with raw carrots, leaving 1-inch headspace.

Add 1 teaspoon of salt per quart to the jar, if desired. Add hot cooking liquid or water, leaving 1-inch headspace. Remove air bubbles and adjust headspace if needed. Wipe rims of jars with a dampened clean paper towel. Adjust lids and process.

Recommended process time for Carrots in a dial-gauge pressure canner						
			Canner Pressure (PSI) at Altitudes of			
Style of Pack	Jar Size	Process Time	0–2,000 ft	2,001–4,000 ft	4,001–6,000 ft	6,001–8,000 ft
Hot and Raw	Pints	25 min	11 lb	12 lb	13 lb	14 lb
	Quarts	30	11	12	13	14

Recommended process time for Carrots in a weighted-gauge pressure canner				
			Canner Pressure (PSI) at Altitudes of	
Style of Pack	Jar Size	Process Time	0–1,000 ft	Above 1,000 ft
Hot and Raw	Pints	25 min	10 lb	15 lb
	Quarts	30	10	15

CORN—CREAM STYLE

Quantity: An average of 20 pounds (in husks) of sweet corn is needed per canner load of 9 pints. A bushel weighs 35 pounds and yields 12 to 20 pints—an average of 2-1/4 pounds per pint.

Quality: Select ears containing slightly immature kernels, or of ideal quality for eating fresh.

Procedure: Husk corn, remove silk, and wash ears. Blanch ears 4 minutes in boiling water. Cut corn from cob at about the center of kernel. Scrape remaining corn from cobs with a table knife.

Hot pack—To each quart of corn and scrapings, in a saucepan, add two cups of boiling water. Heat to boiling. Add 1/2 teaspoon salt to each jar, if desired. Fill hot pint jar with hot corn mixture, leaving 1-inch headspace. Remove air bubbles and adjust headspace if needed. Wipe rims of jars with a dampened clean paper towel. Adjust lids and process.

Recommended process time for Cream Style Corn in a dial-gauge pressure canner

Style of Pack	Jar Size	Process Time	Canner Pressure (PSI) at Altitudes of			
			0–2,000 ft	2,001–4,000 ft	4,001–6,000 ft	6,001–8,000 ft
Hot	Pints	85 min	11 lb	12 lb	13 lb	14 lb

Recommended process time for Cream Style Corn in a weighted-gauge pressure canner

Style of Pack	Jar Size	Process Time	Canner Pressure (PSI) at Altitudes of	
			0–1,000 ft	Above 1,000 ft
Hot	Pints	85 min	10 lb	15 lb

CORN—WHOLE KERNEL

Quantity: An average of 31-1/2 pounds (in husks) of sweet corn is needed per canner load of 7 quarts; an average of 20 pounds is needed per canner load of 9 pints. A bushel weighs 35 pounds and yields 6 to 11 quarts—an average of 4-1/2 pounds per quart.

Quality: Select ears containing slightly immature kernels or of ideal quality for eating fresh. Canning of some sweeter varieties or too immature kernels may cause browning. Can a small amount, check color and flavor before canning large quantities.

Procedure: Husk corn, remove silk, and wash. Blanch 3 minutes in boiling water. Cut corn from cob at about 3/4 the depth of kernel.

Caution: Do not scrape cob.

Hot pack—To each clean quart of kernels in a saucepan, add 1 cup of hot water, heat to boiling and simmer 5 minutes. Add 1 teaspoon of salt per quart to the jar, if desired. Fill hot jars with corn and cooking liquid, leaving 1-inch headspace.

Raw pack—Fill hot jars with raw kernels, leaving 1-inch headspace. Do not shake or press down. Add 1 teaspoon of salt per quart to the jar, if desired.

Add fresh boiling water, leaving 1-inch headspace. Remove air bubbles and adjust headspace if needed. Wipe rims of jars with a dampened clean paper towel. Adjust lids and process.

Recommended process time for Whole Kernel Corn in a dial-gauge pressure canner

Style of Pack	Jar Size	Process Time	Canner Pressure (PSI) at Altitudes of			
			0–2,000 ft	2,001–4,000 ft	4,001–6,000 ft	6,001–8,000 ft
Hot and Raw	Pints	55 min	11 lb	12 lb	13 lb	14 lb
	Quarts	85	11	12	13	14

Recommended process time for Whole Kernel Corn in a weighted-gauge pressure canner

Style of Pack	Jar Size	Process Time	Canner Pressure (PSI) at Altitudes of	
			0–1,000 ft	Above 1,000 ft
Hot and Raw	Pints	55 min	10 lb	15 lb
	Quarts	85	10	15

MIXED VEGETABLES

6 cups sliced carrots
6 cups cut, whole kernel sweet corn
6 cups cut green beans
6 cups shelled lima beans
4 cups whole or crushed tomatoes
4 cups diced zucchini

Yield: 7 quarts

Optional mix—You may change the suggested proportions or substitute other favorite vegetables except leafy greens, dried beans, cream-style corn, squash and sweet potatoes.

Procedure: Except for zucchini, wash and prepare vegetables as described previously for each vegetable. Wash, trim, and slice or cube zucchini; combine all vegetables in a large pot or kettle, and add enough water to cover pieces. Add 1 teaspoon salt per quart to the jar, if desired. Boil 5 minutes and fill hot jars with hot pieces and liquid, leaving 1-inch headspace. Remove air bubbles and adjust headspace if needed. Wipe rims of jars with a dampened clean paper towel. Adjust lids and process.

Recommended process time for Mixed Vegetables in a dial-gauge pressure canner							
			Canner Pressure (PSI) at Altitudes of			
Style of Pack	Jar Size	Process Time	0–2,000 ft	2,001–4,000 ft	4,001–6,000 ft	6,001–8,000 ft
Hot	Pints	75 min	11 lb	12 lb	13 lb	14 lb
	Quarts	90	11	12	13	14

Recommended process time for Mixed Vegetables in a weighted-gauge pressure canner				
			Canner Pressure (PSI) at Altitudes of	
Style of Pack	Jar Size	Process Time	0–1,000 ft	Above 1,000 ft
Hot	Pints	75 min	10 lb	15 lb
	Quarts	90	10	15

MUSHROOMS—WHOLE OR SLICED

Quantity: An average of 14-1/2 pounds is needed per canner load of 9 pints; an average of 7-1/2 pounds is needed per canner load of 9 half-pints—an average of 2 pounds per pint.

Quality: Select only brightly colored, small to medium-size domestic mushrooms with short stems, tight veils (unopened caps), and no discoloration. **Caution: Do not can wild mushrooms.**

Procedure: Trim stems and discolored parts. Soak in cold water for 10 minutes to remove dirt. Wash in clean water. Leave small mushrooms whole; cut large ones. Cover with water in a saucepan and boil 5 minutes. Fill hot jars with hot mushrooms, leaving 1-inch headspace. Add 1/2 teaspoon of salt per pint to the jar, if desired. For better color, add 1/8 teaspoon of ascorbic acid powder, or a 500-milligram tablet of vitamin C. Add fresh hot water, leaving 1-inch headspace. Remove air bubbles and adjust headspace if needed. Wipe rims of jars with a dampened clean paper towel. Adjust lids and process.

Recommended process time for Mushrooms in a dial-gauge pressure canner						
			Canner Pressure (PSI) at Altitudes of			
Style of Pack	Jar Size	Process Time	0–2,000 ft	2,001–4,000 ft	4,001–6,000 ft	6,001–8,000 ft
Hot	Half-pints or Pints	45 min	11 lb	12 lb	13 lb	14 lb

Recommended process time for Mushrooms in a weighted-gauge pressure canner				
			Canner Pressure (PSI) at Altitudes of	
Style of Pack	Jar Size	Process Time	0–1,000 ft	Above 1,000 ft
Hot	Half-pints or Pints	45 min	10 lb	15 lb

OKRA

Quantity: An average of 11 pounds is needed per canner load of 7 quarts; an average of 7 pounds is needed per canner load of 9 pints. A bushel weighs 26 pounds and yields 16 to 18 quarts—an average of 1-1/2 pounds per quart.

Quality: Select young, tender pods. Remove and discard diseased and rust-spotted pods.

Procedure: Wash pods and trim ends. Leave whole or cut into 1-inch pieces. Cover with hot water in a saucepan, boil 2 minutes and drain. Fill hot jars with hot okra and cooking liquid, leaving 1-inch headspace. Add 1 teaspoon of salt per quart to the jar, if desired. Remove air bubbles and adjust headspace if needed. Wipe rims of jars with a dampened clean paper towel. Adjust lids and process.

Recommended process time for Okra in a dial-gauge pressure canner						
			Canner Pressure (PSI) at Altitudes of			
Style of Pack	Jar Size	Process Time	0–2,000 ft	2,001–4,000 ft	4,001–6,000 ft	6,001–8,000 ft
Hot	Pints	25 min	11 lb	12 lb	13 lb	14 lb
	Quarts	40	11	12	13	14

Recommended process time for Okra in a weighted-gauge pressure canner				
			Canner Pressure (PSI) at Altitudes of	
Style of Pack	Jar Size	Process Time	0–1,000 ft	Above 1,000 ft
Hot	Pints	25 min	10 lb	15 lb
	Quarts	40	10	15

PEAS, GREEN OR ENGLISH—SHELLED

It is recommended that sugar snap and Chinese edible pods be frozen for best quality.

Quantity: An average of 31-1/2 pounds (in pods) is needed per canner load of 7 quarts; an average of 20 pounds is needed per canner load of 9 pints. A bushel weighs 30 pounds and yields 5 to 10 quarts—an average of 4-1/2 pounds per quart.

Quality: Select filled pods containing young, tender, sweet seeds. Discard diseased pods.

Procedure: Shell and wash peas. Add 1 teaspoon of salt per quart to the jar, if desired.

Hot pack—Cover with boiling water. Bring to a boil in a saucepan, and boil 2 minutes. Fill hot jars loosely with hot peas, and add cooking liquid, leaving 1-inch headspace.

Raw pack—Fill hot jars with raw peas, add boiling water, leaving 1-inch headspace. Do not shake or press down peas.

Remove air bubbles and adjust headspace if needed. Wipe rims of jars with a dampened clean paper towel. Adjust lids and process.

Recommended process time for Peas, Green or English in a dial-gauge pressure canner

Style of Pack	Jar Size	Process Time	Canner Pressure (PSI) at Altitudes of			
			0–2,000 ft	2,001–4,000 ft	4,001–6,000 ft	6,001–8,000 ft
Hot and Raw	Pints or Quarts	40 min	11 lb	12 lb	13 lb	14 lb

Recommended process time for Peas, Green or English in a weighted-gauge pressure canner

Style of Pack	Jar Size	Process Time	Canner Pressure (PSI) at Altitudes of	
			0–1,000 ft	Above 1,000 ft
Hot and Raw	Pints or Quarts	40 min	10 lb	15 lb

PEPPERS

Hot or sweet, including chiles, jalapeño, and pimiento

Quantity: An average of 9 pounds is needed per canner load of 9 pints. A bushel weighs 25 pounds and yields 20 to 30 pints—an average of 1 pound per pint.

Quality: Select firm yellow, green, or red peppers. Do not use soft or diseased peppers.

Procedure: Select your favorite pepper(s). **Caution: If you choose hot peppers, wear plastic or rubber gloves and do not touch your face while handling or cutting hot peppers. If you do not wear gloves, wash hands thoroughly with soap and water before touching your face or eyes.** Small peppers may be left whole. Large peppers may be quartered. Remove cores and seeds. Slash two or four slits in each pepper, and either blanch in boiling water or blister skins using one of these two methods:

Oven or broiler method to blister skins – Place peppers in a hot oven (400°F) or broiler for 6-8 minutes until skins blister.

Range-top method to blister skins – Cover hot burner, either gas or electric, with heavy wire mesh. Place peppers on burner for several minutes until skins blister.

After blistering skins, place peppers in a pan and cover with a damp cloth. (This will make peeling the peppers easier.) Cool several minutes; peel off skins. Flatten whole peppers. Add 1/2 teaspoon of salt to each pint jar, if desired. Fill hot jars loosely with peppers and add fresh boiling water, leaving 1-inch headspace. Remove air bubbles and adjust headspace if needed. Wipe rims of jars with a dampened clean paper towel. Adjust lids and process.

Recommended process time for Peppers in a dial-gauge pressure canner

Style of Pack	Jar Size	Process Time	Canner Pressure (PSI) at Altitudes of			
			0–2,000 ft	2,001–4,000 ft	4,001–6,000 ft	6,001–8,000 ft
Hot	Half-pints or Pints	35 min	11 lb	12 lb	13 lb	14 lb

Recommended process time for Peppers in a weighted-gauge pressure canner

Style of Pack	Jar Size	Process Time	Canner Pressure (PSI) at Altitudes of	
			0–1,000 ft	Above 1,000 ft
Hot	Half-pints or Pints	35 min	10 lb	15 lb

POTATOES, SWEET—PIECES OR WHOLE

It is not recommended to dry pack sweet potatoes.

Quantity: An average of 17-1/2 pounds is needed per canner load of 7 quarts; an average of 11 pounds is needed per canner load of 9 pints. A bushel weighs 50 pounds and yields 17 to 25 quarts—an average of 2-1/2 pounds per quart.

Quality: Choose small to medium-sized potatoes. They should be mature and not too fibrous. Can within 1 to 2 months after harvest.

Procedure: Wash potatoes and boil or steam until partially soft (15 to 20 minutes). Remove skins. Cut medium potatoes, if needed, so that pieces are uniform in size. **Caution: Do not mash or puree pieces.** Fill hot jars, leaving 1-inch headspace. Add 1 teaspoon salt per quart to the jar, if desired. Cover with your choice of fresh boiling water or syrup (see page 2-5), leaving 1-inch headspace. Remove air bubbles and adjust headspace if needed. Wipe rims of jars with a dampened clean paper towel. Adjust lids and process.

Recommended process time for Sweet Potatoes in a dial-gauge pressure canner

Style of Pack	Jar Size	Process Time	Canner Pressure (PSI) at Altitudes of			
			0–2,000 ft	2,001–4,000 ft	4,001–6,000 ft	6,001–8,000 ft
Hot	Pints	65 min	11 lb	12 lb	13 lb	14 lb
	Quarts	90	11	12	13	14

Recommended process time for Sweet Potatoes in a weighted-gauge pressure canner

Style of Pack	Jar Size	Process Time	Canner Pressure (PSI) at Altitudes of	
			0–1,000 ft	Above 1,000 ft
Hot	Pints	65 min	10 lb	15 lb
	Quarts	90	10	15

POTATOES, WHITE—CUBED OR WHOLE

Quantity: An average of 20 pounds is needed per canner load of 7 quarts; an average of 13 pounds is needed per canner load of 9 pints. A bag weighs 50 pounds and yields 18 to 22 quarts—an average of 2-1/2 to 3 pounds per quart.

Quality: Select small to medium-size mature potatoes of ideal quality for cooking. Tubers stored below 45°F may discolor when canned. Choose potatoes 1 to 2 inches in diameter if they are to be packed whole.

Procedure: Wash and peel potatoes. Place in ascorbic acid solution to prevent darkening (see pages 1-11). If desired, cut into 1/2-inch cubes. Drain. Cook 2 minutes in boiling water and drain again. For whole potatoes, boil 10 minutes and drain. Add 1 teaspoon of salt per quart to the jar, if desired. Fill hot jars with hot potatoes and fresh hot water, leaving 1-inch headspace. Remove air bubbles and adjust headspace if needed. Wipe rims of jars with a dampened clean paper towel. Adjust lids and process.

Recommended process time for White Potatoes in a dial-gauge pressure canner

Style of Pack	Jar Size	Process Time	Canner Pressure (PSI) at Altitudes of			
			0–2,000 ft	2,001–4,000 ft	4,001–6,000 ft	6,001–8,000 ft
Hot	Pints	35 min	11 lb	12 lb	13 lb	14 lb
	Quarts	40	11	12	13	14

Recommended process time for White Potatoes in a weighted-gauge pressure canner

Style of Pack	Jar Size	Process Time	Canner Pressure (PSI) at Altitudes of	
			0–1,000 ft	Above 1,000 ft
Hot	Pints	35 min	10 lb	15 lb
	Quarts	40	10	15

PUMPKINS AND WINTER SQUASH—CUBED

Quantity: An average of 16 pounds is needed per canner load of 7 quarts; an average of 10 pounds is needed per canner load of 9 pints—an average of 2-1/4 pounds per quart.

Quality: Pumpkins and squash should have a hard rind and stringless, mature pulp of ideal quality for cooking fresh. Small size pumpkins (sugar or pie varieties) make better products.

Procedure: Wash, remove seeds, cut into 1-inch-wide slices, and peel. Cut flesh into 1-inch cubes. Boil 2 minutes in water. **Caution: Do not mash or puree.** Fill hot jars with cubes and cooking liquid, leaving 1-inch headspace. Remove air bubbles and adjust headspace if needed. Wipe rims of jars with a dampened clean paper towel. Adjust lids and process.

For making pies, drain jars and strain or sieve the cubes at preparation time.

Recommended process time for Pumpkin and Winter Squash in a dial-gauge pressure canner						
			Canner Pressure (PSI) at Altitudes of			
Style of Pack	Jar Size	Process Time	0–2,000 ft	2,001–4,000 ft	4,001–6,000 ft	6,001–8,000 ft
Hot	Pints	55 min	11 lb	12 lb	13 lb	14 lb
	Quarts	90	11	12	13	14

Recommended process time for Pumpkin and Winter Squash in a weighted-gauge pressure canner				
			Canner Pressure (PSI) at Altitudes of	
Style of Pack	Jar Size	Process Time	0–1,000 ft	Above 1,000 ft
Hot	Pints	55 min	10 lb	15 lb
	Quarts	90	10	15

SOUPS

Vegetable, dried bean or pea, meat, poultry, or seafoods

Caution: Do not add noodles or other pasta, rice, flour, cream, milk or other thickening agents to home canned soups. If dried beans or peas are used, they must be fully rehydrated first.

Procedure: Select, wash, and prepare vegetables, meat, and seafoods as described for the specific foods. Cover meat with water and cook until tender. Cool meat and remove bones. Cook vegetables. For each cup of dried beans or peas, add 3 cups of water, boil 2 minutes, remove from heat, soak 1 hour, and heat to boil.

Drain all foods and combine with meat broth, tomatoes, or water to cover. Boil 5 minutes. **Caution: Do not thicken.** Salt to taste, if desired.

Fill hot jars only halfway with mixture of solids. Add and cover with remaining liquid, leaving 1-inch headspace. Remove air bubbles and adjust headspace if needed. Wipe rims of jars with a dampened clean paper towel. Adjust lids and process.

Recommended process time for Soups in a dial-gauge pressure canner

Style of Pack	Jar Size	Process Time	Canner Pressure (PSI) at Altitudes of			
			0–2,000 ft	2,001–4,000 ft	4,001–6,000 ft	6,001–8,000 ft
Hot	Pints	60* min	11 lb	12 lb	13 lb	14 lb
	Quarts	75*	11	12	13	14

*Caution: Process 100 minutes if soup contains seafoods.

Recommended process time for Soups in a weighted-gauge pressure canner

Style of Pack	Jar Size	Process Time	Canner Pressure (PSI) at Altitudes of	
			0–1,000 ft	Above 1,000 ft
Hot	Pints	60* min	10 lb	15 lb
	Quarts	75*	10	15

*Caution: Process 100 minutes if soup contains seafoods.

SPINACH AND OTHER GREENS

Quantity: An average of 28 pounds is needed per canner load of 7 quarts; an average of 18 pounds is needed per canner load of 9 pints. A bushel weighs 18 pounds and yields 3 to 9 quarts—an average of 4 pounds per quart.

Quality: Can only freshly harvested greens. Discard any wilted, discolored, diseased, or insect-damaged leaves. Leaves should be tender and attractive in color.

Procedure: Wash only small amounts of greens at one time. Drain water and continue rinsing until water is clear and free of grit. Cut out tough stems and midribs. Place 1 pound of greens at a time in cheesecloth bag or blancher basket and steam 3 to 5 minutes or until well wilted. Add 1/2 teaspoon of salt to each quart jar, if desired. Fill hot jars loosely with greens and add fresh boiling water, leaving 1-inch headspace. Remove air bubbles and adjust headspace if needed. Wipe rims of jars with a dampened clean paper towel. Adjust lids and process.

Recommended process time for Spinach and Other Greens in a dial-gauge pressure canner

Style of Pack	Jar Size	Process Time	Canner Pressure (PSI) at Altitudes of			
			0–2,000 ft	2,001–4,000 ft	4,001–6,000 ft	6,001–8,000 ft
Hot	Pints	70 min	11 lb	12 lb	13 lb	14 lb
	Quarts	90	11	12	13	14

Recommended process time for Spinach and Other Greens in a weighted-gauge pressure canner

Style of Pack	Jar Size	Process Time	Canner Pressure (PSI) at Altitudes of	
			0–1,000 ft	Above 1,000 ft
Hot	Pints	70 min	10 lb	15 lb
	Quarts	90	10	15

SQUASH, WINTER — CUBED

Prepare and process according to instructions for "Pumpkin" (see page 4-18).

SUCCOTASH

15 lbs unhusked sweet corn or 3 qts cut whole kernels
14 lbs mature green podded lima beans or 4 qts shelled limas
2 qts crushed or whole tomatoes (optional)

Yield: 7 quarts

Procedure: Wash and prepare fresh produce as described previously for specific vegetables.

Hot pack—Combine all prepared vegetables in a large kettle with enough water to cover the pieces. Add 1 teaspoon salt to each hot quart jar, if desired. Boil succotash gently 5 minutes and fill hot jars with pieces and cooking liquid, leaving 1-inch headspace.

Raw pack—Fill hot jars with equal parts of all prepared vegetables, leaving 1-inch headspace. Do not shake or press down pieces. Add 1 teaspoon salt to each quart jar, if desired. Add fresh boiling water, leaving 1-inch headspace.

Remove air bubbles and adjust headspace if needed. Wipe rims of jars with a dampened clean paper towel. Adjust lids and process.

Recommended process time for Succotash in a dial-gauge pressure canner

Style of Pack	Jar Size	Process Time	Canner Pressure (PSI) at Altitudes of			
			0–2,000 ft	2,001–4,000 ft	4,001–6,000 ft	6,001–8,000 ft
Hot and Raw	Pints	60 min	11 lb	12 lb	13 lb	14 lb
	Quarts	85	11	12	13	14

Recommended process time for Succotash in a weighted-gauge pressure canner

Style of Pack	Jar Size	Process Time	Canner Pressure (PSI) at Altitudes of	
			0–1,000 ft	Above 1,000 ft
Hot and Raw	Pints	60 min	10 lb	15 lb
	Quarts	85	10	15

Complete Guide to
Home Canning

Guide 5
Preparing and Canning Poultry, Red Meats, and Seafoods

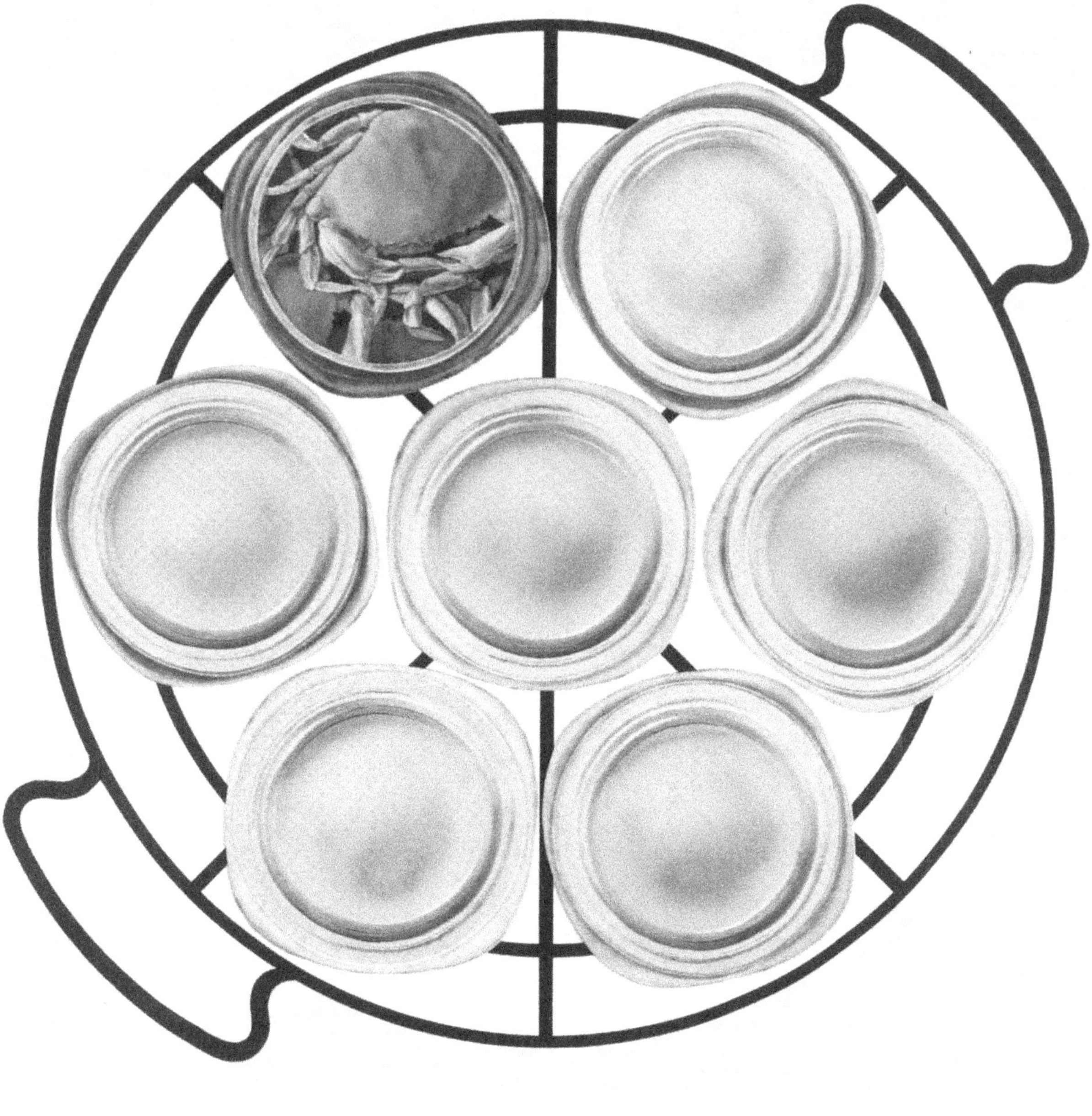

United States Department of Agriculture

National Institute of Food and Agriculture

Guide 5
Preparing and Canning Poultry, Red Meats, and Seafoods

Table of Contents

Section	Page
Chicken or rabbit	5-5
Ground or chopped meat	5-6
Strips, cubes, or chunks of meat	5-6
Meat stock (broth)	5-7
Chile con carne	5-8
Clams	5-9
King and Dungeness crab meat	5-9
Fish in pint jars	5-10
Fish in quart jars	5-11
Oysters	5-12
Smoked fish	5-13
Tuna	5-14

CHICKEN OR RABBIT

Procedure: Choose freshly killed and dressed, healthy animals. Large chickens are more flavorful than fryers. Dressed chicken should be chilled for 6 to 12 hours before canning. Dressed rabbits should be soaked 1 hour in water containing 1 tablespoon of salt per quart, and then rinsed. Remove excess fat. Cut the chicken or rabbit into suitable sizes for canning. Can with or without bones. The hot pack is preferred for best liquid cover and quality during storage. Natural poultry fat and juices are usually not enough to cover the meat in raw packs.

Hot pack—Boil, steam, or bake meat until about two-thirds done. Add 1 teaspoon salt per quart to the jar, if desired. Fill hot jars with pieces and hot broth, leaving 1-1/4 inch headspace. Remove air bubbles and adjust headspace if needed.

Raw pack—Add 1 teaspoon salt per quart, if desired. Fill hot jars loosely with raw meat pieces, leaving 1-1/4-inch headspace. Do not add liquid.

Wipe rims of jars with a dampened clean paper towel. Adjust lids and process.

Recommended process time for Chicken or Rabbit in a dial-gauge pressure canner

Style of Pack	Jar Size	Process Time	Canner Pressure (PSI) at Altitudes of			
			0–2,000 ft	2,001–4,000 ft	4,001–6,000 ft	6,001–8,000 ft
Without Bones:						
Hot and Raw	Pints	75 min	11 lb	12 lb	13 lb	14 lb
	Quarts	90	11	12	13	14
With Bones:						
Hot and Raw	Pints	65 min	11 lb	12 lb	13 lb	14 lb
	Quarts	75	11	12	13	14

Recommended process time for Chicken or Rabbit in a weighted-gauge pressure canner

Style of Pack	Jar Size	Process Time	Canner Pressure (PSI) at Altitudes of	
			0–1,000 ft	Above 1,000 ft
Without Bones:				
Hot and Raw	Pints	75 min	10 lb	15 lb
	Quarts	90	10	15
With Bones:				
Hot and Raw	Pints	65 min	10 lb	15 lb
	Quarts	75	10	15

GROUND OR CHOPPED MEAT

Bear, beef, lamb, pork, sausage, veal, venison

Procedure: Choose fresh, chilled meat. With venison, add one part high-quality pork fat to three or four parts venison before grinding. Use freshly made sausage, seasoned with salt and cayenne pepper (sage may cause a bitter off-flavor). Shape chopped meat into patties or balls or cut cased sausage into 3- to 4-inch links. Cook until lightly browned. Ground meat may be sauteed without shaping. Remove excess fat. Fill hot jars with pieces. Add boiling meat broth, tomato juice, or water, leaving 1-inch headspace. Remove air bubbles and adjust headspace if needed. Add 1 teaspoon of salt per quart to the jars, if desired. Wipe rims of jars with a dampened clean paper towel. Adjust lids and process.

Recommended process time for Ground or Chopped Meat in a dial-gauge pressure canner

Style of Pack	Jar Size	Process Time	Canner Pressure (PSI) at Altitudes of			
			0–2,000 ft	2,001–4,000 ft	4,001–6,000 ft	6,001–8,000 ft
Hot	Pints	75 min	11 lb	12 lb	13 lb	14 lb
	Quarts	90	11	12	13	14

Recommended process time for Ground or Chopped Meat in a weighted-gauge pressure canner

Style of Pack	Jar Size	Process Time	Canner Pressure (PSI) at Altitudes of	
			0–1,000 ft	Above 1,000 ft
Hot	Pints	75 min	10 lb	15 lb
	Quarts	90	10	15

STRIPS, CUBES, OR CHUNKS OF MEAT

Bear, beef, lamb, pork, veal, venison

Procedure: Choose high quality chilled meat. Remove excess fat. Soak strong-flavored wild meats for 1 hour in brine water containing 1 tablespoon of salt per quart. Rinse. Remove large bones. The hot pack is preferred for best liquid cover and quality during storage. The natural amount of fat and juices in today's leaner meat cuts are usually not enough to cover most of the meat in raw packs.

Hot pack—Precook meat until rare by roasting, stewing, or browning in a small amount of fat. Add 1 teaspoon of salt per quart to the jar, if desired. Fill hot jars with pieces and add boiling broth, meat drippings, water, or tomato juice (especially with wild game), leaving 1-inch headspace. Remove air bubbles and adjust headspace if needed.

Raw pack—Add 1 teaspoon of salt per quart to the jar, if desired. Fill hot jars with raw meat pieces, leaving 1-inch headspace. Do not add liquid.

Wipe rims of jars with a dampened clean paper towel. Adjust lids and process.

Recommended process time for Strips, Cubes, or Chunks of Meat in a dial-gauge pressure canner					
			Canner Pressure (PSI) at Altitudes of			
Style of Pack	Jar Size	Process Time	0–2,000 ft	2,001–4,000 ft	4,001–6,000 ft	6,001–8,000 ft
Hot and Raw	Pints	75 min	11 lb	12 lb	13 lb	14 lb
	Quarts	90	11	12	13	14

Recommended process time for Strips, Cubes, or Chunks of Meat in a weighted-gauge pressure canner					
			Canner Pressure (PSI) at Altitudes of	
Style of Pack	Jar Size	Process Time	0–1,000 ft	Above 1,000 ft
Hot and Raw	Pints	75 min	10 lb	15 lb
	Quarts	90	10	15

MEAT STOCK (BROTH)

Beef: Beef: Saw or crack fresh trimmed beef bones (with meat removed) to enhance extraction of flavor. Rinse bones and place in a large stockpot, cover bones with water. Place cover on pot and simmer 3 to 4 hours. Remove bones and cool broth; skim off excess fat and discard. If desired, remove any tiny amount of meat tidbits still clinging to bones and add back to the broth. Reheat broth to boiling and fill jars, leaving 1-inch headspace. Wipe rims of jars with a dampened clean paper towel. Adjust lids and process.

Chicken or turkey: Place large carcass bones (with meat removed) in a large stockpot. Add enough water to cover bones. Cover pot and simmer 30 to 45 minutes or until any remaining tidbits of meat on bones easily fall off. Remove bones, cool broth and discard excess fat. If desired, remove any tiny amount of meat trimmings still clinging to bones and add back to the broth. Reheat broth to boiling and fill jars, leaving 1-inch headspace. Wipe rims of jars with a dampened clean paper towel. Adjust lids and process.

Recommended process time for Meat Stock in a dial-gauge pressure canner					
			Canner Pressure (PSI) at Altitudes of			
Style of Pack	Jar Size	Process Time	0–2,000 ft	2,001–4,000 ft	4,001–6,000 ft	6,001–8,000 ft
Hot	Pints	20 min	11 lb	12 lb	13 lb	14 lb
	Quarts	25	11	12	13	14

Recommended process time for Meat Stock in a weighted-gauge pressure canner					
			Canner Pressure (PSI) at Altitudes of	
Style of Pack	Jar Size	Process Time	0–1,000 ft	Above 1,000 ft
Hot	Pints	20 min	10 lb	15 lb
	Quarts	25	10	15

CHILE CON CARNE

3 cups dried pinto or red kidney beans
5-1/2 cups water
5 tsp salt (separated)
3 lbs ground beef
1-1/2 cups chopped onions
1 cup chopped peppers of your choice (optional)
1 tsp black pepper
3 to 6 tbsp chili powder
2 quarts crushed or whole tomatoes

Yield: 9 pints

Procedure: Wash beans thoroughly and place them in a 2 qt. saucepan. Add cold water to a level of 2 to 3 inches above the beans and soak 12 to 18 hours. Drain and discard water. Combine beans with 5-1/2 cups of fresh water and 2 teaspoons salt. Bring to a boil. Reduce heat and simmer 30 minutes. Drain and discard water. Brown ground beef, chopped onions, and peppers (if desired), in a skillet. Drain off fat and add 3 teaspoons salt, pepper, chili powder, tomatoes and drained cooked beans. Simmer 5 minutes. **Caution: Do not thicken.** Fill hot jars, leaving 1-inch headspace. Remove air bubbles and adjust headspace if needed. Wipe rims of jars with a dampened clean paper towel. Adjust lids and process.

Recommended process time for Chile Con Carne in a dial-gauge pressure canner

Style of Pack	Jar Size	Process Time	Canner Pressure (PSI) at Altitudes of			
			0–2,000 ft	2,001–4,000 ft	4,001–6,000 ft	6,001–8,000 ft
Hot	Pints	75 min	11 lb	12 lb	13 lb	14 lb

Recommended process time for Chile Con Carne in a weighted-gauge pressure canner

Style of Pack	Jar Size	Process Time	Canner Pressure (PSI) at Altitudes of	
			0–1,000 ft	Above 1,000 ft
Hot	Pints	75 min	10 lb	15 lb

CLAMS

Whole or minced

Procedure: Keep clams live on ice until ready to can. Scrub shells thoroughly and rinse, steam 5 minutes, and open. Remove clam meat. Collect and save clam juice. Wash clam meat in water containing 1 teaspoon of salt per quart. Rinse and cover clam meat with boiling water containing 2 tablespoons of lemon juice or 1/2 teaspoon of citric acid per gallon. Boil 2 minutes and drain. To make minced clams, grind clams with a meat grinder or food processor. Fill hot jars loosely with pieces and add hot clam juice and boiling water if needed, leaving 1-inch headspace. Remove air bubbles and adjust headspace if needed. Wipe rims of jars with a dampened clean paper towel. Adjust lids and process.

Recommended process time for Clams in a dial-gauge pressure canner

Style of Pack	Jar Size	Process Time	Canner Pressure (PSI) at Altitudes of			
			0–2,000 ft	2,001–4,000 ft	4,001–6,000 ft	6,001–8,000 ft
Hot	Half-pints	60 min	11 lb	12 lb	13 lb	14 lb
	Pints	70	11	12	13	14

Recommended process time for Clams in a weighted-gauge pressure canner

Style of Pack	Jar Size	Process Time	Canner Pressure (PSI) at Altitudes of	
			0–1,000 ft	Above 1,000 ft
Hot	Half-pints	60 min	10 lb	15 lb
	Pints	70	10	15

KING AND DUNGENESS CRAB MEAT

It is recommended that blue crab meat be frozen instead of canned for best quality. Crab meat canned according to the following procedure may have a distinctly acidic flavor and freezing is the preferred method of preservation at this time.

Procedure: Keep live crabs on ice until ready to can. Wash crabs thoroughly, using several changes of cold water. Simmer crabs 20 minutes in water containing cup of lemon juice and 2 tablespoons of salt (or up to 1 cup of salt, if desired) per gallon. Cool in cold water, drain, remove back shell, then remove meat from body and claws. Soak meat 2 minutes in cold water containing 2 cups of lemon juice or 4 cups of white vinegar, and 2 tablespoons of salt (or up to 1 cup of salt, if desired) per gallon. Drain and squeeze crab meat to remove excess moisture. Fill hot half-pint jars with 6 ounces of crab meat and pint jars with 12 ounces, leaving 1-inch headspace. Add 1/2 teaspoon of citric acid or 2 tablespoons of lemon juice to each half-pint jar, or 1 teaspoon of citric acid or 4 tablespoons of lemon juice per pint jar. Cover with fresh boiling water, leaving 1-inch headspace. Remove air bubbles and adjust headspace if needed. Wipe rims of jars with a dampened clean paper towel. Adjust lids and process.

Recommended process time for King and Dungeness Crab Meat in a dial-gauge pressure canner

Style of Pack	Jar Size	Process Time	Canner Pressure (PSI) at Altitudes of			
			0–2,000 ft	2,001–4,000 ft	4,001–6,000 ft	6,001–8,000 ft
See above	Half-pints	70 min	11 lb	12 lb	13 lb	14 lb
	Pints	80	11	12	13	14

Recommended process time for King and Dungeness Crab Meat in a weighted-gauge pressure canner

Style of Pack	Jar Size	Process Time	Canner Pressure (PSI) at Altitudes of	
			0–1,000 ft	Above 1,000 ft
See above	Half-pints	70 min	10 lb	15 lb
	Pints	80	10	15

FISH in Pint Jars

Blue, mackerel, salmon, steelhead, trout, and other fatty fish except tuna

Caution: Bleed and eviscerate fish immediately after catching, never more than 2 hours after they are caught. Keep cleaned fish on ice until ready to can.

Note: Glass-like crystals of struvite, or magnesium ammonium phosphate, sometime form in canned salmon. There is no way for the home canner to prevent these crystals from forming, but they usually dissolve when heated and are safe to eat.

Procedure: If the fish is frozen, thaw it in the refrigerator before canning. Rinse the fish in cold water. You can add vinegar to the water (2 tablespoons per quart) to help remove slime. Remove head, tail, fins, and scales; it is not necessary to remove the skin. You can leave the bones in most fish because the bones become very soft and are a good source of calcium. For halibut, remove the head, tail, fins, skin, and the bones. Wash and remove all blood. Refrigerate all fish until you are ready to pack in jars.

Split fish lengthwise, if desired. Cut cleaned fish into 3-1/2-inch lengths. If the skin has been left on the fish, pack the fish skin out, for a nicer appearance or skin in, for easier jar cleaning. Fill hot pint jars, leaving 1-inch headspace. Add 1 teaspoon of salt per pint, if desired. Do not add liquids. Carefully clean the jar rims with a clean, damp paper towel; wipe with a dry paper towel to remove any fish oil. Adjust lids and process. Fish in half-pint or 12-ounce jars would be processed for the same amount of time as pint jars.

Recommended process time for Fish in Pint Jars in a dial-gauge pressure canner

Style of Pack	Jar Size	Process Time	Canner Pressure (PSI) at Altitudes of			
			0–2,000 ft	2,001–4,000 ft	4,001–6,000 ft	6,001–8,000 ft
Raw	Pints	100 min	11 lb	12 lb	13 lb	14 lb

Recommended process time for Fish in Pint Jars in a weighted-gauge pressure canner

Style of Pack	Jar Size	Process Time	Canner Pressure (PSI) at Altitudes of	
			0–1,000 ft	Above 1,000 ft
Raw	Pints	100 min	10 lb	15 lb

FISH in Quart Jars

Blue, mackerel, salmon, steelhead, trout, and other fatty fish except tuna

Note: Glass-like crystals of struvite, or magnesium ammonium phosphate, sometime form in canned salmon. There is no way for the home canner to prevent these crystals from forming, but they usually dissolve when heated and are safe to eat.

Caution: Bleed and eviscerate fish immediately after catching, never more than 2 hours after they are caught. Keep cleaned fish on ice until ready to can.

Procedure: If the fish is frozen, thaw it in the refrigerator before canning. Rinse the fish in cold water. You can add vinegar to the water (2 tablespoons per quart) to help remove slime. Remove head, tail, fins, and scales; it is not necessary to remove the skin. You can leave the bones in most fish because the bones become very soft and are a good source of calcium. For halibut, remove the head, tail, fins, skin, and the bones. Wash and remove all blood. Refrigerate all fish until you are ready to pack in jars.

Cut the fish into jar-length filets or chunks of any size. The one-quart straight-sided mason-type jar is recommended. If the skin has been left on the fish, pack the fish skin out, for a nicer appearance or skin in, for easier jar cleaning. Pack solidly into hot quart jars, leaving 1-inch headspace. If desired, run a plastic knife around the inside of the jar to align the product; this allows firm packing of fish.

> For most fish, no liquid, salt, or spices need to be added, although seasonings or salt may be added for flavor (1 to 2 teaspoons salt per quart, or amount desired).

> For halibut, add up to 4 tablespoons of vegetable or olive oil per quart jar if you wish. The canned product will seem moister. However, the oil will increase the caloric value of the fish.

Carefully clean the jar rims with a clean, damp paper towel; wipe with a dry paper towel to remove any fish oil. Adjust lids and process.

Processing Change for Quart Jars: The directions for operating the pressure canner during processing of quart jars are different from those for processing pint jars, so please read the following carefully. It is critical to product safety that the processing directions are followed exactly. When you are ready to process your jars of fish, add 3 quarts of water to the pressure canner. Put the rack in the bottom of canner and place closed jars on the rack. Fasten the canner cover securely, but do not close the lid vent. Heat the canner on high for 20 minutes. If steam comes through the open vent in a steady stream at the end of 20 minutes, allow it to escape for an additional 10 minutes. If steam does not come through the open vent in a steady stream at the end of 20 minutes, keep heating the canner until it does. Then allow the steam to escape for an additional 10 minutes to vent the canner. This step removes air from inside the canner so the temperature is the same throughout the canner. *The total time it takes to heat and vent the canner should never be less than 30 minutes. The total time may be more than 30 minutes if you have tightly packed jars, cold fish, or larger sized canners.* **For safety's sake, you must have a complete, uninterrupted 160 minutes (2 hours and 40 minutes) at a minimum pressure required for your altitude. Write down the time at the beginning of the process and the time when the process will be finished.**

Recommended process time for Fish in Quart Jars in a dial-gauge pressure canner						
			Canner Pressure (PSI) at Altitudes of			
Style of Pack	Jar Size	Process Time	0–2,000 ft	2,001–4,000 ft	4,001–6,000 ft	6,001–8,000 ft
Raw	Quarts	160 min	11 lb	12 lb	13 lb	14 lb

Recommended process time for Fish in Quart Jars in a weighted-gauge pressure canner				
			Canner Pressure (PSI) at Altitudes of	
Style of Pack	Jar Size	Process Time	0–1,000 ft	Above 1,000 ft
Raw	Quarts	160 min	10 lb	15 lb

OYSTERS

Procedure: Keep live oysters on ice until ready to can. Wash shells. Heat 5 to 7 minutes in preheated oven at 400°F. Cool briefly in ice water. Drain, open shell, and remove meat. Wash meat in water containing 1/2 cup salt per gallon. Drain. Add 1/2 teaspoon salt to each pint, if desired. Fill hot half-pint or pint jars with drained oysters and cover with fresh boiling water, leaving 1-inch headspace. Remove air bubbles and adjust headspace if needed. Wipe rims of jars with a dampened clean paper towel. Adjust lids and process.

Recommended process time for Oysters in a dial-gauge pressure canner

Style of Pack	Jar Size	Process Time	Canner Pressure (PSI) at Altitudes of			
			0–2,000 ft	2,001–4,000 ft	4,001–6,000 ft	6,001–8,000 ft
See above	Half-pints or Pints	75 min	11 lb	12 lb	13 lb	14 lb

Recommended process time for Oysters in a weighted-gauge pressure canner

Style of Pack	Jar Size	Process Time	Canner Pressure (PSI) at Altitudes of	
			0–1,000 ft	Above 1,000 ft
See above	Half-pints or Pints	75 min	10 lb	15 lb

SMOKED FISH

Salmon, rockfish and flatfish (sole, cod, flounder) and other fish

Caution: Safe processing times for other smoked seafoods have not been determined. Those products should be frozen. Smoking of fish should be done by tested methods. Lightly smoked fish is recommended for canning because the smoked flavor will become stronger and the flesh drier after processing. However, because it has not yet been cooked, do not taste lightly smoked fish before canning.

Follow these recommended canning instructions carefully. Use a 16 to 22 quart pressure canner for this procedure; do not use smaller pressure saucepans. Safe processing times have not been determined. Do not use jars larger than one pint. Half-pints could be safely processed for the same length of time as pints, but the quality of the product may be less acceptable.

Procedure: If smoked fish has been frozen, thaw in the refrigerator until no ice crystals remain before canning. If not done prior to smoking, cut fish into pieces that will fit vertically into pint canning jars, leaving 1-inch headspace. Pack smoked fish vertically into hot jars, leaving 1-inch headspace between the pieces and the top rim of the jar. The fish may be packed either loosely or tightly. Do not add liquid to the jars. Clean jar rims with a clean, damp paper towel. Adjust lids and process.

Processing Change for Smoked Fish: The directions for filling the pressure canner for processing smoked fish are different than those for other pressure canning, so please read the following carefully. **It is critical to product safety that the processing directions are followed exactly.** When you are ready to process your jars of smoked fish, measure 4 quarts (16 cups) of cool tap water and pour into the pressure canner. (**Note:** The water level probably will reach the screw bands of pint jars.) **Do not decrease the amount of water or heat the water before processing begins.** Place prepared, closed jars on the rack in the bottom of the canner, and proceed as with usual pressure canning instructions.

Recommended process time for Smoked Fish in a dial-gauge pressure canner

Style of Pack	Jar Size	Process Time	Canner Pressure (PSI) at Altitudes of			
			0–2,000 ft	2,001–4,000 ft	4,001–6,000 ft	6,001–8,000 ft
See above	Pints	110 min	11 lb	12 lb	13 lb	14 lb

Recommended process time for Smoked Fish in a weighted-gauge pressure canner

Style of Pack	Jar Size	Process Time	Canner Pressure (PSI) at Altitudes of	
			0–1,000 ft	Above 1,000 ft
See above	Pints	110 min	10 lb	15 lb

TUNA

Tuna may be canned either precooked or raw. Precooking removes most of the strong-flavored oils. The strong flavor of dark tuna flesh affects the delicate flavor of white flesh. Many people prefer not to can dark flesh. It may be used as pet food.

Note: Glass-like crystals of struvite, or magnesium ammonium phosphate, sometime form in canned tuna. There is no way for the home canner to prevent these crystals from forming, but they usually dissolve when heated and are safe to eat.

Procedure: Keep tuna on ice until ready to can. Remove viscera and wash fish well in cold water. Allow blood to drain from stomach cavity. Place fish belly down on a rack or metal tray in the bottom of a large baking pan. Cut tuna in half crosswise, if necessary. Precook fish by baking at 250°F for 2-1/2 to 4 hours (depending on size) or at 350°F for 1 hour. The fish may also be cooked in a steamer for 2 to 4 hours. If a thermometer is used, cook to a 165° to 175°F internal temperature. Refrigerate cooked fish overnight to firm the meat. Peel off the skin with a knife, removing blood vessels and any discolored flesh. Cut meat away from bones; cut out and discard all bones, fin bases, and dark flesh. Quarter. Cut quarters crosswise into lengths suitable for half-pint or pint jars. Fill into hot jars, pressing down gently to make a solid pack. Tuna may be packed in water or oil, whichever is preferred. Add water or oil to jars, leaving 1-inch headspace. Remove air bubbles and adjust headspace if needed. Add 1/2 teaspoon of salt per half-pint or 1 teaspoon of salt per pint, if desired. Carefully clean the jar rims with a clean, damp paper towel; wipe with a dry paper towel to remove any fish oil. Adjust lids and process.

Recommended process time for Tuna in a dial-gauge pressure canner

Style of Pack	Jar Size	Process Time	Canner Pressure (PSI) at Altitudes of			
			0–2,000 ft	2,001–4,000 ft	4,001–6,000 ft	6,001–8,000 ft
See above	Half-pints or Pints	100 min	11 lb	12 lb	13 lb	14 lb

Recommended process time for Tuna in a weighted-gauge pressure canner

Style of Pack	Jar Size	Process Time	Canner Pressure (PSI) at Altitudes of	
			0–1,000 ft	Above 1,000 ft
See above	Half-pints or Pints	100 min	10 lb	15 lb

Complete Guide to
Home Canning

Guide 6
Preparing and Canning Fermented Foods and Pickled Vegetables

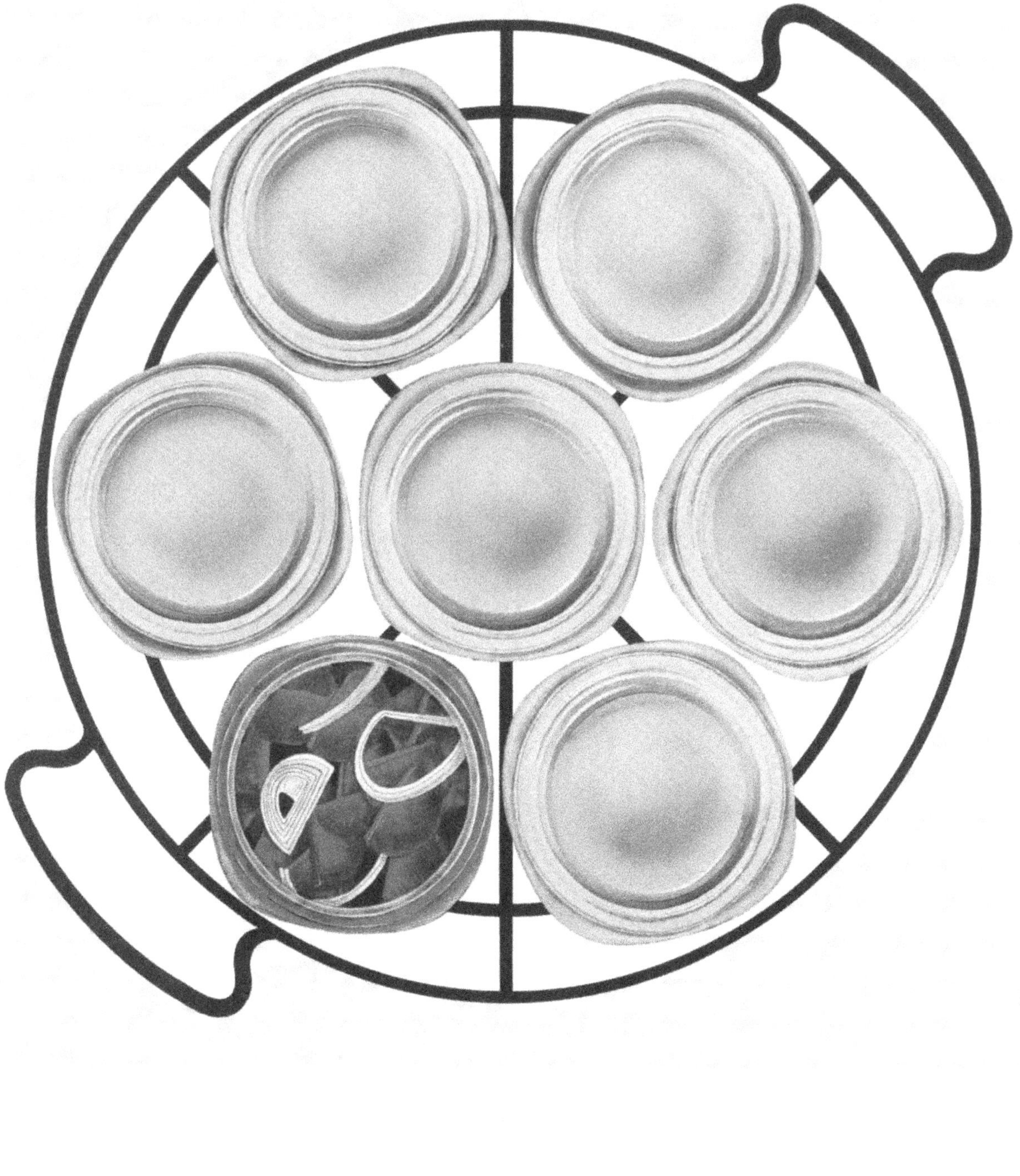

United States Department of Agriculture

National Institute of Food and Agriculture

Guide 6
Preparing and Canning Fermented Foods and Pickled Vegetables

Table of Contents

Section	Page
Selection of fresh cucumbers	6-5
Low-temperature pasteurization treatment	6-5
Suitable containers, covers, and weights for fermenting foods	6-6
Salts used in pickling	6-7
Fermented foods	**6-7**
Dill pickles	6-7
Sauerkraut	6-8
Cucumber Pickles	**6-9**
Bread-and-butter pickles	6-9
Quick fresh-pack dill pickles	6-10
Sweet gherkin pickles	6-10
14-day sweet pickles	6-11
Quick sweet pickles	6-12
Other Vegetable Pickles	**6-13**
Pickled asparagus	6-13
Pickled dilled beans	6-14
Pickled three-bean salad	6-14
Pickled beets	6-15
Pickled carrots	6-16
Pickled baby carrots	6-16
Pickled cauliflower or Brussels sprouts	6-17
Chayote and jicama slaw	6-17
Bread-and-butter pickled jicama	6-18
Marinated whole mushrooms	6-18
Pickled dilled okra	6-19
Pickled pearl onions	6-20
Marinated peppers	6-20
Pickled bell peppers	6-21
Pickled hot peppers	6-22
Pickled jalapeño pepper rings	6-23
Pickled yellow pepper rings	6-24
Pickled sweet green tomatoes	6-24
Pickled mixed vegetables	6-25
Pickled bread-and-butter zucchini	6-26

Pickled Vegetable Relishes 6-26
    Chayote and pear relish 6-26
    Piccalilli 6-27
    Pickle relish 6-28
    Pickled corn relish 6-28
    Pickled green tomato relish 6-29
    Pickled horseradish sauce 6-30
    Pickled pepper-onion relish 6-30
    Spicy jicama relish 6-30
    Tangy tomatillo relish 6-31

Pickled Foods for Special Diets 6-32
    No sugar added pickled beets 6-32
    No sugar added sweet pickle cucumber slices 6-33
    Reduced-sodium sliced dill pickles 6-34
    Reduced-sodium sliced sweet pickles 6-34

Selection of fresh cucumbers

Quantity: An average of 14 pounds is needed per canner load of 7 quarts; an average of 9 pounds is needed per canner load of 9 pints. A bushel weighs 48 pounds and yields 16 to 24 quarts—an average of 2 pounds per quart.

Quality: Select firm cucumbers of the appropriate size: about 1-1/2 inches for gherkins and 4 inches for dills. Use odd-shaped and more mature cucumbers for relishes and bread-and-butter style pickles.

Low-temperature pasteurization treatment

The following treatment results in a better product texture but must be carefully managed to avoid possible spoilage. Place jars in a canner filled half way with warm (120° to 140°F) water. Then, add hot water to a level 1 inch above jars. Heat the water enough to maintain 180° to 185°F water temperature for 30 minutes. Check with a candy or jelly thermometer to be certain that the water temperature is at least 180°F during the entire 30 minutes. Temperatures higher than 185°F may cause unnecessary softening of pickles. **Caution: Use only when recipe indicates.**

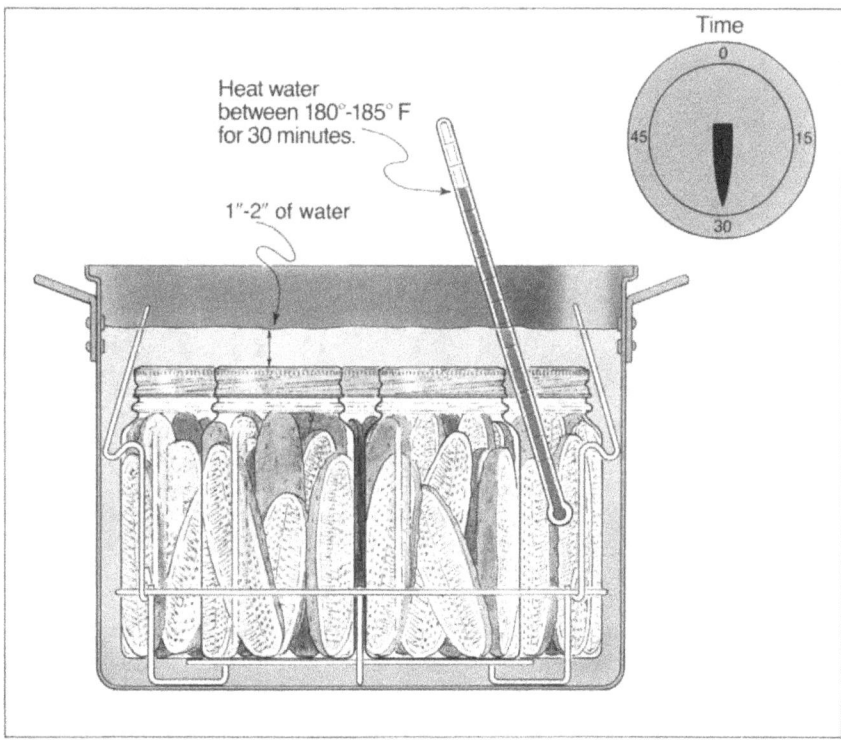

Suitable containers, covers, and weights for fermenting food

A 1-gallon container is needed for each 5 pounds of fresh vegetables. Therefore, a 5-gallon stone crock is of ideal size for fermenting about 25 pounds of fresh cabbage or cucumbers. Food-grade plastic and glass containers are excellent substitutes for stone crocks. Other 1- to 3-gallon non-food-grade plastic containers may be used if lined inside with a clean food-grade plastic bag. **Caution: Be certain that foods contact only food-grade plastics. Do not use garbage bags or trash liners.** Fermenting sauerkraut in quart and half-gallon Mason jars is an acceptable practice, but may result in more spoilage losses.

Cabbage and cucumbers must be kept 1 to 2 inches under brine while fermenting. After adding prepared vegetables and brine, insert a suitably sized dinner plate or glass pie plate inside the fermentation container. The plate must be slightly smaller than the container opening, yet large enough to cover most of the shredded cabbage or cucumbers. To keep the plate under the brine, weight it down with 2 to 3 sealed quart jars filled with water. Covering the container opening with a clean, heavy bath towel helps to prevent contamination from insects and molds while the vegetables are fermenting. Fine quality fermented vegetables are also obtained when the plate is weighted down with a very large clean, plastic bag filled with 3 quarts of water containing

4-1/2 tablespoons of canning or pickling salt. Be sure to seal the plastic bag. Freezer bags sold for packaging turkeys are suitable for use with 5-gallon containers.

The fermentation container, plate, and jars must be washed in hot sudsy water, and rinsed well with very hot water before use.

Salts used in pickling

Use of canning or pickling salt is recommended. Fermented and nonfermented pickles may be safely made using either iodized or noniodized table salt. However, noncaking materials added to table salts may make the brine cloudy. Flake salt varies in density and is not recommended for use.

Reduced-sodium salts, for example mixtures of sodium and potassium chloride, may be used in quick pickle recipes, as indicated in this guide. The pickles may, however, have a slightly different taste than expected. **Caution: Use of reduced-sodium salt in fermented pickle recipes is not recommended.**

Fermented foods

DILL PICKLES

Use the following quantities for each gallon capacity of your container.

4 lbs of 4-inch pickling cucumbers
2 tbsp dill seed or 4 to 5 heads fresh or dry dill weed
1/2 cup salt
1/4 cup vinegar (5%)
8 cups water and one or more of the following ingredients:
  2 cloves garlic (optional)
  2 dried red peppers (optional)
  2 tsp whole mixed pickling spices (optional)

Procedure: Wash cucumbers. Cut 1/16-inch slice off blossom end and discard. Leave 1/4-inch of stem attached. Place half of dill and spices on bottom of a clean, suitable container (see page 6-6). Add cucumbers, remaining dill, and spices. Dissolve salt in vinegar and water and pour over cucumbers. Add suitable cover and weight. Store where temperature is between 70° and 75°F for about 3 to 4 weeks while fermenting. Temperatures of 55° to 65°F are acceptable, but the fermentation will take 5 to 6 weeks. Avoid temperatures above 80°F, or pickles will become too soft during fermentation. Fermenting pickles cure slowly. Check the container several times a week and promptly remove surface scum or mold. **Caution: If the pickles become soft, slimy, or develop a disagreeable odor, discard them.** Fully fermented pickles may be stored in the original container for about 4 to 6 months, provided they are refrigerated and surface scum and molds are removed regularly. Canning fully fermented pickles is a better way to store them. To can them, pour the brine into a pan, heat slowly to a boil, and simmer 5 minutes. Filter brine through paper coffee filters to reduce cloudiness, if desired. Fill hot jar with pickles and hot brine, leaving 1/2-inch headspace. Remove air bubbles and adjust headspace if needed. Wipe rims of jars with a dampened clean paper towel. Adjust lids and process as below, or use the low temperature pasteurization treatment described on page 6-5.

Recommended process time for Dill Pickles in a boiling-water canner				
		Process Time at Altitudes of		
Style of Pack	Jar Size	0–1,000 ft	1,001–6,000 ft	Above 6,000 ft
Raw	Pints	10 min	15	20
	Quarts	15	20	25

SAUERKRAUT

25 lbs cabbage
3/4 cup canning or pickling salt

Quality: For the best sauerkraut, use firm heads of fresh cabbage. Shred cabbage and start kraut between 24 and 48 hours after harvest.

Yield: About 9 quarts

Procedure: Work with about 5 pounds of cabbage at a time. Discard outer leaves. Rinse heads under cold running water and drain. Cut heads in quarters and remove cores. Shred or slice to a thickness of a quarter. Put cabbage in a suitable fermentation container (see page 6-6), and add 3 tablespoons of salt. Mix thoroughly, using clean hands. Pack firmly until salt draws juices from cabbage. Repeat shredding, salting, and packing until all cabbage is in the container. Be sure it is deep enough so that its rim is at least 4 or 5 inches above the cabbage. If juice does not cover cabbage, add boiled and cooled brine (1-1/2 tablespoons of salt per quart of water). Add plate and weights; cover container with a clean bath towel. Store at 70° to 75°F while fermenting. At temperatures between 70° and 75°F, kraut will be fully fermented in about 3 to 4 weeks; at 60° to 65°F, fermentation may take 5 to 6 weeks. At temperatures lower than 60°F, kraut may not ferment. Above 75°F, kraut may become soft.

If you weigh the cabbage down with a brine-filled bag, do not disturb the crock until normal fermentation is completed (when bubbling ceases). If you use jars as weight, you will have to check the kraut two to three times each week and remove scum if it forms. Fully fermented kraut may be kept tightly covered in the refrigerator for several months or it may be canned as follows:

Hot pack—Bring kraut and liquid slowly to a boil in a large kettle, stirring frequently. Remove from heat and fill hot jars rather firmly with kraut and juices, leaving 1/2-inch headspace.

Raw pack—Fill hot jars firmly with kraut and cover with juices, leaving 1/2-inch headspace.

Remove air bubbles and adjust headspace if needed. Wipe rims of jars with a dampened clean paper towel. Adjust lids and process.

Recommended process time for Sauerkraut in a boiling-water canner					
		Process Time at Altitudes of			
Style of Pack	Jar Size	0– 1,000 ft	1,001– 3,000 ft	3,001– 6,000 ft	Above 6,000 ft
Hot	Pints	10 min	15	15	20
	Quarts	15	20	20	25
Raw	Pints	20	25	30	35
	Quarts	25	30	35	40

Cucumber pickles

BREAD-AND-BUTTER PICKLES

6 lbs of 4- to 5-inch pickling cucumbers
8 cups thinly sliced onions (about 3 pounds)
1/2 cup canning or pickling salt
4 cups vinegar (5%)
4-1/2 cups sugar
2 tbsp mustard seed
1-1/2 tbsp celery seed
1 tbsp ground turmeric
1 cup pickling lime (optional) for use in variation below for making firmer pickles

Yield: About 8 pints

Procedure: Wash cucumbers. Cut 1/16-inch off blossom end and discard. Cut into 3/16-inch slices. Combine cucumbers and onions in a large bowl. Add salt. Cover with 2 inches crushed or cubed ice. Refrigerate 3 to 4 hours, adding more ice as needed.

Combine remaining ingredients in a large pot. Boil 10 minutes. Drain and add cucumbers and onions and slowly reheat to boiling. Fill hot pint jars with slices and cooking syrup, leaving 1/2-inch headspace. Remove air bubbles and adjust headspace if needed. Wipe rims of jars with a dampened clean paper towel. Adjust lids and process as below or use low-temperature pasteurization treatment described on page 6-5.

Variation for firmer pickles: Wash cucumbers. Cut 1/16-inch off blossom end and discard. Cut into 3/16-inch slices. Mix 1 cup pickling lime and 1/2 cup salt to 1 gallon water in a 2- to 3-gallon crock or enamelware container. **Caution: Avoid inhaling lime dust while mixing the lime-water solution.** Soak cucumber slices in lime water for 12 to 24 hours, stirring occasionally. Remove from lime solution, rinse, and resoak 1 hour in fresh cold water. Repeat the rinsing and soaking steps two more times. Handle carefully, as slices will be brittle. Drain well. With this variation, the onions are not limed.

Storage: After processing and cooling, jars should be stored 4 to 5 weeks to develop ideal flavor.

Variation: Squash bread-and-butter pickles. Substitute slender (1 to 1-1/2 inches in diameter) zucchini or yellow summer squash for cucumbers. Do not use the liming variation.

Recommended process time for Bread-and-Butter Pickles in a boiling-water canner

Style of Pack	Jar Size	Process Time at Altitudes of		
		0–1,000 ft	1,001–6,000 ft	Above 6,000 ft
Hot	Pints or Quarts	10 min	15	20

QUICK FRESH-PACK DILL PICKLES

8 lbs of 3- to 5-inch pickling cucumbers
2 gals water
1-1/4 cups canning or pickling salt (divided)
1-1/2 qts vinegar (5%)
1/4 cup sugar
2 qts water
2 tbsp whole mixed pickling spice
about 3 tbsp whole mustard seed (1 tsp per pint jar)
about 14 heads of fresh dill (1-1/2 heads per pint jar) or
    4-1/2 tbsp dill seed (1-1/2 tsp per pint jar)

Yield: About 7 to 9 pints

Procedure: Wash cucumbers. Cut 1/16-inch slice off blossom end and discard, but leave 1/4-inch of stem attached. Dissolve 3/4 cup salt in 2 gallons water. Pour over cucumbers and let stand 12 hours. Drain. Combine vinegar, 1/2 cup salt, sugar, and 2 quarts water. Add mixed pickling spices tied in a clean white cloth. Heat to boiling. Fill hot jars with cucumbers. Add 1 tsp mustard seed and 1-1/2 heads fresh dill per pint. Cover with boiling pickling solution, leaving 1/2-inch headspace. Remove air bubbles and adjust headspace if needed. Wipe rims of jars with a dampened clean paper towel. Adjust lids and process as below or use the low-temperature pasteurization treatment described on page 6-5.

Recommended process time for Quick Fresh-Pack Dill Pickles in a boiling-water canner

Style of Pack	Jar Size	Process Time at Altitudes of		
		0–1,000 ft	1,001–6,000 ft	Above 6,000 ft
Raw	Pints	10 min	15	20
	Quarts	15	20	25

SWEET GHERKIN PICKLES

7 lbs cucumbers (1-1/2 inch or less)
1/2 cup canning or pickling salt
8 cups sugar
6 cups vinegar (5%)
3/4 tsp turmeric
2 tsp celery seeds
2 tsp whole mixed pickling spice

2 cinnamon sticks
1/2 tsp fennel (optional)
2 tsp vanilla (optional)

Yield: About 6 to 7 pints

Procedure: Wash cucumbers. Cut 1/16-inch slice off blossom end and discard, but leave 1/4-inch of stem attached. Place cucumbers in large container and cover with boiling water. Six to 8 hours later, and again on the second day, drain and cover with 6 quarts of fresh boiling water containing 1/4-cup salt. On the third day, drain and prick cucumbers with a table fork. Combine and bring to a boil 3 cups vinegar, 3 cups sugar, turmeric, and spices. Pour over cucumbers. Six to 8 hours later, drain and save the pickling syrup. Add another 2 cups each of sugar and vinegar and reheat to boil. Pour over pickles. On the fourth day, drain and save syrup. Add another 2 cups sugar and 1 cup vinegar. Heat to boiling and pour over pickles. Drain and save pickling syrup 6 to 8 hours later. Add 1 cup sugar and 2 tsp vanilla and heat to boiling. Fill hot sterile pint jars (see page 1-14) with pickles and cover with hot syrup, leaving 1/2-inch headspace. Remove air bubbles and adjust headspace if needed. Wipe rims of jars with a dampened clean paper towel. Adjust lids and process as below, or use the low temperature pasteurization treatment described on page 6-5.

Recommended process time for Sweet Gherkin Pickles in a boiling-water canner

Style of Pack	Jar Size	Process Time at Altitudes of		
		0–1,000 ft	1,001–6,000 ft	Above 6,000 ft
Raw	Pints	5 min	10	15

14-DAY SWEET PICKLES

Can be canned whole, in strips, or in slices

4 lbs of 2- to 5-inch pickling cucumbers
    (If packed whole, use cucumbers of uniform size)
3/4 cup canning or pickling salt
    (Separated—1/4 cup on each of the 1st, 3rd, and 5th days)
2 tsp celery seed
2 tbsp mixed pickling spices
5-1/2 cups sugar
4 cups vinegar (5%)

Yield: About 5 to 9 pints

Procedure: Wash cucumbers. Cut 1/16-inch slice off blossom end and discard, but leave 1/4-inch of stem attached. Place whole cucumbers in suitable 1-gallon container (see page 6-6). Add 1/4 cup canning or pickling salt to 2 quarts water and bring to a boil. Pour over cucumbers. Add suitable cover and weight. Place clean towel over container and keep the temperature at about 70°F. **On the third and fifth days,** drain salt water and discard. Rinse cucumbers and rescald cover and weight. Return cucumbers to container. Add 1/4 cup salt to 2 quarts fresh water and boil. Pour over cucumbers. Replace cover and weight, and re-cover with clean towel. **On the seventh day,** drain salt water and discard. Rinse cucumbers and rescald containers, cover, and weight. Slice or strip cucumbers, if desired, and return to container. Place celery seed and pickling spices in small cheesecloth bag. Combine 2 cups sugar and 4 cups vinegar in a saucepan. Add spice bag, bring to a boil and pour pickling solution over cucumbers. Add cover and weight, and re-cover with clean towel. **On each of the next six days,** drain syrup and spice bag and save. Add 1/2 cup sugar each day and bring to a boil in a saucepan. Remove cucumbers and rinse. Scald container, cover, and weight daily. Return cucumbers to container, add boiled syrup, cover, weight, and re-cover with towel. **On the 14th day,** drain syrup into saucepan. Fill hot sterile pint jars (see page 1-14) or clean hot quart jars, leaving 1/2-inch headspace. Add 1/2 cup sugar to syrup and bring to boil. Remove spice bag. Pour hot syrup over cucumbers, leaving 1/2-inch headspace. Remove air bubbles and adjust headspace if needed. Wipe rims of jars with a dampened clean paper towel. Adjust lids and process as below or use low-temperature pasteurization treatment described on page 6-5.

Recommended process time for 14-Day Sweet Pickles in a boiling-water canner

Style of Pack	Jar Size	Process Time at Altitudes of		
		0–1,000 ft	1,001–6,000 ft	Above 6,000 ft
Raw	Pints	5 min	10	15
	Quarts	10	15	20

QUICK SWEET PICKLES

May be canned as either strips or slices

8 lbs of 3- to 4-inch pickling cucumbers
1/3 cup canning or pickling salt
4-1/2 cups sugar
3-1/2 cups vinegar (5%)
2 tsp celery seed
1 tbsp whole allspice
2 tbsp mustard seed
1 cup pickling lime (optional) for use in variation below for making firmer pickles

Yield: About 7 to 9 pints

Procedure: Wash cucumbers. Cut 1/16-inch off blossom end and discard, but leave 1/4 inch of stem attached. Slice or cut in strips, if desired. Place in bowl and sprinkle with 1/3 cup salt. Cover with 2 inches of crushed or cubed ice. Refrigerate 3 to 4 hours. Add more ice as needed. Drain well.

Combine sugar, vinegar, celery seed, allspice, and mustard seed in 6-quart kettle. Heat to boiling.

Hot pack—Add cucumbers and heat slowly until vinegar solution returns to boil. Stir occasionally to make sure mixture heats evenly. Fill sterile jars, leaving 1/2-inch headspace.

Raw pack—Fill hot jars, leaving 1/2-inch headspace. Add hot pickling syrup, leaving 1/2-inch headspace.

Remove air bubbles and adjust headspace if needed. Wipe rims of jars with a dampened clean paper towel. Adjust lids and process as below or use the low temperature pasteurization treatment described on page 6-5.

Variation for firmer pickles: Wash cucumbers. Cut 1/1 6-inch off blossom end and discard, but leave 1/4-inch of stem attached. Slice or strip cucumbers. Mix 1 cup pickling lime and 1/2 cup salt to 1 gallon water in a 2- to 3-gallon crock or enamelware container. **Caution: Avoid inhaling lime dust while mixing the lime-water solution.** Soak cucumber slices or strips in lime water solution for 12 to 24 hours, stirring occasionally. Remove from lime solution and rinse and resoak 1 hour in fresh cold water. Repeat the rinsing and resoaking two more times. Handle carefully because slices or strips will be brittle. Drain well.

Recommended process time for Quick Sweet Pickles in a boiling-water canner

Style of Pack	Jar Size	Process Time at Altitudes of		
		0–1,000 ft	1,001–6,000 ft	Above 6,000 ft
Hot	Pints or Quarts	5 min	10	15
Raw	Pints	10	15	20
	Quarts	15	20	25

Storage: After processing and cooling, jars should be stored 4 to 5 weeks to develop ideal flavor.

Variation: Add 2 slices of raw whole onion to each jar before filling with cucumbers.

Other vegetable pickles

PICKLED ASPARAGUS

Yield: 6 wide-mouth pint jars

10 lbs asparagus
6 large garlic cloves
4-1/2 cups water
4-1/2 cups white distilled vinegar (5%)
6 small hot peppers (optional)
1/2 cup canning salt
3 tsp dill seed

Yield: 7 12-ounce jars

7 lbs asparagus
7 large garlic cloves
3 cups water
3 cups white distilled vinegar (5%)
7 small hot peppers (optional)
1/3 cup canning salt
2 tsp dill seed

Procedure: Wash asparagus well, but gently, under running water. Cut stems from the bottom to leave spears with tips that fit into the canning jar, leaving a little more than 1/2-inch headspace. Peel and wash garlic cloves. Place a garlic clove at the bottom of each jar, and tightly pack asparagus into hot jars with the blunt ends down. In an 8-quart saucepot, combine water, vinegar, hot peppers (optional), salt and dill seed. Bring to a boil. Place one hot pepper (if used) in each jar over asparagus spears. Pour boiling hot pickling brine over spears, leaving 1/2-inch headspace. Remove air bubbles and adjust headspace if needed. Wipe rims of jars with a dampened clean paper towel. Adjust lids and process.

		Process Time at Altitudes of		
Style of Pack	Jar Size	0–1,000 ft	1,001–6,000 ft	Above 6,000 ft
Raw	12-ounce or Pints	10 min	15	20

Recommended process time for Pickled Asparagus in a boiling-water canner

PICKLED DILLED BEANS

4 lbs fresh tender green or yellow beans (5 to 6 inches long)
8 to 16 heads fresh dill
8 cloves garlic (optional)
1/2 cup canning or pickling salt
4 cups white vinegar (5%)
4 cups water
1 tsp hot red pepper flakes (optional)

Yield: About 8 pints

Procedure: Wash and trim ends from beans and cut to 4-inch lengths. In each hot sterile pint jar (see page 1-14), place 1 to 2 dill heads and, if desired, 1 clove of garlic. Place whole beans upright in jars, leaving 1/2-inch headspace. Trim beans to ensure proper fit, if necessary. Combine salt, vinegar, water, and pepper flakes (if desired). Bring to a boil. Add hot solution to beans, leaving 1/2-inch headspace. Remove air bubbles and adjust headspace if needed. Wipe rims of jars with a dampened clean paper towel. Adjust lids and process.

Recommended process time for Pickled Dilled Beans in a boiling-water canner

		Process Time at Altitudes of		
Style of Pack	Jar Size	0–1,000 ft	1,001–6,000 ft	Above 6,000 ft
Raw	Pints	5 min	10	15

PICKLED THREE-BEAN SALAD

1-1/2 cups cut and blanched green or yellow beans (prepared as below)
1-1/2 cups canned, drained, red kidney beans
1 cup canned, drained garbanzo beans
1/2 cup peeled and thinly sliced onion (about 1 medium onion)
1/2 cup trimmed and thinly sliced celery (1-1/2 medium stalks)
1/2 cup sliced green peppers (1/2 medium pepper)
1/2 cup white vinegar (5%)
1/4 cup bottled lemon juice
3/4 cup sugar
1/4 cup oil
1/2 tsp canning or pickling salt
1-1/4 cups water

Yield: About 5 to 6 half-pints

Procedure: Wash and snap off ends of fresh beans. Cut or snap into 1- to 2-inch pieces. Blanch 3 minutes and cool immediately. Rinse kidney beans with tap water and drain again. Prepare and measure all other vegetables. Combine vinegar, lemon juice, sugar, and water and bring to a boil. Remove from heat. Add oil and salt and mix well. Add beans, onions, celery, and green pepper to solution and bring to a simmer. Marinate 12 to 14 hours in refrigerator, then heat entire mixture to a boil. Fill hot jars with solids. Add hot liquid, leaving 1/2-inch headspace. Remove air bubbles and adjust headspace if needed. Wipe rims of jars with a dampened clean paper towel. Adjust lids and process.

		Process Time at Altitudes of		
Style of Pack	Jar Size	0–1,000 ft	1,001–6,000 ft	Above 6,000 ft
Hot	Half-pints or Pints	15 min	20	25

Recommended process time for Pickled Three-Bean Salad in a boiling-water canner

PICKLED BEETS

7 lbs of 2- to 2-1/2-inch diameter beets
4 cups vinegar (5%)
1-1/2 tsp canning or pickling salt
2 cups sugar
2 cups water
2 cinnamon sticks
12 whole cloves
4 to 6 onions (2- to 2-1/2-inch diameter), if desired

Yield: About 8 pints

Procedure: Trim off beet tops, leaving 1 inch of stem and roots to prevent bleeding of color. Wash thoroughly. Sort for size. Cover similar sizes together with boiling water and cook until tender (about 25 to 30 minutes). **Caution: Drain and discard liquid.** Cool beets. Trim off roots and stems and slip off skins. Slice into 1/4-inch slices. Peel and thinly slice onions. Combine vinegar, salt, sugar, and fresh water. Put spices in cheesecloth bag and add to vinegar mixture. Bring to a boil. Add beets and onions. Simmer 5 minutes. Remove spice bag. Fill hot jars with beets and onions, leaving 1/2-inch headspace. Add hot vinegar solution, allowing 1/2-inch headspace. Remove air bubbles and adjust headspace if needed. Wipe rims of jars with a dampened clean paper towel. Adjust lids and process.

Variation: For pickled whole baby beets, follow above directions but use beets that are 1-to 1-1/2 inches in diameter. Pack whole; do not slice. Onions may be omitted.

Recommended process time for **Pickled Beets** in a boiling-water canner

Style of Pack	Jar Size	Process Time at Altitudes of			
		0–1,000 ft	1,001–3,000 ft	3,001–6,000 ft	Above 6,000 ft
Hot	Pints or Quarts	30 min	35	40	45

PICKLED CARROTS

2-3/4 lbs peeled carrots (about 3-1/2 lbs as purchased)
5-1/2 cups white vinegar (5%)
1 cup water
2 cups sugar
2 tsp canning salt
8 tsp mustard seed
4 tsp celery seed

Yield: About 4 pints

Procedure: Wash and peel carrots. Cut into rounds that are approximately 1/2-inch thick. Combine vinegar, water, sugar and canning salt in an 8-quart Dutch oven or stockpot. Bring to a boil and boil 3 minutes. Add carrots and bring back to a boil. Then reduce heat to a simmer and heat until half-cooked (about 10 minutes). Meanwhile, place 2 teaspoons mustard seed and 1 teaspoon celery seed into each empty hot pint jar. Fill jars with hot carrots, leaving 1-inch headspace. Fill with hot pickling liquid, leaving 1/2-inch headspace. Remove air bubbles and adjust headspace if needed. Wipe rims of jars with a dampened clean paper towel. Adjust lids and process.

Recommended process time for **Pickled Carrots** in a boiling-water canner

Style of Pack	Jar Size	Process Time at Altitudes of		
		0–1,000 ft	1,001–6,000 ft	Above 6,000 ft
Hot	Pints	15 min	20	25

PICKLED BABY CARROTS

Procedure: Follow directions for Pickled Carrots, using 8-1/2 cups peeled baby carrots, leaving them whole, and use the same process time.

PICKLED CAULIFLOWER OR BRUSSELS SPROUTS

12 cups of 1- to 2-inch cauliflower flowerets or small Brussels sprouts
4 cups white vinegar (5%)
2 cups sugar
2 cups thinly sliced onions
1 cup diced sweet red peppers
2 tbsp mustard seed
1 tbsp celery seed
1 tsp turmeric
1 tsp hot red pepper flakes

Yield: About 9 half-pints

Procedure: Wash cauliflower flowerets or Brussels sprouts (remove stems and blemished outer leaves) and boil in salt water (4 tsp canning salt per gallon of water) for 3 minutes for cauliflower and 4 minutes for Brussels sprouts. Drain and cool. Combine vinegar, sugar, onion, diced red pepper, and spices in large saucepan. Bring to a boil and simmer 5 minutes. Distribute onion and diced pepper among jars. Fill hot jars with pieces and pickling solution, leaving 1/2-inch headspace. Remove air bubbles and adjust headspace if needed. Wipe rims of jars with a dampened clean paper towel. Adjust lids and process.

Recommended process time for Pickled Cauliflower or Brussels Sprouts in a boiling-water canner

Style of Pack	Jar Size	Process Time at Altitudes of		
		0–1,000 ft	1,001–6,000 ft	Above 6,000 ft
Hot	Half-pints or Pints	10 min	15	20

CHAYOTE AND JICAMA SLAW

4 cups julienned jicama
4 cups julienned chayote
2 cups finely chopped red bell pepper
2 finely chopped hot peppers
2-1/2 cups water
2-1/2 cups cider vinegar (5%)
1/2 cup white sugar
3-1/2 tsp canning salt
1 tsp celery seed (optional)

Yield: About 6 half-pints

Procedure: Caution: Wear plastic or rubber gloves and do not touch your face while handling or cutting hot peppers. If you do not wear gloves, wash hands thoroughly with soap and water before touching your face or eyes. Wash, peel and thinly julienne jicama and chayote, discarding the seed of the chayote. In an 8-quart Dutch oven or stockpot, combine all ingredients except chayote. Bring to a boil and boil for 5 minutes. Reduce heat to simmering and add chayote. Bring back to a boil and then turn heat off. Fill hot solids into hot half-pint jars, leaving 1/2-inch headspace. Cover with boiling cooking liquid, leaving 1/2-inch headspace. Remove air bubbles and adjust headspace if needed. Wipe rims of jars with a dampened clean paper towel. Adjust lids and process.

Recommended process time for Chayote and Jicama Slaw in a boiling-water canner				
		Process Time at Altitudes of		
Style of Pack	Jar Size	0– 1,000 ft	1,001– 6,000 ft	Above 6,000 ft
Hot	Half-pints	15 min	20	25

BREAD-AND-BUTTER PICKLED JICAMA

14 cups cubed jicama
3 cups thinly sliced onion
1 cup chopped red bell pepper
4 cups white vinegar (5%)
4-1/2 cups sugar
2 tbsp mustard seed
1 tbsp celery seed
1 tsp ground turmeric

Yield: About 6 pints

Procedure: Combine vinegar, sugar and spices in a 12-quart Dutch oven or large saucepot. Stir and bring to a boil. Stir in prepared jicama, onion slices, and red bell pepper. Return to a boil, reduce heat and simmer 5 minutes. Stir occasionally. Fill hot solids into hot pint jars, leaving 1/2-inch headspace. Cover with boiling cooking liquid, leaving 1/2-inch headspace. Remove air bubbles and adjust headspace if needed. Wipe rims of jars with a dampened clean paper towel. Adjust lids and process.

Recommended process time for Bread-and-Butter Pickled Jicama in a boiling-water canner				
		Process Time at Altitudes of		
Style of Pack	Jar Size	0– 1,000 ft	1,001– 6,000 ft	Above 6,000 ft
Hot	Pints	15 min	20	25

MARINATED WHOLE MUSHROOMS

7 lbs small whole mushrooms
1/2 cup bottled lemon juice
2 cups olive or salad oil
2-1/2 cups white vinegar (5%)
1 tbsp oregano leaves
1 tbsp dried basil leaves
1 tbsp canning or pickling salt

1/2 cup finely chopped onions
1/4 cup diced pimiento
2 cloves garlic, cut in quarters
25 black peppercorns

Yield: About 9 half-pints

Procedure: Select very fresh unopened mushrooms with caps less than 1-1/4 inch in diameter. Wash. Cut stems, leaving 1/4 inch attached to cap. Add lemon juice and water to cover. Bring to boil. Simmer 5 minutes. Drain mushrooms. Mix olive oil, vinegar, oregano, basil, and salt in a saucepan. Stir in onions and pimiento and heat to boiling. Place 1/4 garlic clove and 2-3 peppercorns in a half-pint jar. Fill hot jars with mushrooms and hot, well-mixed oil/vinegar solution, leaving 1/2-inch headspace. Remove air bubbles and adjust headspace if needed. Wipe rims of jars with a dampened clean paper towel. Adjust lids and process.

Recommended process time for Marinated Whole Mushrooms in a boiling-water canner

Style of Pack	Jar Size	Process Time at Altitudes of			
		0–1,000 ft	1,001–3,000 ft	3,001–6,000 ft	Above 6,000 ft
Hot	Half-pints	20 min	25	30	35

PICKLED DILLED OKRA

7 lbs small okra pods
6 small hot peppers
4 tsp dill seed
8 to 9 garlic cloves
2/3 cup canning or pickling salt
6 cups water
6 cups vinegar (5%)

Yield: About 8 to 9 pints

Procedure: Wash and trim okra. Fill hot jars firmly with whole okra, leaving 1/2-inch headspace. Place 1 garlic clove in each jar. Combine salt, hot peppers, dill seed, water, and vinegar in large saucepan and bring to a boil. Pour hot pickling solution over okra, leaving 1/2-inch headspace. Remove air bubbles and adjust headspace if needed. Wipe rims of jars with a dampened clean paper towel. Adjust lids and process.

Recommended process time for Pickled Dilled Okra in a boiling-water canner

Style of Pack	Jar Size	Process Time at Altitudes of		
		0–1,000 ft	1,001–6,000 ft	Above 6,000 ft
Hot	Pints	10 min	15	20

PICKLED PEARL ONIONS

8 cups peeled white pearl onions
5-1/2 cups white vinegar (5%)
1 cup water
2 tsp canning salt
2 cups sugar
8 tsp mustard seed
4 tsp celery seed

Yield: About 3 to 4 pints

Procedure: To peel onions, place a few at a time in a wire-mesh basket or strainer, dip in boiling water for 30 seconds, then remove and place in cold water for 30 seconds. Cut a 1/16th-inch slice from the root end, and then remove the peel and cut 1/16th-inch from the other end of the onion. Combine vinegar, water, salt and sugar in an 8-quart Dutch oven or stockpot. Bring to a boil and boil 3 minutes. Add peeled onions and bring back to a boil. Reduce heat to a simmer and heat until half-cooked (about 5 minutes). Meanwhile, place 2 teaspoons mustard seed and 1 teaspoon celery seed into each empty hot pint jar. Fill with hot onions, leaving 1 inch headspace. Fill with hot pickling liquid, leaving 1/2-inch headspace. Remove air bubbles and adjust headspace if needed. Wipe rims of jars with a dampened clean paper towel. Adjust lids and process.

Recommended process time for Pickled Pearl Onions in a boiling-water canner

Style of Pack	Jar Size	Process Time at Altitudes of		
		0–1,000 ft	1,001–6,000 ft	Above 6,000 ft
Hot	Pints	10 min	15	20

MARINATED PEPPERS

Bell, Hungarian, banana, or jalapeño

4 lbs firm peppers*
1 cup bottled lemon juice
2 cups white vinegar (5%)
1 tbsp oregano leaves
1 cup olive or salad oil
1/2 cup chopped onions
2 cloves garlic, quartered (optional)
2 tbsp prepared horseradish (optional)

* Note: It is possible to adjust the intensity of pickled jalapeño peppers by using all hot jalapeño peppers (hot style), or blending with sweet and mild peppers (medium or mild style).

    For hot style: Use 4 lbs jalapeño peppers.

    For medium style: Use 2 lbs jalapeño peppers and 2 lbs sweet and mild peppers.

    For mild style: Use 1 lb jalapeño peppers and 3 lbs sweet and mild peppers.

Yield: About 9 half-pints

Procedure: Select your favorite pepper. **Caution: If you select hot peppers, wear plastic or rubber gloves and do not touch your face while handling or cutting hot peppers. If you do not wear gloves, wash hands thoroughly with soap and water before touching your face or eyes.** Peppers may be left whole. Large peppers may be quartered. Wash, slash two to four slits in each pepper, and blanch in boiling water or blister skins on tough-skinned hot peppers using one of these two methods:

Oven or broiler method to blister skins – Place peppers in a hot oven (400°F) or under a broiler for 6 to 8 minutes until skins blister.

Range-top method to blister skins – Cover hot burner (either gas or electric) with heavy wire mesh. Place peppers on burner for several minutes until skins blister.

After blistering skins, place peppers in a pan and cover with a damp cloth. (This will make peeling the peppers easier.) Cool several minutes; peel off skins. Flatten whole peppers. Mix all remaining ingredients in a saucepan and heat to boiling. Place 1/4 garlic clove (optional) and 1/4 teaspoon salt in each hot half-pint jar or 1/2 teaspoon per pint. Fill hot jars with peppers. Add hot, well-mixed oil/pickling solution over peppers, leaving 1/2-inch headspace. Remove air bubbles and adjust headspace if needed. Wipe rims of jars with a dampened clean paper towel. Adjust lids and process.

Recommended process time for Marinated Peppers in a boiling-water canner

Style of Pack	Jar Size	Process Time at Altitudes of		
		0–1,000 ft	1,001–6,000 ft	Above 6,000 ft
Raw	Half-pints or Pints	15 min	20	25

PICKLED BELL PEPPERS

7 lbs firm bell peppers
3-1/2 cups sugar
3 cups vinegar (5%)
3 cups water
9 cloves garlic
4-1/2 tsp canning or pickling salt

Yield: About 9 pints

Procedure: Wash peppers, cut into quarters, remove cores and seeds, and cut away any blemishes. Slice peppers in strips. Boil sugar, vinegar, and water for 1 minute. Add peppers and bring to a boil. Place 1/2 clove of garlic and 1/4 teaspoon salt in each hot sterile half-pint jar; double the amounts for pint jars. Add pepper strips and cover with hot vinegar mixture, leaving 1/2-inch headspace. Remove air bubbles and adjust headspace if needed. Wipe rims of jars with a dampened clean paper towel. Adjust lids and process.

Recommended process time for Pickled Bell Peppers in a boiling-water canner				
		Process Time at Altitudes of		
Style of Pack	Jar Size	0–1,000 ft	1,001–6,000 ft	Above 6,000 ft
Hot	Half-pints or Pints	5 min	10	15

PICKLED HOT PEPPERS

Hungarian, banana, chile, jalapeño

4 lbs hot long red, green, or yellow peppers
3 lbs sweet red and green peppers, mixed
5 cups vinegar (5%)
1 cup water
4 tsp canning or pickling salt
2 tbsp sugar
2 cloves garlic

Yield: About 9 pints

Procedure: Caution: Wear plastic or rubber gloves and do not touch your face while handling or cutting hot peppers. If you do not wear gloves, wash hands thoroughly with soap and water before touching your face or eyes. Wash peppers. If small peppers are left whole, slash 2 to 4 slits in each. Quarter large peppers. Blanch in boiling water or blister skins on tough-skinned hot peppers using one of these two methods:

Oven or broiler method to blister skins – Place peppers in a hot oven (400°F) or under a broiler for 6 to 8 minutes until skins blister.

Range-top method to blister skins – Cover hot burner (either gas or electric) with heavy wire mesh. Place peppers on burner for several minutes until skins blister.

After blistering skins, place peppers in a pan and cover with a damp cloth. (This will make peeling the peppers easier.) Cool several minutes; peel off skins. Flatten small peppers. Quarter large peppers. Fill hot jars with peppers, leaving 1/2-inch headspace. Combine and heat other ingredients to boiling and simmer 10 minutes. Remove garlic. Add hot pickling solution over peppers, leaving 1/2-inch headspace. Remove air bubbles and adjust headspace if needed. Wipe rims of jars with a dampened clean paper towel. Adjust lids and process.

Recommended process time for Pickled Hot Peppers in a boiling-water canner

Style of Pack	Jar Size	0–1,000 ft	1,001–6,000 ft	Above 6,000 ft
Raw	Half-pints or Pints	10 min	15	20

PICKLED JALAPEÑO PEPPER RINGS

3 lbs jalapeño peppers
1-1/2 cups pickling lime
1-1/2 gallons water
7-1/2 cups cider vinegar (5%)
1-3/4 cups water
2-1/2 tbsp canning salt
3 tbsp celery seed
6 tbsp mustard seed

Yield: About 6 pint jars

Procedure: Caution: Wear plastic or rubber gloves and do not touch your face while handling or cutting hot peppers. If you do not wear gloves, wash hands thoroughly with soap and water before touching your face or eyes. Wash peppers well and slice into 1/4-inch thick slices. Discard stem end. Mix 1-1/2 cups pickling lime with 1-1/2 gallons water in a stainless steel, glass or food grade plastic container. Avoid inhaling lime dust while mixing the lime-water solution. Soak pepper slices in the lime water, in refrigerator, for 18 hours, stirring occasionally (12 to 24 hours may be used). Drain lime solution from soaked pepper rings. Rinse peppers gently but thoroughly with water. Cover pepper rings with fresh cold water and soak, in refrigerator, 1 hour. Drain water from peppers. Repeat the rinsing, soaking and draining steps two more times. Drain thoroughly at the end. Place 1 tablespoon mustard seed and 1-1/2 teaspoons celery seed in the bottom of each hot pint jar. Pack drained pepper rings into the jars, leaving 1/2-inch headspace. Bring cider vinegar, 1-3/4 cups water and canning salt to a boil over high heat. Ladle boiling hot brine solution over pepper rings in jars, leaving 1/2-inch headspace. Remove air bubbles and adjust headspace if needed. Wipe rims of jars with a dampened clean paper towel. Adjust lids and process.

Recommended process time for Pickled Jalapeño Rings in a boiling-water canner

Style of Pack	Jar Size	0–1,000 ft	1,001–6,000 ft	Above 6,000 ft
Hot	Pints	10 min	15	20

PICKLED YELLOW PEPPER RINGS

2-1/2 to 3 lbs yellow (banana) peppers
2 tbsp celery seed
4 tbsp mustard seed
5 cups cider vinegar (5%)
1-1/4 cups water
5 tsp canning salt

Yield: About 4 pint jars

Procedure: Caution: Wear plastic or rubber gloves and do not touch your face while handling or cutting hot peppers. If you do not wear gloves, wash hands thoroughly with soap and water before touching your face or eyes. Wash peppers well and remove stem end; slice peppers into 1/4-inch thick rings. Place 1/2 tablespoon celery seed and 1 tablespoon mustard seed in the bottom of each empty hot pint jar. Fill pepper rings into jars, leaving 1/2-inch headspace. In a 4-quart Dutch oven or saucepan, combine the cider vinegar, water and salt; heat to boiling. Cover pepper rings with boiling pickling liquid, leaving 1/2-inch headspace. Remove air bubbles and adjust headspace if needed. Wipe rims of jars with a dampened clean paper towel. Adjust lids and process.

Recommended process time for Pickled Yellow Pepper Rings in a boiling-water canner

Style of Pack	Jar Size	Process Time at Altitudes of		
		0–1,000 ft	1,001–6,000 ft	Above 6,000 ft
Hot	Pints	10 min	15	20

PICKLED SWEET GREEN TOMATOES

10 to 11 lbs of green tomatoes (16 cups sliced)
2 cups sliced onions
1/4 cup canning or pickling salt
3 cups brown sugar
4 cups vinegar (5%)
1 tbsp mustard seed
1 tbsp allspice
1 tbsp celery seed
1 tbsp whole cloves

Yield: About 9 pints

Procedure: Wash and slice tomatoes and onions. Place in bowl, sprinkle with 1/4 cup salt, and let stand 4 to 6 hours. Drain. Heat and stir sugar in vinegar until dissolved. Tie mustard seed, allspice, celery seed, and cloves in a spice bag. Add to vinegar with tomatoes and onions. If needed, add minimum water to cover pieces. Bring to boil and simmer 30 minutes, stirring as needed to prevent burning. Tomatoes should be tender and transparent when properly cooked. Remove spice bag. Fill hot jar with solids and cover with hot pickling solution, leaving 1/2-inch headspace. Remove air bubbles and adjust headspace if needed. Wipe rims of jars with a dampened clean paper towel. Adjust lids and process.

Recommended process time for Pickled Sweet Green Tomatoes in a boiling-water canner

Style of Pack	Jar Size	Process Time at Altitudes of		
		0–1,000 ft	1,001–6,000 ft	Above 6,000 ft
Hot	Pints	10 min	15	20
	Quarts	15	20	25

PICKLED MIXED VEGETABLES

4 lbs of 4- to 5-inch pickling cucumbers, washed, and cut into 1-inch slices (cut off 1/16 inch from blossom end and discard)
2 lbs peeled and quartered small onions
4 cups cut celery (1-inch pieces)
2 cups peeled and cut carrots (1/2-inch pieces)
2 cups cut sweet red peppers (1/2-inch pieces)
2 cups cauliflower flowerets
5 cups white vinegar (5%)
1/4 cup prepared mustard
1/2 cup canning or pickling salt
3-1/2 cups sugar
3 tbsp celery seed
2 tbsp mustard seed
1/2 tsp whole cloves
1/2 tsp ground turmeric

Yield: About 10 pints

Procedure: Combine vegetables, cover with 2 inches of cubed or crushed ice, and refrigerate 3 to 4 hours. In 8-quart kettle, combine vinegar and mustard and mix well. Add salt, sugar, celery seed, mustard seed, cloves, turmeric. Bring to a boil. Drain vegetables and add to hot pickling solution. Cover and slowly bring to boil. Drain vegetables but save pickling solution. Fill vegetables in hot sterile pint jars, or hot quarts, leaving 1/2-inch headspace. Add pickling solution, leaving 1/2-inch headspace. Remove air bubbles and adjust headspace if needed. Wipe rims of jars with a dampened clean paper towel. Adjust lids and process.

Recommended process time for Pickled Mixed Vegetables in a boiling-water canner

Style of Pack	Jar Size	Process Time at Altitudes of		
		0–1,000 ft	1,001–6,000 ft	Above 6,000 ft
Hot	Pints	5 min	10	15
	Quarts	10	15	20

PICKLED BREAD-AND-BUTTER ZUCCHINI

16 cups fresh zucchini, sliced
4 cups onions, thinly sliced
1/2 cup canning or pickling salt
4 cups white vinegar (5%)
2 cups sugar
4 tbsp mustard seed
2 tbsp celery seed
2 tsp ground turmeric

Yield: About 8 to 9 pints

Procedure: Cover zucchini and onion slices with 1 inch of water and salt. Let stand 2 hours and drain thoroughly. Combine vinegar, sugar, and spices. Bring to a boil and add zucchini and onions. Simmer 5 minutes and fill hot jars with mixture and pickling solution, leaving 1/2-inch headspace. Remove air bubbles and adjust headspace if needed. Wipe rims of jars with a dampened clean paper towel. Adjust lids and process or use low-temperature pasteurization treatment described on page 6-5.

Recommended process time for Pickled Bread-and-Butter Zucchini in a bolling-water canner				
		Process Time at Altitudes of		
Style of Pack	Jar Size	0–1,000 ft	1,001–6,000 ft	Above 6,000 ft
Hot	Pints or Quarts	10 min	15	20

Pickled vegetable relishes

CHAYOTE AND PEAR RELISH

3-1/2 cups peeled, cubed chayote
3-1/2 cups peeled, cubed Seckel pears
2 cups chopped red bell pepper
2 cups chopped yellow bell pepper
3 cups finely chopped onion
2 Serrano peppers, finely chopped
2-1/2 cups cider vinegar (5%)
1-1/2 cups water
1 cup white sugar
2 tsp canning salt
1 tsp ground allspice
1 tsp ground pumpkin pie spice

Yield: About 5 pint jars

Procedure: Caution: Wear plastic or rubber gloves and do not touch your face while handling or cutting hot peppers. If you do not wear gloves, wash hands thoroughly with soap and water before touching your face or eyes. Wash, peel and cut chayote and pears into

1/2-inch cubes, discarding cores and seeds. Chop onions and peppers. Combine vinegar, water, sugar, salt and spices in a Dutch oven or large saucepot. Bring to a boil, stirring to dissolve sugar. Add chopped onions and peppers; return to a boil and boil for 2 minutes, stirring occasionally. Add cubed chayote and pears; return to the boiling point and turn off heat. Fill the hot solids into hot pint jars, leaving 1-inch headspace. Cover with boiling cooking liquid, leaving 1/2-inch headspace. Remove air bubbles and adjust headspace if needed. Wipe rims of jars with a dampened clean paper towel. Adjust lids and process.

Recommended process time for Chayote Pear Relish in a boiling-water canner

Style of Pack	Jar Size	Process Time at Altitudes of		
		0–1,000 ft	1,001–6,000 ft	Above 6,000 ft
Hot	Pints	15 min	20	25

PICCALILLI

6 cups chopped green tomatoes
1-1/2 cups chopped sweet red peppers
1-1/2 cups chopped green peppers
2-1/4 cups chopped onions
7-1/2 cups chopped cabbage
1/2 cup canning or pickling salt
3 tbsp whole mixed pickling spice
4-1/2 cups vinegar (5%)
3 cups brown sugar

Yield: About 9 half-pints

Procedure: Wash, chop, and combine vegetables with 1/2 cup salt. Cover with hot water and let stand 12 hours. Drain and press in a clean white cloth to remove all possible liquid. Tie spices loosely in a spice bag and add to combined vinegar and brown sugar and heat to a boil in a sauce pan. Add vegetables and boil gently 30 minutes or until the volume of the mixture is reduced by one-half. Remove spice bag. Fill hot sterile jars (see page 1-14), with hot mixture, leaving 1/2-inch headspace. Remove air bubbles and adjust headspace if needed. Wipe rims of jars with a dampened clean paper towel. Adjust lids and process.

Recommended process time for Piccalilli in a boiling-water canner

Style of Pack	Jar Size	Process Time at Altitudes of		
		0–1,000 ft	1,001–6,000 ft	Above 6,000 ft
Hot	Half-pints or Pints	5 min	10	15

PICKLE RELISH

3 qts chopped cucumbers
3 cups each of chopped sweet green and red peppers
1 cup chopped onions
3/4 cup canning or pickling salt
4 cups ice
8 cups water
2 cups sugar
4 tsp each of mustard seed, turmeric, whole allspice, and whole cloves
6 cups white vinegar (5%)

Yield: About 9 pints

Procedure: Add cucumbers, peppers, onions, salt, and ice to water and let stand 4 hours. Drain and re-cover vegetables with fresh ice water for another hour. Drain again. Combine spices in a spice or cheesecloth bag. Add spices to sugar and vinegar. Heat to boiling and pour mixture over vegetables. Cover and refrigerate 24 hours. Heat mixture to boiling and fill hot into hot jars, leaving 1/2-inch headspace. Remove air bubbles and adjust headspace if needed. Wipe rims of jars with a dampened clean paper towel. Adjust lids and process.

Recommended process time for Pickle Relish in a boiling-water canner				
		Process Time at Altitudes of		
Style of Pack	Jar Size	0–1,000 ft	1,001–6,000 ft	Above 6,000 ft
Hot	Half-pints or Pints	10 min	15	20

PICKLED CORN RELISH

10 cups fresh whole kernel corn (16 to 20 medium-size ears), or
    six 10-ounce packages of frozen corn
2-1/2 cups diced sweet red peppers
2-1/2 cups diced sweet green peppers
2-1/2 cups chopped celery
1-1/4 cups diced onions
1-3/4 cups sugar
5 cups vinegar (5%)
2-1/2 tbsp canning or pickling salt
2-1/2 tsp celery seed
2-1/2 tbsp dry mustard
1-1/4 tsp turmeric

Yield: About 9 pints

Procedure: Boil ears of corn 5 minutes. Dip in cold water. Cut whole kernels from cob or use six 10-ounce frozen packages of corn. Combine peppers, celery, onions, sugar, vinegar, salt, and celery seed in a saucepan. Bring to boil and simmer 5 minutes, stirring occasionally. Mix mustard and turmeric in 1/2 cup of the simmered mixture. Add this mixture and corn to the hot mixture.

Simmer another 5 minutes. If desired, thicken mixture with flour paste (1/4 cup flour blended in 1/4 cup water) and stir frequently. Fill hot jars with hot mixture, leaving 1/2-inch headspace. Remove air bubbles and adjust headspace if needed. Wipe rims of jars with a dampened clean paper towel. Adjust lids and process.

Recommended process time for Pickled Corn Relish in a boiling-water canner

Style of Pack	Jar Size	Process Time at Altitudes of		
		0–1,000 ft	1,001–6,000 ft	Above 6,000 ft
Hot	Half-pints or Pints	15 min	20	25

PICKLED GREEN TOMATO RELISH

10 lbs small, hard green tomatoes
1-1/2 lbs red bell peppers
1-1/2 lbs green bell peppers
2 lbs onions
1/2 cup canning or pickling salt
1 qt water
4 cups sugar
1 qt vinegar (5%)
1/3 cup prepared yellow mustard
2 tbsp cornstarch

Yield: About 7 to 9 pints

Procedure: Wash and coarsely grate or finely chop tomatoes, peppers, and onions. Dissolve salt in water and pour over vegetables in large kettle. Heat to boiling and simmer 5 minutes. Drain in colander. Return vegetables to kettle. Add sugar, vinegar, mustard, and cornstarch. Stir to mix. Heat to boiling and simmer 5 minutes. Fill hot sterile pint jars (see page 1-14) with hot relish, leaving 1/2-inch headspace. Remove air bubbles and adjust headspace if needed. Wipe rims of jars with a dampened clean paper towel. Adjust lids and process.

Recommended process time for Pickled Green Tomato Relish in a boiling-water canner

Style of Pack	Jar Size	Process Time at Altitudes of		
		0–1,000 ft	1,001–6,000 ft	Above 6,000 ft
Hot	Pints	5 min	10	15

PICKLED HORSERADISH SAUCE

2 cups (3/4 lb) freshly grated horseradish
1 cup white vinegar (5%)
1/2 tsp canning or pickling salt
1/4 tsp powdered ascorbic acid

Yield: About 2 half-pints

Procedure: The pungency of fresh horseradish fades within 1 to 2 months, even when refrigerated. Therefore, make only small quantities at a time. Wash horseradish roots thoroughly and peel off brown outer skin. The peeled roots may be grated in a food processor or cut into small cubes and put through a food grinder. Combine ingredients and fill into sterile jars (see page 1-14), leaving 1/4-inch headspace. Seal jars tightly and store in a refrigerator.

PICKLED PEPPER-ONION RELISH

6 cups finely chopped onions
3 cups finely chopped sweet red peppers
3 cups finely chopped green peppers
1-1/2 cups sugar
6 cups vinegar (5%), preferably white distilled
2 tbsp canning or pickling salt

Yield: About 9 half-pints

Procedure: Wash and chop vegetables. Combine all ingredients and boil gently until mixture thickens and volume is reduced by one-half (about 30 minutes). Fill hot sterile jars (see page 1-14) with hot relish, leaving 1/2-inch headspace, and seal tightly. Store in refrigerator and use within one month. **Caution: If extended storage is desired, this product must be processed.**

Recommended process time for Pickled Pepper-Onion Relish in a boiling-water canner				
		Process Time at Altitudes of		
Style of Pack	Jar Size	0–1,000 ft	1,001–6,000 ft	Above 6,000 ft
Hot	Half-pints or Pints	5 min	10	15

SPICY JICAMA RELISH

9 cups diced jicama (you will need about 4 pounds purchased jicama)
1 tbsp whole mixed pickling spice
1 two-inch stick cinnamon
8 cups white vinegar (5%)
4 cups sugar
2 tsp crushed red pepper
4 cups diced yellow bell pepper

4-1/2 cups diced red bell pepper
4 cups chopped onion
2 fresh fingerhot peppers (about 6 inches each), finely chopped and partially seeded

Yield: About 7 pint jars

Procedure: Caution: Wear plastic or rubber gloves and do not touch your face while handling or cutting hot peppers. If you do not wear gloves, wash hands thoroughly with soap and water before touching your face or eyes. Wash, peel and trim jicama; dice. Place pickling spice and cinnamon on a clean, double-layer, 6-inch-square piece of 100% cotton cheesecloth. Bring corners together and tie with a clean string. (Or use a purchased muslin spice bag.) In a 4-quart Dutch oven or saucepot, combine pickling spice bag, vinegar, sugar, and crushed red pepper. Bring to boiling, stirring to dissolve sugar. Stir in diced jicama, sweet peppers, onion and fingerhots. Return mixture to boiling. Reduce heat and simmer, covered, over medium-low heat about 25 minutes. Discard spice bag. Fill relish into hot pint jars, leaving 1/2-inch headspace. Cover with hot pickling liquid, leaving 1/2-inch headspace. Remove air bubbles and adjust headspace if needed. Wipe rims of jars with a dampened clean paper towel. Adjust lids and process.

Recommended process time for Spicy Jicama Relish in a boiling-water canner					
		Process Time at Altitudes of			
Style of Pack	Jar Size	0–1,000 ft	1,001–3,000 ft	3,001–6,000 ft	Above 6,000 ft
Hot	Pints	20 min	25	30	35

TANGY TOMATILLO RELISH

12 cups chopped tomatillos
3 cups finely chopped jicama
3 cups chopped onion
6 cups chopped plum-type tomatoes
1-1/2 cups chopped green bell pepper
1-1/2 cups chopped red bell pepper
1-1/2 cups chopped yellow bell pepper
1 cup canning salt
2 qts water
6 tbsp whole mixed pickling spice
1 tbsp crushed red pepper flakes (optional)
6 cups sugar
6-1/2 cups cider vinegar (5%)

Yield: About 6 or 7 pints

Procedure: Remove husks from tomatillos and wash well. Peel jicama and onion. Wash all vegetables well before trimming and chopping. Place chopped tomatillos, jicama, onion, tomatoes, and all bell peppers in a 4-quart Dutch oven or saucepot. Dissolve canning salt in water. Pour over prepared vegetables. Heat to boiling; simmer 5 minutes. Drain thoroughly through a cheesecloth-lined strainer (until no more water drips through, about 15 to 20 minutes). Place pickling spice and optional red pepper flakes on a clean, double-layer, 6 inch-square piece of 100% cotton cheesecloth. Bring corners together and tie with a clean string. (Or use a purchased muslin spice bag.) Mix sugar, vinegar and spices (in cheesecloth bag) in a saucepan; bring to a boil. Add drained vegetables. Return to boil; reduce heat and simmer, uncovered, 30 minutes. Remove spice bag. Fill hot relish mixture into hot pint jars, leaving 1/2-inch headspace. Remove air bubbles and adjust headspace if needed. Wipe rims of jars with a dampened clean paper towel. Adjust lids and process.

Recommended process time for Tangy Tomatillo Relish in a boiling-water canner				
		Process Time at Altitudes of		
Style of Pack	Jar Size	0–1,000 ft	1,001–6,000 ft	Above 6,000 ft
Hot	Pints	15 min	20	25

Pickled foods for special diets

NO SUGAR ADDED PICKLED BEETS

7 lbs of 2- to 2-1/2-inch diameter beets
4 to 6 onions (2- to 2-1/2-inch diameter), if desired
6 cups white vinegar (5 percent)
1-1/2 tsp canning or pickling salt
2 cups Splenda®
3 cups water
2 cinnamon sticks
12 whole cloves

Yield: About 8 pints

Procedure: Trim off beet tops, leaving 1 inch of stem and roots to prevent bleeding of color. Wash thoroughly. Sort for size. Cover similar sizes together with boiling water and cook until tender (about 25 to 30 minutes). **Caution: Drain and discard liquid.** Cool beets. Trim off roots and stems and slip off skins. Slice into 1/4-inch slices. Peel, wash and thinly slice onions. Combine vinegar, salt, Splenda®, and 3 cups fresh water in large Dutch oven. Tie cinnamon sticks and cloves in cheesecloth bag and add to vinegar mixture. Bring to a boil. Add beets and onions. Simmer 5 minutes. Remove spice bag. Fill hot beets and onion slices into hot pint jars, leaving 1/2-inch headspace. Cover with boiling vinegar solution, leaving 1/2-inch headspace. Remove air bubbles and adjust headspace if needed. Wipe rims of jars with a dampened clean paper towel. Adjust lids and process.

Variation: *Pickled whole baby beets* - Follow the directions above but use beets that are no more than 1- to 1-1/2 inches in diameter. Pack whole after cooking, trimming and peeling; do not slice.

Recommended process time for **No Sugar Added Pickled Beets** in a boiling-water canner					
		Process Time at Altitudes of			
Style of Pack	Jar Size	0–1,000 ft	1,001–3,000 ft	3,001–6,000 ft	Above 6,000 ft
Hot	Pints	30 min	35	40	45

NO SUGAR ADDED SWEET PICKLE CUCUMBER SLICES

3-1/2 lbs of pickling cucumbers
boiling water to cover sliced cucumbers
4 cups cider vinegar (5%)
1 cup water
3 cups Splenda®
1 tbsp canning salt
1 tbsp mustard seed
1 tbsp whole allspice
1 tbsp celery seed
4 one-inch cinnamon sticks

Yield: About 4 or 5 pint jars

Procedure: Wash cucumbers. Slice 1/16th-inch off the blossom ends and discard. Slice cucumbers into 1/4-inch thick slices. Pour boiling water over the cucumber slices and let stand 5 to 10 minutes. Drain off the hot water and pour cold water over the cucumbers. Let cold water run continuously over the cucumber slices, or change water frequently until cucumbers are cooled. Drain slices well. Mix vinegar, 1 cup water, Splenda® and all spices in a 10-quart Dutch oven or stockpot. Bring to a boil. Add drained cucumber slices carefully to the boiling liquid and return to a boil. Place one cinnamon stick in each empty hot jar, if desired. Fill hot pickle slices into hot pint jars, leaving 1/2-inch headspace. Cover with boiling pickling brine, leaving 1/2-inch headspace. Remove air bubbles and adjust headspace if needed. Wipe rims of jars with a dampened clean paper towel. Adjust lids and process.

Recommended process time for **No Sugar Added Sweet Cucumber Pickle Slices** in a boiling-water canner				
		Process Time at Altitudes of		
Style of Pack	Jar Size	0–1,000 ft	1,001–6,000 ft	Above 6,000 ft
Hot	Pints	10 min	15	20

REDUCED-SODIUM SLICED DILL PICKLES

4 lbs (3- to 5-inch) pickling cucumbers
6 cups vinegar (5%)
6 cups sugar
2 tbsp canning or pickling salt
1-1/2 tsp celery seed
1-1/2 tsp mustard seed
2 large onions, thinly sliced
8 heads fresh dill

Yield: About 8 pints

Procedure: Wash cucumbers. Cut 1/16-inch slice off blossom end and discard. Cut cucumbers in 1/4-inch slices. Combine vinegar, sugar, salt, celery, and mustard seeds in large saucepan. Bring mixture to boiling. Place 2 slices of onion and 1/2 dill head on bottom of each hot pint jar. Fill hot jars with cucumber slices, leaving 1/2-inch headspace. Add 1 slice of onion and 1/2 dill head on top. Pour hot pickling solution over cucumbers, leaving 1/4-inch headspace. Remove air bubbles and adjust headspace if needed. Wipe rims of jars with a dampened clean paper towel. Adjust lids and process.

Recommended process time for Reduced-Sodium Sliced Dill Pickles in a boiling-water canner

Style of Pack	Jar Size	Process Time at Altitudes of		
		0–1,000 ft	1,001–6,000 ft	Above 6,000 ft
Raw	Pints	15 min	20	25

REDUCED-SODIUM SLICED SWEET PICKLES

4 lbs (3- to 4-inch) pickling cucumbers

Brining solution:
1 qt distilled white vinegar (5%)
1 tbsp canning or pickling salt
1 tbsp mustard seed
1/2 cup sugar

Canning syrup:
1-2/3 cups distilled white vinegar (5%)
3 cups sugar
1 tbsp whole allspice
2-1/4 tsp celery seed

Yield: About 4 to 5 pints

Procedure: Wash cucumbers and cut 1/16 inch off blossom end, and discard. Cut cucumbers into 1/4-inch slices. Combine all ingredients for canning syrup in a saucepan and bring to boiling. Keep syrup hot until used. In a large kettle, mix the ingredients for the brining solution. Add the cut cucumbers, cover, and simmer until the cucumbers change color from bright to dull green (about 5 to 7 minutes). Drain the cucumber slices. Fill hot jars, and cover with hot canning syrup leaving 1/2-inch headspace. Remove air bubbles and adjust headspace if needed. Wipe rims of jars with a dampened clean paper towel. Adjust lids and process.

Recommended process time for Reduced-Sodium Sliced Sweet Pickles in a boiling-water canner				
		Process Time at Altitudes of		
Style of Pack	Jar Size	0–1,000 ft	1,001–6,000 ft	Above 6,000 ft
Hot	Pints	10 min	15	20

Complete Guide to
Home Canning

Guide 7
Preparing and Canning Jams and Jellies

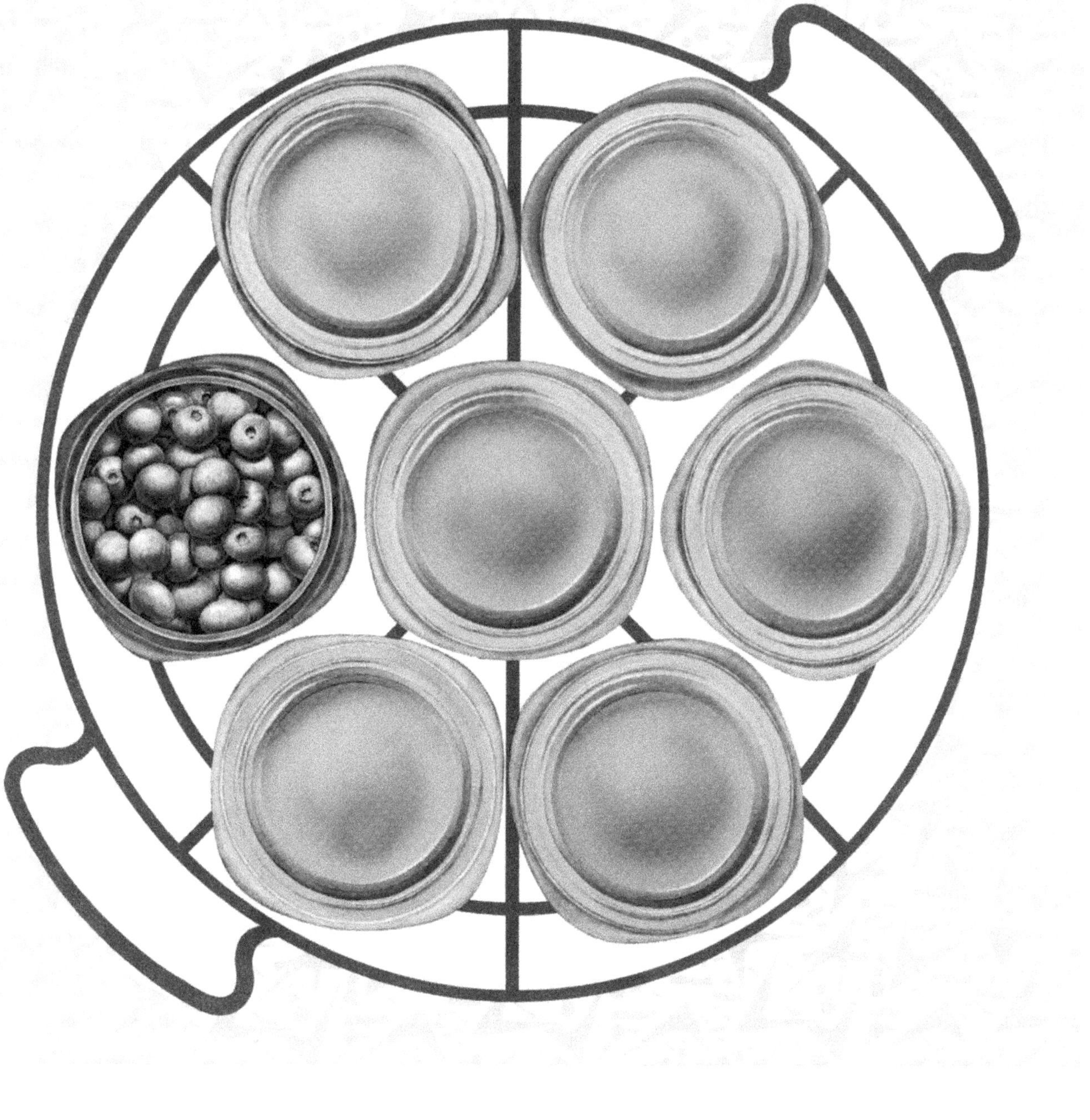

United States Department of Agriculture

National Institute of Food and Agriculture

Guide 7
Preparing and Canning Jams and Jellies

Table of Contents

Section	Page
Making jelly without added pectin	7-5
Extracting juices and making jelly	7-5
Making jam without added pectin	7-6
Making Jams and Jellies with Added Pectin	**7-7**
Pear-apple jam	7-8
Strawberry-rhubarb jelly	7-8
Blueberry-spice jam	7-9
Grape-plum jelly	7-10
Golden pepper jelly	7-10
Making Reduced-Sugar Fruit Spreads	**7-11**
Peach-pineapple spread	7-11
Refrigerated apple spread (made with gelatin)	7-12
Refrigerated grape spread (made with gelatin)	7-12
Remaking soft jellies	7-13

Making jelly without added pectin

Use only firm fruits naturally high in pectin. Select a mixture of about 3/4 ripe and 1/4 underripe fruit. Do not use commercially canned or frozen fruit juices. Their pectin content is too low. Wash all fruits thoroughly before cooking. Crush soft fruits or berries; cut firmer fruits into small pieces. Using the peels and cores adds pectin to the juice during cooking. Add water to fruits that require it, as listed in the table of ingredients below. Put fruit and water in large saucepan and bring to a boil. Then simmer according to the times below until fruit is soft, while stirring to prevent scorching. One pound of fruit should yield at least 1 cup of clear juice.

Extracting juices and making jelly

To Extract Juice			Ingredients Added to Each Cup of Strained Juice		Yield from 4 Cups of Juice (Half-pints)
	Cups of Water to be Added per Pound of Fruit	Minutes to Simmer Fruit before Extracting Juice	Sugar (Cups)	Lemon Juice (Tsp)	
Apples	1	20 to 25	3/4	1-1/2 (optional)	4 to 5
Blackberries	None or 1/4	5 to 10	3/4 to 1	None	7 to 8
Crab apples	1	20 to 25	1	None	4 to 5
Grapes	None or 1/4	5 to 10	3/4 to 1	None	8 to 9
Plums	1/2	15 to 20	3/4	None	8 to 9

When fruit is tender, strain through a colander, then strain through a double layer of cheesecloth or a jelly bag. Allow juice to drip through, using a stand or colander to hold the bag. Pressing or squeezing the bag or cloth will cause cloudy jelly.

Using no more than 6 to 8 cups of extracted fruit juice at a time, measure fruit juice, sugar, and lemon juice according to the ingredients in the table above and heat to boiling. Stir until the sugar is dissolved. Boil over high heat to the jellying point. To test jelly for doneness, use one of the following methods.

Temperature test—Use a jelly or candy thermometer and boil until mixture reaches the following temperatures at altitudes of:

Sea Level	1,000 ft	2,000 ft	3,000 ft	4,000 ft	5,000 ft	6,000 ft	7,000 ft	8,000 ft
220°F	218°F	216°F	214°F	212°F	211°F	209°F	207°F	205°F

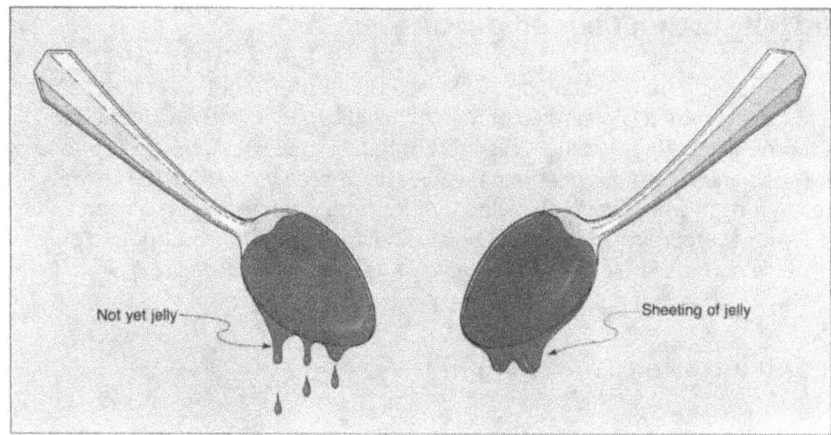

Sheet or spoon test—Dip a cool metal spoon into the boiling jelly mixture. Raise the spoon about 12 inches above the pan (out of steam). Turn the spoon so the liquid runs off the side. The jelly is done when the syrup forms two drops that flow together and sheet or hang off the edge of the spoon.

Remove from heat and quickly skim off foam. Fill sterile jars (see page 1-14) with jelly. Use a measuring cup or ladle the jelly through a wide-mouthed funnel, leaving 1/4 inch headspace. Wipe rims of jars with a dampened clean paper towel. Adjust lids and process.

Recommended process time for Jelly without Added Pectin in a boiling-water canner				
		Process Time at Altitudes of		
Style of Pack	Jar Size	0–1,000 ft	1,001–6,000 ft	Above 6,000 ft
Hot	Half-pints or Pints	5 min	10	15

Making jam without added pectin

Wash and rinse all fruits thoroughly before cooking. Do not soak. For best flavor, use fully ripe fruit. Remove stems, skins, and pits from fruit; cut into pieces and crush. For berries, remove stems and blossoms and crush. Seedy berries may be put through a sieve or food mill. Measure crushed fruit into large saucepan using the ingredient quantities specified in the table below.

Ingredient Quantities				
Fruit	Cups Crushed Fruit	Cups Sugar	Tbsp Lemon Juice	Yield (Half-pints)
Apricots	4 to 4-1/2	4	2	5 to 6
Berries *	4	4	0	3 to 4
Peaches	5-1/2 to 6	4 to 5	2	6 to 7

*Includes blackberries, boysenberries, dewberries, gooseberries, loganberries, raspberries, and strawberries

Add sugar and bring to a boil while stirring rapidly and constantly. Continue to boil until mixture thickens. Use one of the following tests to determine when jams and jellies are ready to fill. Remember to allow for thickening during cooling.

Temperature test—Use a jelly or candy thermometer and boil until mixture reaches the temperature for your altitude (see page 7-5).

Refrigerator test—Remove the jam mixture from the heat. Pour a small amount of boiling jam on a cold plate and put it in the freezing compartment of a refrigerator for a few minutes. If the mixture gels, it is ready to fill.

Remove from heat and skim off foam quickly. Fill sterile jars (see page 1-14) with jam. Use a measuring cup or ladle the jam through a wide-mouthed funnel, leaving 1/4 inch headspace. Wipe rims of jars with a dampened clean paper towel. Adjust lids and process.

Recommended process time for Jam without Added Pectin in a boiling-water canner

Style of Pack	Jar Size	Process Time at Altitudes of		
		0–1,000 ft	1,001–6,000 ft	Above 6,000 ft
Hot	Half-pints or Pints	5 min	10	15

Making Jams and Jellies with Added Pectin

Fresh fruits and juices as well as commercially canned or frozen fruit juice can be used with commercially prepared powdered or liquid pectins. The order of combining ingredients depends on the type of pectin used. Complete directions for a variety of fruits are provided with packaged pectin. Jelly or jam made with added pectin requires less cooking and generally gives a larger yield. These products have more natural fruit flavors, too. In addition, using added pectin eliminates the need to test hot jellies and jams for proper gelling. Adding 1/2 teaspoon of butter or margarine with the juice and pectin will reduce foaming. However, these may cause off-flavor in long-term storage of jellies and jams. Recipes available using packaged pectin include:

Jellies—Apple, crab apple, blackberry, boysenberry, dewberry, currant, elderberry, grape, mayhaw, mint, peach, plum, black or red raspberry, loganberry, rhubarb, and strawberry.

Jams—Apricot, blackberry, boysenberry, dewberry, loganberry, red raspberry, youngberry, blueberry, cherry, currant, fig, gooseberry, grape, orange marmalade, peach, pear, plum, rhubarb, strawberry, and spiced tomato.

Be sure to use pre-sterilized Mason canning jars, self-sealing two-piece lids, and a 5-minute process (corrected for altitude, as necessary) in boiling water. (See page 1-30 about spoilage of jams and jellies.)

Purchase fresh pectin each year. Old pectin may result in poor gels. Follow the instructions with each package and process as below:

Recommended process time for Jellies and Jam with Added Pectin in a boiling-water canner				
		Process Time at Altitudes of		
Style of Pack	Jar Size	0–1,000 ft	1,001–6,000 ft	Above 6,000 ft
Hot	Half-pints or Pints	5 min	10	15

Following are a few additional jelly and jam recipes for use with packaged pectin.

PEAR-APPLE JAM

2 cups peeled, cored, and finely chopped pears (about 2 lbs)
1 cup peeled, cored, and finely chopped apples
6-1/2 cups sugar
1/4 tsp ground cinnamon
1/3 cup bottled lemon juice
6 oz liquid pectin

Yield: About 7 to 8 half-pints

Procedure: Crush apples and pears in a large saucepan and stir in cinnamon. Thoroughly mix sugar and lemon juice with fruits and bring to a boil over high heat, stirring constantly. Immediately stir in pectin. Bring to a full rolling boil and boil hard 1 minute, stirring constantly. Remove from heat, quickly skim off foam, and fill sterile jars (see page 1-14) leaving 1/4-inch headspace. Wipe rims of jars with a dampened clean paper towel. Adjust lids and process.

Recommended process time for Pear-Apple Jam in a boiling-water canner				
		Process Time at Altitudes of		
Style of Pack	Jar Size	0–1,000 ft	1,001–6,000 ft	Above 6,000 ft
Hot	Half-pints or Pints	5 min	10	15

STRAWBERRY-RHUBARB JELLY

1-1/2 lbs red stalks of rhubarb
1-1/2 qts ripe strawberries
1/2 tsp butter or margarine to reduce foaming (optional)
6 cups sugar
6 oz liquid pectin

Yield: About 7 half-pints

Procedure: Wash and cut rhubarb into 1-inch pieces and blend or grind. Wash, stem, and crush strawberries, one layer at a time, in a saucepan. Place both fruits in a jelly bag or double layer of cheesecloth and gently squeeze out juice. Measure 3-1/2 cups of juice into a large saucepan. Add butter and sugar, thoroughly mixing into juice. Bring to a boil over high heat, stirring constantly. Immediately stir in pectin. Bring to a full rolling boil and boil hard 1 minute, stirring constantly. Remove from heat, quickly skim off foam, and fill sterile jars (see page 1-14), leaving 1/4-inch headspace. Wipe rims of jars with a dampened clean paper towel. Adjust lids and process.

Recommended process time for Strawberry-Rhubarb Jelly in a boiling-water canner

Style of Pack	Jar Size	Process Time at Altitudes of		
		0–1,000 ft	1,001–6,000 ft	Above 6,000 ft
Hot	Half-pints or Pints	5 min	10	15

BLUEBERRY-SPICE JAM

2-1/2 pints ripe blueberries
1 tbsp lemon juice
1/2 tsp ground nutmeg or cinnamon
5-1/2 cups sugar
3/4 cup water
1 box (1-3/4 oz) powdered pectin

Yield: About 5 half-pints

Procedure: Wash and thoroughly crush blueberries, one layer at a time, in a saucepan. Add lemon juice, spice, and water. Stir in pectin and bring to a full rolling boil over high heat, stirring frequently. Add the sugar and return to a full rolling boil. Boil hard for 1 minute, stirring constantly. Remove from heat, quickly skim off foam, and fill sterile jars (see page 1-14), leaving 1/4-inch headspace. Wipe rims of jars with a dampened clean paper towel. Adjust lids and process.

Recommended process time for Blueberry-Spice Jam in a boiling-water canner

Style of Pack	Jar Size	Process Time at Altitudes of		
		0–1,000 ft	1,001–6,000 ft	Above 6,000 ft
Hot	Half-pints or Pints	5 min	10	15

GRAPE-PLUM JELLY

3-1/2 lbs ripe plums
3 lbs ripe Concord grapes
1 cup water
1/2 tsp butter or margarine to reduce foaming (optional)
8-1/2 cups sugar
1 box (1-3/4 oz) powdered pectin

Yield: About 10 half-pints

Procedure: Wash and pit plums; do not peel. Thoroughly crush the plums and grapes, one layer at a time, in a saucepan with water. Bring to a boil, cover, and simmer 10 minutes. Strain juice through a jelly bag or double layer of cheesecloth. Measure sugar and set aside. Combine 6-1/2 cups of juice with butter and pectin in large saucepan. Bring to a hard boil over high heat, stirring constantly. Add the sugar and return to a full rolling boil. Boil hard for 1 minute, stirring constantly. Remove from heat, quickly skim off foam, and fill sterile jars (see page 1-14), leaving 1/4-inch headspace. Wipe rims of jars with a dampened clean paper towel. Adjust lids and process.

Recommended process time for Grape-Plum Jelly in a boiling-water canner				
		Process Time at Altitudes of		
Style of Pack	Jar Size	0–1,000 ft	1,001–6,000 ft	Above 6,000 ft
Hot	Half-pints or Pints	5 min	10	15

GOLDEN PEPPER JELLY

5 cups chopped yellow bell peppers (about 4 large fleshy peppers as purchased)
½ cup chopped Serrano chile peppers (about 5 peppers as purchased)
1-1/2 cups white distilled vinegar (5%)
5 cups sugar
1 pouch (3 oz.) liquid pectin

Yield: About 5 half-pint jars

Procedure: Caution: Wear plastic or rubber gloves and do not touch your face while handling or cutting hot peppers. If you do not wear gloves, wash hands thoroughly with soap and water before touching your face or eyes. Wash all peppers thoroughly; remove stems and seeds from the peppers. Do not remove the membrane from the hot peppers, since the remaining capsaicin for pepper heat is located there. Place sweet and hot peppers in a blender or food processor. Add enough of the vinegar to puree the peppers, then puree. Combine the pepper-vinegar puree and remaining vinegar into an 8- or 10-quart saucepan. Heat to a boil; then boil 10 minutes to extract flavors and color. Remove from heat and strain through a jelly bag into a bowl. (The jelly bag is preferred; several layers of cheesecloth may also be used.) Measure 2-1/4 cups of the strained pepper-vinegar juice back into the saucepan. Stir in sugar until dissolved and return mixture to a boil. Add the pectin, return to a full rolling boil and boil hard for 1 minute, stirring constantly. Remove from heat, quickly skim off any foam, and fill into sterile jars (see page 1-14), leaving 1/4-inch headspace. Wipe rims of jars with a dampened clean paper towel. Adjust lids and process.

Notes: The use of yellow peppers gives this jelly a light golden color. Other colored sweet peppers can be substituted, but these will provide a different jelly color. Other hot peppers can also be substituted. It is best to start with a mild hot pepper flavor and increase it to suit personal tastes. If properly prepared, the jelly will have a mildly firm set; it is best to use half-pint jars.

Recommended process time for Golden Pepper Jelly in a boiling-water canner

Style of Pack	Jar Size	Process Time at Altitudes of		
		0–1,000 ft	1,001–6,000 ft	Above 6,000 ft
Hot	Half-pints	5 min	10	15

Making Reduced-Sugar Fruit Spreads

A variety of fruit spreads may be made that are tasteful, yet lower in sugars and calories than regular jams and jellies. The following are recipes for reduced-sugar fruit spreads. Gelatin may be used as a thickening agent, as indicated in two of the following recipes. Sweet fruits, apple juice, spices, and/or a liquid, low-calorie sweetener are used to provide the sweet flavor of the fruit spreads. When gelatin is used in the recipe, the jars of spread should not be processed. They should be refrigerated and used within 4 weeks.

PEACH-PINEAPPLE SPREAD

4 cups drained peach pulp (procedure as below)
2 cups drained unsweetened crushed pineapple
1/4 cup bottled lemon juice
2 cups sugar (optional)

This recipe may be made with any combination of peaches, nectarines, apricots, and plums.

This recipe may be made without sugar or with up to 2 cups, according to taste or preference. Non-nutritive sweeteners may be added. If aspartame (a low-calorie nutritive sweetener) is used, the sweetening power of aspartame may be lost within 3 to 4 weeks.

Yield: 5 to 6 half-pints

Procedure: Thoroughly wash 4 to 6 pounds of firm, ripe peaches. Drain well. Peel and remove pits. Grind fruit flesh with a medium or coarse blade, or crush with a fork (do not use a blender). Place ground or crushed fruit in a 2-quart saucepan. Heat slowly to release juice, stirring constantly, until fruit is tender. Place cooked fruit in a jelly bag or strainer lined with four layers of cheesecloth. Allow juice to drip about 15 minutes. Save the juice for jelly or other uses. Measure 4 cups of drained fruit pulp for making spread. Combine the 4 cups of pulp, pineapple, and lemon juice in a 4-quart saucepan. Add up to 2 cups of sugar, if desired, and mix well. Heat and boil gently for 10 to 15 minutes, stirring enough to prevent sticking. Fill hot jars quickly, leaving 1/4-inch headspace. Wipe rims of jars with a dampened clean paper towel. Adjust lids and process.

Recommended process time for Peach-Pineapple Spread in a boiling-water canner					
		Process Time at Altitudes of			
Style of Pack	Jar Size	0–1,000 ft	1,001–3,000 ft	3,001–6,000 ft	Above 6,000 ft
Hot	Half-pints	15 min	20	20	25
	Pints	20	25	30	35

REFRIGERATED APPLE SPREAD (made with gelatin)

2 tbsp unflavored gelatin powder
1 qt bottle unsweetened apple juice
2 tbsp bottled lemon juice
2 tbsp liquid low-calorie sweetener
Food coloring, if desired

Yield: 4 half-pints

Procedure: In a saucepan, soften the gelatin in the apple and lemon juices. To dissolve gelatin, bring to a full rolling boil and boil 2 minutes. Remove from heat. Stir in sweetener and food coloring, if desired. Fill jars, leaving 1/4-inch headspace. Wipe rims of jars with a dampened clean paper towel. Adjust lids. Do not process or freeze. **Caution: Store in refrigerator and use within 4 weeks.**

Optional: For spiced apple jelly, add 2 sticks of cinnamon and 4 whole cloves to mixture before boiling. Remove both spices before adding the sweetener and food coloring.

REFRIGERATOR GRAPE SPREAD (made with gelatin)

2 tbsp unflavored gelatin powder
1 bottle (24 oz) unsweetened grape juice
2 tbsp bottled lemon juice
2 tbsp liquid low-calorie sweetener

Yield: 3 half-pints

Procedure: In a saucepan, soften the gelatin in the grape and lemon juices. Bring to a full rolling boil to dissolve gelatin. Boil 1 minute and remove from heat. Stir in sweetener. Fill hot jars quickly, leaving 1/4-inch headspace. Wipe rims of jars with a dampened clean paper towel. Adjust lids. Do not process or freeze. **Caution: Store in refrigerator and use within 4 weeks.**

Remaking soft jellies

Measure jelly to be recooked. Work with no more than 4 to 6 cups at a time.

To remake with powdered pectin: For each quart of jelly, mix 1/4 cup sugar, 1/2 cup water, 2 tablespoons bottled lemon juice, and 4 teaspoons powdered pectin. Bring to a boil while stirring. Add jelly and bring to a rolling boil over high heat, stirring constantly. Boil hard 1/2 minute. Remove from heat, quickly skim foam off jelly, and fill sterile jars (see page 1-14), leaving 1/4-inch headspace. Wipe rims of jars with a dampened clean paper towel. Adjust new lids and process.

To remake with liquid pectin: For each quart of jelly, measure 3/4 cup sugar, 2 tablespoons bottled lemon juice, and 2 tablespoons liquid pectin. Bring jelly only to boil over high heat, while stirring. Remove from heat and quickly add the sugar, lemon juice, and pectin. Bring to a full rolling boil, stirring constantly. Boil hard for 1 minute. Quickly skim off foam and fill sterile jars (see page 1-14), leaving 1/4-inch headspace. Wipe rims of jars with a dampened clean paper towel. Adjust new lids and process.

To remake without added pectin: For each quart of jelly, add 2 tablespoons bottled lemon juice. Heat to boiling and boil for 3 to 4 minutes. Use one of the tests described on page 7-5 to determine jelly doneness. Remove from heat, quickly skim off foam, and fill sterile jars (see page 1-14), leaving 1/4-inch headspace. Wipe rims of jars with a dampened clean paper towel. Adjust new lids and process.

Recommended process time for Remade Soft Jellies in a boiling-water canner

Style of Pack	Jar Size	Process Time at Altitudes of		
		0–1,000 ft	1,001–6,000 ft	Above 6,000 ft
Hot	Half-pints or Pints	5 min	10	15